MW00791536

"Barb Maiberger's new book lands in therapist's hands at just the right time. Tackling recent challenges such as the COVID pandemic and social upheavals, she leverages her own personal experiences of shock, stress, and pressured adaptations to a changing world with grace and courage. What results is a book that not only gives voice to the stress and suffering of these last few years, but also makes something useful out of it. Full of practical strategies and examples, she guides us both personally and professionally in how to work remotely; everything from how to light your room to how to observe and treat clients through a computer monitor, to how to take care of your body as it sits in front of the screen for hours at a time. My aching back and aching heart thank you!"

Christine Caldwell, Ph.D., LPC, BC-DMT, ACS
Professor Emeritus, Naropa University, Somatic Counseling Psychology

"In *Remote Together*, Barb Maiberger offers challenged therapists practical and compassionate support in two important arenas—working online and including the body. Barb's gentle, relatable wisdom and compassion is soothing, heartful, and authentic. Barb shares practical tips that support us to bring our healing practices online without fear of losing connection. Simultaneously she is introducing the basics of integrating the body into psychotherapeutic work. May You Soar, the title of the final section, exemplifies the joyous tone of the whole book."

Susan Aposhyan
Founder Body-Mind Psychotherapy and Embodied Spirituality Online, Author of *Body-Mind Psychotherapy*, *Natural Intelligence*, and *Heart Open, Body Awake*

"Barb Maiberger's *Remote Together* offers a careful examination of what can and has gone wrong with the transition to remote therapy. She explores how we can discover what has gone wrong for each one of us psychotherapists, through a compassionate approach to really exploring how the old strategies are not just failing some of us, but most of us. She shows how she and countless other therapists have been impacted by the pandemic and the transition to remote therapy has fundamentally changed private practice. She offers a loving look at how we can develop new kinds of self-care through self-awareness and by re-learning how to listen and really care for ourselves and our bodies in the present moment. Her experiences as a dancer, somatic psychotherapist, and EMDR trainer inform her ability to help each psychotherapist practice listening to their body, to their longings, to their anxieties, and to their childhood voices while turning a loving eye toward the care and feeding of their soul."

Kekuni Minton, Ph.D
Co-author of *Trauma and the Body: A Sensorimotor Approach to Psychotherapy*

"As an EMDR therapist who has worked to resource my clients throughout a profoundly chaotic time in the world, I couldn't be more grateful for this timely book. Barb Maiberger has written a guide that is authentic, compassionate, and wise, but also filled with practical applications for therapists working to navigate the ever-changing world of telehealth. If you are a therapist, this is a must have book."

Aundi Kolber MA, LPC, NCC
Therapist & Author of *Try Softer* and *The Try Softer Guided Journey*

"Negotiating the unfamiliar path of virtual therapy has caught most psychotherapists off guard; about nine out of ten have reported in 2011 that they needed help, especially to maintain self-care. For all virtual therapy providers, I recommend Barb Maiberger's warm and practical book. We are first introduced to Barb's personal journey as she reveals her own awkwardness and fear while faced with the pandemic, then how she adapted some of the somatic practices she has pioneered so that clinical colleagues could also have access to simple but powerful self-help tools. There is a lot of creativity and love in this book."

John Hartung
Colorado Center for Alternative Psychology

"Cutting edge, vulnerable & highly relevant. . . Maiberger acknowledges the very human challenges psychotherapists have faced spontaneously shifting their entire businesses online overnight while simultaneously walking alongside clients amidst the shared trauma of a global pandemic. Through empathic storytelling, the author shares real life examples of therapists' struggles as well as offers numerous invaluable somatic tools and practices for therapists to create more confidence, connection, flow, creativity and care for themselves and clients."

Katie Asmus MA, LPC, BMP
Somatic, Nature-based EMDR, Psychotherapist and University faculty, and founder of Somatic Wilderness Therapy Institute

REMOTE TOGETHER

REMOTE TOGETHER

A Therapist's Guide to Cultivating a Sustainable Practice

BARB MAIBERGER

Bodymind Press

Remote Together: A Therapist's Guide to Cultivating a Sustainable Practice

Cover Design and Layout by Adelle Dittman
Cover Photo Image by Young B. Kim
Author Photograph by Alisha Light

Published by Bodymind Press, an imprint of Integrated Body Mind
Therapy, Inc., 4696 Broadway, Suite 3, Boulder, Colorado 80304.
For more information visit https://bodymindpress.com

ISBN: 978-0-578-97900-7 (paperback)
ISBN: 978-0-578-97901-4 (ebook)
ISBN: 978-0-578-99542-7 (hardcover)

....

To my fellow therapists, thank you for being essential members of your community. Remember you are not alone in your struggles, and support is all around you.

....

CONTENTS

PRACTICES

ACKNOWLEDGMENTS

Since I was 4 years old, I have been a dancer. Dance has been a part of my life for as long as I can remember. Dance is how I make meaning of the world and how I express myself. In the beginning, dance was just a fun part of my life, and, over the years, it has become a foundation of how I think, move and behave personally and professionally. Many of my dance instructors helped me see that life is about movement, and without movement, we wouldn't be alive. Over the years, I have taught dance, massage therapy, somatic psychology, and now EMDR therapy. Whatever I'm teaching, I find ways to dance with the material. In writing this book, I discovered that my dance world came alive and informed me of concepts that I wanted to share with you, *dear reader*.

I couldn't use this dance language if it weren't for my mother, who enrolled me in my first dance class at age four. She sacrificed so much, all so that I could pursue my dance career, spending countless hours driving me to rehearsals, buying costumes that were too expensive for our family's budget, and sitting through every performance as one of my biggest fans. I am indebted to her for helping me find my love of dance.

I am grateful to Stella J. Becker, who is no longer with us, my first dance instructor who ingrained in me that dance was an expression of being alive. To this day, I remember her face beaming with pride as my passion came alive on stage. I know she is smiling down at me now as she sees how much I've grown and integrated dance into my life so fully.

As my passion for dance grew, I attended the Ohio State University and majored in dance performance. There, my dance instructors taught me about the quality of movement, the structure of a dance, and the intricacies of each step's timing, pacing, and dynamics. I am grateful to all the teachers at OSU, especially Vicki Blaine and Karen Bell, who saw my potential as a dancer and nurtured my desire to perform. They taught me that through practice, the bodymind could be trained to perform intricate steps, laying down a foundation for being flexible, adaptable, and creative. Performances rarely go perfectly and having a solid foundation in place allows for the magic to happen on stage no matter what. I am thankful for these skills because they guide me as a psychotherapist in being present, aware, and in the moment as sessions unfold for clients' experiences.

After college, my professional dance career took off with me performing in a company in Pittsburgh and then in New York City. All the choreographers I worked with helped shape my understanding of movement, emotion, and expression. They challenged me to dig deeper, be authentic, and be fully present. I learned a hard lesson as a professional dancer: if you ignore your body's warning signals and something doesn't feel right, it can lead to a serious injury, which is what happened to me. While I was injured and unable to dance, I started exploring the world of massage therapy, which I loved just as much as dance. I became energized to learn about the body in a new way and decided to leave the field of dance as my profession. Through massage therapy, I began to appreciate how the body moves and that taking care of the body is not a choice, it is essential. I started to understand that there is a deep connection between the body and the mind, and the two are intricately linked. As I worked with my clients, many started to recall being abused in their childhoods. My curiosity got the best of me, and I ended up taking an excellent somatic psychotherapy training with Pat Ogden, whose pioneering work has influenced thousands of therapists around the world. Through this training, I decided that understanding somatic psychology more fully was something I wanted to pursue and am grateful to Pat for encouraging me to go further with my studies.

After moving from New York City to Boulder, I began to study somatic psychology at Naropa University just for fun. Kekuni Minton, who also works with Pat Ogden, was my instructor and planted the seed to pursue a master's degree in somatic psychology. With his help, I enrolled in the master's program at Naropa University. I am thankful to all my instructors at Naropa , especially Christine Caldwell, Susan Aposhyan, Kekuni Minton, and Ryan Kennedy, for their teaching as well as their guidance to follow my passions in learning how to work with trauma. Their influences are felt throughout this book, and I am forever grateful for their openness to sharing their wisdom and knowledge with me.

After graduate school, I continued my journey on how to work with trauma by learning EMDR therapy. I am thankful to Francine Shapiro for discovering this powerful modality of healing trauma and sharing it with the world. I was lucky enough to connect with Molly Gierasch, an EMDR trainer in

Boulder, Colorado, who, upon meeting me, asked me to work with her. Under her guidance, I honed my skills as an EMDR therapist and consultant, eventually becoming an EMDR trainer myself. Molly influenced me to bring more of my somatic psychology knowledge into the world of EMDR therapy and I am grateful she believed in me.

As my skills as an EMDR therapist and consultant grew, the therapists I was consulting with encouraged me to write my first book, *EMDR Essentials: A Guide for Clients and Therapists*. This book was written for clients to learn what EMDR therapy is and what to expect from this therapeutic modality and has also helped therapists find ways to explain a complex psychotherapeutic modality in simpler terms. Next, I started developing advanced workshops for EMDR therapists with colleagues of mine who specialized in somatic psychology and EMDR therapy. I want to express thanks to Dr. Arielle Schwartz, Katie Asmus, and John Gray for developing meaningful advanced workshops with me so that EMDR therapists with no somatic background could gain more insights and skills to incorporate into their practices. Dr. Arielle Schwartz approached me about turning our workshops into a book, and I am grateful that she pursued this idea with me. Our book, *EMDR Therapy and Somatic Psychology: Interventions to Enhance Embodiment in Trauma Treatment*, took shape and was published in 2018. Our voices together have helped thousands of therapists and their clients become more embodied in their EMDR therapy practices.

Now, as I approached writing my third book, I was impacted by COVID-19 pandemic, and so have focused my work on helping therapists take care of themselves before, during, and after remote therapy sessions in an embodied way. As I started writing this book, I found myself unsure how to express what I knew was inside me. I felt that I had to be professional in how I wrote but knew my personal voice somehow needed to be included. As I shared my writings with a good friend, Jannett Matusiak, who is a beautiful writer, she encouraged me to write more from my personal voice to make the book more intimate, heartfelt, and embodied in my writing. I was scared to be this vulnerable, and I appreciate her gentle encouragement to take that risk. Her guidance changed the shape of the book, and I appreciate her being honest with her feedback. I also am indebted to Janette for helping me find Jesaka Long, my editor. When I first met Jesaka, my body resonated from head to toe that this woman would understand me, honor my words, and help guide me on this journey of writing another book. Her open heart, gentle guidance, and sensitive feedback helped me heal a deep wound around writing and accept that my personal voice was okay to share with the world. I am grateful that she has come into my life and now become an integral part of my support team.

In finding my voice through writing this book, I want to thank all the therapists who I have the honor and privilege of working with. Their experiences teach me daily and I am grateful they put their trust in me to guide and support them through their struggles as well as their successes. These therapists inspire me daily, give me purpose to my work, and make this book a reality.

Through writing this book, I found it essential to reach

out to my support team more regularly to help me find my center, ground, and support my process. I want to thank Dr. Sam Berne, a holistic eye doctor, who helped me take better care of my eyes as I struggled with sitting in front of a computer all day long. His belief that our eyes are a vital organ in the body needing attention and care inspires me to be gentler and more loving with my eyes. His wisdom is shared in this book so that others may incorporate simple practices to take better care of their eyes too.

I also want to thank Tanya Coon and Robyn Outram, who work remotely with me by challenging my limitations, helping me heal my traumas, and focusing my body, mind, and spirit to handle the ups and downs in my life. Their support, trust, and faith give me the strength to continue my journey of being authentic in my interactions and growing up into being the best version of myself I can be. As they have modeled to me that remote healing can be powerful, it has given me the courage to help therapists feel that connection is possible in remote therapy.

Through the process of writing, I took the risk of having two colleagues, Erin Staniszeski and Sarah Rose, both highly skilled therapists and consultants, give me feedback on whether therapists would find value in this book. I am grateful they selflessly took time out of their busy lives to read this early work and to let me know they were excited about my ideas and couldn't wait for the completed version. These two women are beautiful souls on this earth who bring tons of laughter into my life while also providing the support I need professionally. I want to thank them for being such an important part of my life.

I also want to thank my business coach, Craig Revord, who encourages me to be Big, Bold, Barb in everything I do. He has helped me face my fears, continue to think outside of the box, and follow my true passions. His support helped me have the courage to write this book, be vulnerable, and not hold back from sharing my ideas with a larger community.

On a more personal note, I want to thank my good friend, Dotty Uhl, who listens to me complain about how hard it is to write, lets me cry when I feel overwhelmed, and laughs with me until my cheeks hurt so bad I'm begging her to stop. She is a true friend who stands by my side, has witnessed the pains and joys throughout my life, and is there for me whenever I need. She is a true gift in my life.

Last, I could have never completed this book without the incredible support of my loving husband, Young Kim. He knew I was going to write this book even before I did. When we were first quarantined from due to the pandemic, he took a photo of me doing my first remote consultation session without me knowing it. When I completed the first draft of this book, and I started wondering what image I wanted on the cover, he looked at me and said, "I know exactly what should be on the cover; it's a photo of you." I welled up with tears knowing that he had been holding onto this secret for months, waiting for the right moment to surprise me. When he showed me the photo, I fell in love with it and knew that it had to be on the cover. I am deeply indebted to him for his willingness to brainstorm with me for hours, helping me formulate my ideas more succinctly, and encouraging me to finish this project. I appreciate his openness and willingness for me to share his experiences living in a systemic racist society that has caused tremendous pain for him. Young continues to be one of the most influential people in my life, and I can't imagine my world without him. He makes me a better person just by knowing him, and I am fortunate that we are business partners, and in a loving marriage. I look forward to spending more years together being playful, joyful, and, of course, full of dance.

INTRODUCTION

....

Therapy is a sacred dance between therapist and client.

....

FINDING HOPE

It is exactly one year from the day the COVID-19 Pandemic shutdown my training business for 3 months, where I find myself crying, wondering how I would survive this challenging time. I'm on my way home from work when I look at my phone and see twenty texts—which only happens when something terrible has happened. All of the messages say the same thing: "Are you okay?!!!" I am confused, wondering what on earth is going on? The last time something like this occurred, Boulder was flooding while I slept, and I had no idea until I saw all the texts asking how I was doing. Now, when I get home, I ask my husband Young what's going on, and he tells me there's been a shooting. We turn on the news and stare at the screen. I'm feeling dizzy, nauseous, and sad that ten people's lives were taken in just a blink of an eye. I do not believe this could happen in Boulder, my home, my safe place. My body shakes and trembles; tears stream down my face as I grieve the lost lives and realize it could have been me in *that* grocery store.

The mass shooting changed my world once again, leaving me struggling to find balance in a world full of violence, hate, and fear that's invaded my sense of safety—just like the unknown virus that had turned my life upside down in 2020. The day after the shooting, I had consultations scheduled that I needed to find a way to show up for even though I wanted to stay in bed and pull the covers over my head. My heart was heavy, grieving with pain; fear coursed through my body; and a sense of hopelessness took over. After a year of dealing with the pandemic's debilitating effects, I was once again feeling unstable and incapable of showing up for others. All I wanted to do was cancel my sessions and figure out how I was going take care of myself.

As I took a deep breath and attempted to face my day, I realized I was seeing a group of therapists who were in my training a year ago when I had to abruptly shut it down because it wasn't safe to finish in person. These therapists had not only completed their EMDR training during a pandemic but had continued to study, learn, and support each other while developing their skills. I felt a special bond with this group of therapists because they hung in with me as I struggled to learn how to complete their training in a remote setting. My learning curve was steep, and these brave therapists stood by my side, had compassion for my struggles, and continued to trust that I would help them learn EMDR therapy no matter what happened. These therapists were warriors who are strong, willing to face their fears, and be vulnerable with each other. I had to trust that they would once again have compassion for me as I struggled to show up for their consultation.

I started the session by telling them I was grieving, struggling, and not at 100% because of the mass shooting that occurred yesterday. I worried as I admitted my feelings that they would judge me and that I would disappoint them somehow. What happened next surprised me: they thanked me for modeling how to show up and be real even when it is challenging. As I owned my struggles and allowed myself to be vulnerable, they let themselves be vulnerable too. We were human beings existing together remotely, connecting in the safety of our group. I am so grateful to these therapists for showing me the power of being present and what that can do to foster connection, support, and a deep understanding of the human condition. I hope these therapists know that they teach me every time I work with them, that they are a gift, and that I treasure our interactions. It's therapists like these that give me a reason to get up every day and do what I do, which is sharing with them how to connect, be present, and create safety together during remote therapy.

In a world that feels unstable, people are traumatized daily. Trauma can be debilitating and, without help, can fester like an untreated wound. I struggle when I see trivial things like people fighting over PlayStations or hoarding paper products out of fear of not having enough for themselves. I am horrified by the violence I see on social media of people beating and killing other human beings because of their race, or because of the aftereffects from mass shootings. People are in pain and that pain sometimes spills over and permeates like a virus in communities, causing harm to others. When trauma is unattended, people operate from the most primitive part of their brain—a part that is not rational but rather wired for survival. These out-of-control reactions ripple across the nation through our communities, impacting families in debilitating ways and disrupting our sense of safety.

When I see these violent stories in the news, or I hear therapists in consultation sharing the traumas their clients are experiencing, I often feel anger, pain, and sadness. I long for a safe world. Through my own traumas, I can sometimes lose my sense of compassion and have to slow down my responses so that I can remind myself people are in pain, sometimes alone and suffering with unresolved traumas locked in their bodies and brains just like me.

Through my consulting with therapists, I have seen many of you struggle with the same issues I have of how to navigate what's happening in your personal life while still showing up for your professional life. Know that the stress you are under is real, palpable, and can sometimes rock you to your core, leaving you to feel that whatever you're dealing with is too big to handle. I want you to know that you are not alone and that other therapists are going through the same thing as you. Let yourself find a safe place where you can express yourself with other therapists who can help you not feel so alone, isolated, or feeling like you are carrying the weight of the world on your shoulders. By making yourself available to your clients' pains, you may feel the impact from the energy exchanged between you. Your own wellbeing can be at risk. This energy exchange can take a toll on you mentally, emotionally, physically, and spiritually if you don't reach out and get the support you need.

It's imperative to learn how to keep your practices sustainable, for yourself and your clients, especially as the need—and demand—for remote therapy continues. Even as COVID-19 vaccines provide hope, articles are published every day that show our nation is experiencing a mental health crisis from the isolation, fear, and unknowns that have come from communities having this virus. This news increases the demand for remote therapy so much that many therapists I know have a three-to-six-month waitlist. Many of you are overextending to meet the need of this crisis, stretching yourself too thin by seeing too many clients, adding to your sense of physical, mental, emotional, and spiritual exhaustion. Feeling guilty because the demand is so great will not serve any of your clients if you overextend yourself. Knowing how many clients you can safely see in a day is essential to honor and respect yourself, helping you remain vital in the dance of therapy. Trust that the gift of remote therapy is that clients can now broaden their search beyond your community and get the help they need. If you aren't currently offering remote therapy, it's very likely your clients will ask you to incorporate it into your practice.

I've had the honor of many of you trusting me to guide you in finding ways to take better care of yourselves as you provide remote therapy for your clients. In return, you keep teaching me that daily practices are not optional; rather, they are necessary to keep us vital, present, and capable of sustaining a remote therapy practice. As remote therapy becomes a standard part of offering psychotherapy, you'll need more support to handle the complexities of taking care of yourself through this process. You have to find ways to make remote therapy accessible, viable, and sustainable for both you and your clients. Putting more attention and care into how you prepare before, during, and after your remote therapy sessions is not an option; instead, it is essential to your wellbeing.

If you are the last on your "to-do" list, you may be over-giving in your sessions, which can lead to you feeling alone, empty, and burdened from taking on too much responsibility that isn't yours to take on. You have to create a way to put yourself first on your "to-do" list by practicing daily ways that refuel, replenish, and renew your bodymind. Taking time to practice regularly before, during, and after your remote therapy sessions can help you regulate your nervous system to be more adaptable, flexible, and resilient. The strain that inherently arises from remote sessions will be mitigated better through these practices, thus leading to less fatigue and burnout. Taking time to make sure you are a priority on your "to-do" list is essential in being able to sustain your remote therapy practice.

I have been sharing the practices detailed in this book with therapists during the pandemic, witnessing them embrace, embody, and change how they approach remote therapy. These therapists have reported they feel less fear and better rested at the end of the day and look forward to seeing their clients just like when they were doing in-person sessions. As these therapists have connected to their bodies and minds, they've found ways to help their clients do the same. A key component of this is trusting that the computer is a conduit for connection that can be felt, seen, and experienced in powerful ways. Those therapists who are seeking regular consultation, supervision, and their own therapy seem to be handling the pandemic's challenges better because they are note alone; rather, they are together with peers getting the support they need. They are tapping into a community that validates their experience, providing the support and nurturing that helps give them the confidence that remote therapy is an effective way of offering therapy. As they begin to emerge from the pandemic, they will also be better prepared to incorporate remote therapy as an ongoing part of their practice.

Therapists who are trying to do this work alone without any support are experiencing more remote fatigue, compassion fatigue, and burnout. It takes what I call "allies"—a community of mentors, colleagues, healers, family, and friends—to make it possible for therapists to be resilient in handling the unknowns sure to come tomorrow, next week, or even next year for themselves and their clients.

If you are suffering and feeling alone, now is the time to reach out and find ways to get support and gather your community. Get consultation, supervision, or your own therapy to work through any blocks or unresolved childhood traumas that may be impacting your work, or to learn how to handle times when your community is traumatized in unthinkable ways. Remember, you are human, just like your clients, and you need to get as much support as your clients do. As you better prepare yourself and your clients for remote therapy (whether you're just getting started or planning for the long-term), you will experience a greater sense of confidence as well as more energy, and joy in your work.

The field of psychotherapy has changed forever because of the pandemic and has changed you in the process. I realize for some of you there are real barriers that will prevent you from integrating remote therapy into your practices. Some clients do not have access to computers, high speed internet, or struggle with language barriers. These significant hurdles are a bigger, systemic issue and we don't any have clear answers or solutions. We do need to acknowledge them, but it shouldn't stop you from offering therapy remotely for clients who do have access. If you are changing your practice or learning how to work remotely, incorporating the practices in this book can help you have a sustainable remote therapy practice. I know that once the pandemic is over, many of you will return to your therapy offices, relieved to get back to "normal." On the other hand, some of you may have found that there are benefits to offering remote therapy and will never go back to in-person sessions or may develop a hybrid model of offering both options to your clients. There is no right or wrong to this decision. You need to find what best fits your life and how you work. I do encourage you consider all of your possibilities and not shut off an option like remote therapy because of fears it's not as effective as in-person therapy.

As you continue with your purpose of helping clients transform their pain, see if you can enjoy the practices detailed in this book to support you in providing safe, connected, and effective ways of doing remote therapy sessions. Each step of this remote therapy dance has been laid out for you to try on, explore, and tap into your intuition so that you can nurture your body and soul. This book also brings you the experiences of your fellow therapists, which hopefully assures you that we can support each other: we are remote together. By paying attention to your and your clients' nervous systems, you'll take better care of yourself, have more energy for your work, and be capable of giving more compassion to your clients. As you integrate these practices into your life, you'll eliminate remote fatigue and find a sustainable way to feel supported together as you offer remote therapy sessions.

FINDING MY DANCE

After a long day of work, I sat across from my business partner Young—who happens to also be my husband—and I said to him, "How did we get here?" Our lives had changed in the blink of an eye because of COVID-19, a horrific world crisis. As we struggled to understand what had happened, our conversations reflected how we felt like we were living in a nightmare, swirling around in a rocky storm, and our hope that tomorrow we would wake up to find that our lives were back to normal. I would wake up with energy, ready to go to my office to teach and consult, while Young worked in our home office to keep our business running smoothly. We would wake up to find each day was different from the next, yet oddly somehow the same; it was a new *abnormal* every day. Time seemed to have stretched in a surreal way like a Salvador Dali painting, leaving us confused about what day, month, or even year it was.

Regardless of the day, we felt stuck in that rocky storm— and now our ship had lots of holes in it, and every time we thought we had patched one hole, there was another one that would pop up, demanding attention. Before the pandemic, our ship was sailing smoothly in a rhythm that allowed us to flow gently with the waves. Now, Young and I were out of sync, making huge decisions daily that exhausted us beyond our capacities. Each decision, each change instigated by the pandemic felt debilitating and like a blow to our ship.

For the last 10 years we have offered EMDR trainings to therapists around the country as well as consultation to help them build their skills in EMDR therapy from a somatic approach. These trainings typically are held in large spaces with up to 30 people per training, and because of being quarantined, we could no longer offer those trainings safely and keep the standards of the CDC codes. Our trainings were immediately shut down, leaving us floundering about how we would financially survive this storm.

Not teaching impacted my sense of who I am in the world, my purpose, and my mission. I felt as if I had my hands tied behind my back, and any forward movement came screeching to a halt. There were days I felt so overwhelmed by the world's enormous pain that I didn't feel I could make a good decision with the business. I struggled to take care of myself, including deciding what to eat and what to wear; figuring out the next steps for our business was beyond my capacity. My ability to tolerate this pain in my body consumed me to the point I would sometimes wake up sobbing uncontrollably with no idea how I could function that day. This pain I was feeling was highly disorganizing and distressing. I was confused, anxious, panicky, and grieving for my loss. I knew that I had to find a way to regulate my nervous system better and avoid being swallowed by the stormy ocean waters.

Under quarantine orders, I moved my office into Young's home office to keep myself safe. The move was challenging for both of us. He felt I was invading his space, that my presence was distracting and disorienting for him. Meanwhile, I couldn't find a place for all the things I needed to function daily without interrupting his flow. I am used to a large space in my own office that I have all to myself when not teaching. I like to spread all my projects out across a table, organizing myself for the day. Then, at the end of the day, I put everything back into its assigned place so I have a fresh start the next morning. Being in someone else's space created new challenges that neither of us liked. In an instant, we both felt lost, with nothing grounding us. I was highly anxious, full of fear of the unknown. My nervous system felt wired—like I was ready to jump out of my skin—and I couldn't find rest in my body.

Our home transformed into a workplace 24-hours a day, and we lost our boundaries between work and home. All of our trainings were disrupted at the same time, causing chaos and confusion. We had no idea how long the COVID virus would last or when we could get back to normal. Our workflow was overwhelming, choppy, and hard to organize. Making a tough decision on how to proceed with each training became tedious, complicated, and tremendously stressful. We found ourselves working longer hours, with little to show for it. Exhausted, our self-care suffered because of the urgency to get things back to normal, which was utterly impossible. We became short-tempered with each other and found we had little tolerance for what the other person wanted or needed. In simply trying to survive, we lost our connection to who we were as individuals, as a married couple, and as business partners. We found that our nervous systems were struggling to regulate with no end in sight for the pandemic. Our stress levels were beyond what was possible or right for either one of us to tolerate—like so many other couples. We quickly learned we needed a new way to communicate, one that would be kind and compassionate as we worked independently yet together under the same roof. This new language had to create safety for both of us, and we realized that language was through dance.

Young and I met years ago and fell in love on the dance floor while dancing Argentine tango. Dancing became our place for pure expression of love, joy, and passion. When we dance, we have huge grins on our faces from the pure pleasure of being with each other, of communicating in this nonverbal way. Now, due to the pandemic, we had to find a new vocabulary, to create a different kind of dance separately yet still together. We had to coordinate our movements within a limited space so that both of us had a voice. Part of the dance was figuring out who was leading or following at different times. We had to see which one of us had more energy to push and which one of us needed to have a gentler flow. This dance had to make room for both of us to be equal yet autonomous. This familiar yet new language helped us find a rhythm that worked for both of us. Our movements turned into a beautiful improvisation that made our interactions joyful, playful, more at ease. We found ways to communicate that were respectful and honored each other's needs and wants. We improvised our new dance every day, which fueled our curiosity and led to an overflowing of creative ideas to support our business. It brought more support to each of our nervous systems, helping us find more relaxation in our bodies, relieving some of the pain and discomfort. We learned that we had to take our time and sense our bodies in relationship to ourselves *and* each other. This is how we found a new way to communicate during the quarantine.

As I struggled to find balance personally and professionally, therapists were reaching out to me, wondering how to do EMDR therapy remotely. I was inundated with questions from therapists struggling to learn a new way of working. This transition from in-person to remote sessions felt insurmountable to many therapists because they were experiencing so much at one time. Not only did they have to deal with the realities of the pandemic's impact on their families, they also had to cope with moving their offices into their homes as well as learning how to use new technology, and then making sure they practiced therapy safely. Accepting this new abnormal was complicated and hard to navigate for many of them.

Opening my inbox, I would stare at all the emails and questions, feeling my body freeze from my overwhelm. Answering each of these emails one by one was just too much for me to handle by myself. I knew that I had the answers therapists were looking for, and I needed a way to reach them that could ground both myself and them at the same time. I had to first snap out of my daze from trauma and loss, then ground myself using all the somatic skills essential for therapists to be effective.

Once I was grounded and felt the support from my body, I was able to see what struggles therapists were experiencing and how exactly to respond. I decided to write a blog post entitled "The 8 Phases of Remote EMDR Therapy." In this blog post, I compiled all the questions that EMDR therapists asked and wrote a step-by-step guide to offering remote sessions safely.

My heart and soul poured into every word I wrote so that the blog was genuine, and real. As therapists began learning how to do remote therapy, I asked each of them to step into their power and lead by example by not running away from this new challenge. Therapists were out of their comfort zones, and my job was to help them see that I believed in them and their ability to handle this challenge. The response to this blog post was tremendous, and many therapists thanked me for guiding them on their journey into this unknown world of remote therapy.

Once I wrote the remote EMDR therapy blog post, I let therapists know that I was more available for remote consultation since I could no longer offer trainings. I wanted to provide as much support as possible because I could see that therapists were in distress, feeling alone and isolated due to their struggles. As I started consulting more, I discovered that even though I had mapped out steps for therapists in the blog post, many still struggled with the "how to," not feeling equipped to implement these changes. Many of these therapists' resistance to offering remote therapy led them to shut their therapy practices, hoping that normalcy would return quickly. I understood this resistance deeply since I struggled for years, making my practice remote even before the pandemic started. And then, during the pandemic, I had to adapt my business again.

The first time I faced the idea of taking my practice remote, I felt very attached to my work and only offered in-person sessions since my focus was on somatic therapy. Ultimately, working with people strictly in-person was limiting the growth of my business. I could only teach or consult with therapists who were more local, meaning either I had to travel to them, or they had to travel to me. Travel issues then constrained the business and limited where and how I worked. It was impossible to work with therapists interested in consulting with me who lived out of state unless I switched to remote sessions.

Over the years, Young has been my leader, gently guiding me to try something new and branch out of the small, comfortable, safe zone of how I like to work. I had to face my fears and embrace the big scary world of technology. However, by overcoming my fears to learn and grow through using technology, our business expanded, and we were able to hire more remote workers. Our remote workers, including a customer support person, a lawyer, accountant, and graphic designer, created more support for the two of us. As the business expanded, our consultants also found working remotely more convenient. It was easier for them to fit more work into their schedules thanks to less travel time. We were able to work with therapists across the country and provide services to a more diverse population. By creating this support foundation, we could concentrate on what our gifts were within the business and avoid white knuckling tasks that drained us mentally and emotionally.

One of my most significant roadblocks to achieving this change was embracing that healing and connection can occur in many forms. The practice of healing is both evolutionary and also inevitable because the ability to heal is vital and innate to all living beings. Human beings require safety, empathy, and compassion to heal themselves. For most human civilizations, this typically happened in-person, making proximity to a healer vital for communities to survive. As humans evolved, developing language and writing, the practice of healing could shared over long distances, with many communities, and passed through generation after generation. The rise of remote communications technology made it possible for the practice of healing and finding a connection available to anyone, anywhere, anytime. Remote therapy may be the answer for people suffering right now, providing the ability to remain connected even in times of social distancing, masks, and restrictions to that connection. Therefore, feeling a connection *is* possible and can be a game-changer for therapists if they genuinely understand that remote therapy can make it a reality.

With this understanding of how healing works, I knew I had to figure out why many therapists resisted remote therapy and then resource them so they could find value in this work. Remote therapy is not a new concept and has been around for years. There is research (Varker, Brank, Ward, Terhaag & Phelps, 2019) to support remote therapy as viable and effective for working with anxiety, depression, and posttraumatic stress disorder. My job was to help therapists understand that what they have to offer right now, at this moment, is valuable. They could not wait until that "someday" came, to get back in the office for in-person sessions. Clients needed treatment right then—and they will continue to need remote therapy in the future.

Along with collecting all the questions therapists had regarding the "how to" of remote therapy, I began to track that therapists struggled to show up for their sessions physically, mentally, emotionally, and spiritually. They were exhausted, scared, and dysregulated. Therapists were so busy worrying about their clients that they weren't even aware that *they* were struggling to breathe, to be grounded in their bodies, or to acknowledge that they were afraid for themselves as the pandemic impacted their lives. It became clear to me there were significant emotional issues at play. I had to figure out which specific issues were exhausting the therapists and give them skills to help them feel more in control of their fear, anxieties, and worries. For me to help them professionally, the therapists needed to slow down and identify what was happening for them personally.

I quickly learned that the blog post I wrote merely scratched the surface of what was going on for the therapists contacting me. It wasn't just remote EMDR therapy they feared; they needed somatic skills that could regulate and ground their own nervous systems. My skills as a somatic psychotherapist were being called upon to help therapists become more aware of what was happening inside their own bodies, minds, and spirits; to feel connected to themselves and their clients. Therapists needed to become grounded, emotionally stable, and remain confident in their skills while helping their clients feel safe, connected, and supported in remote therapy.

Many therapists do not have somatic skills because countless schools do not include somatic work in their curriculum or even require it to conduct therapy. I've found over the years, as a teacher and consultant, that therapists are hungry for somatic work and are shocked when they discover that they didn't learn this in school. When therapists begin to understand there is wisdom in the body, they begin to view their clients and themselves more holistically, addressing all aspects of a person. Right now, in the field of psychotherapy, there has been a significant shift, and somatic psychology is beginning to get the recognition it deserves. When I was getting my master's back in the 1990s somatic psychology was seen as strange, weird, and quite frankly not well respected. Over time these views have changed, particularly with the work of Bessel van der Kolk, a world-renowned trauma expert, showing there is neuroscience backing up the importance of why the body is essential in therapy (2015). With this recognition, therapists around the world are now searching and longing for more somatic interventions to incorporate into their practice.

By creating a safe place for therapists to express their overwhelming feelings, I helped them recognize how the pandemic impacted them personally and professionally. The challenges therapists faced were real and difficult to manage by themselves. Like so many people, therapists lost feeling safe in their offices and had to work from home, encountering new challenges with their families and therapy practices. Learning how to use technology made some therapists feel their sessions were cold and distant, making it hard to connect with their clients. For some therapists, these challenges initially felt insurmountable, leaving them traumatized as they were trying to do the work. Many therapists' fears took over to the point where they forgot the skills they already possessed, resulting in them feeling helpless and incompetent.

Through consulting with therapists, I found that the more open and vulnerable I was with my struggles, the more it humanized me, and the therapists began opening up to me on a deeper level. I shared how I regulate my nervous system before, during, and after sessions, which seemed like new information for them. My mission was to show them that the pandemic impacted *everyone*—including us—on deep levels. They had to turn their focus inward, acknowledge what was happening for them, and find resources that helped them feel strong, competent, and capable of conducting remote therapy. Only then would they be able to help their clients deal with the chaos, anxiety, fears, and dysregulation of their nervous systems.

As clients came into sessions feeling unsettled due to the pandemic changes, the racial unrest in their communities, and the instability and chaos from political upheaval, their stories matched the therapists' same experiences. Remote traumatization occurred daily as we all watched social media feeds, where disturbing images of people being murdered, harassed, or bullied, or dying from COVID-19 impacted clients and therapists profoundly. Social distancing, wearing masks, and getting our temperatures taken were becoming a part of our new abnormal. The ability to touch, sense, and feel other humans was taken away on a profound level, leaving many to feel alone, isolated, and fearful of their surroundings. The therapists' traumas matched those of their clients, making it difficult for many therapists to manage. Without awareness and resourcing, therapists were experiencing extreme exhaustion by the end of the day.

What became clear to me was that therapists needed more support than ever. They needed grounding, guidance, and a safe place to express their fears, worries, and the pains that made it so hard to show up as an effective therapist. Therapists can feel like they must have it all together, be perfect, and never make mistakes with their clients. They are not superhumans; instead, they are human beings going through life with real struggles just like their clients.

As therapists felt safe enough with me to share what was happening for them, I began to identify patterns hindering and hurting therapists in their remote therapy practices. Many were putting on a brave face that everything was okay, when, really, they were suffering, feeling alone, and falling apart inside. While trying to deal with the stressors of learning a new way of working, sharing matching traumas with their clients, and feeling that they didn't have the skills to do remote sessions, therapists also forgot to take care of themselves. For some, their normal routines were disrupted entirely, were no longer working, or were nonexistent. Consequently, therapists felt like they were running on empty and found it challenging to have compassion for their clients. All of these challenges were contributing to their extreme exhaustion and remote fatigue.

My job required three key components: (1) help therapists recognize that they have been impacted immensely by the pandemic: (2) guide them in offering remote sessions that were alive, dynamic, and fulfilling; (3) support them in connecting to themselves so as to replenish their bodies and minds. Just as I had to reconnect myself to my body and find skills that could regulate me all day, I had to help therapists figure out what they could do before, during, and after their remote sessions.

Through this connection, therapists reported a shift, believing that remote therapy could be done safely in a grounded and supported way that allowed them to increase their ability to be more present with their clients. As a result, these therapists' remote fatigue began to lessen, and they felt more in control, capable, and competent with their work. Therapists also discovered that as they deepened their connection to themselves, they would feel more connected with their clients—even though they were looking at a computer screen. The work they engaged in with me helped them begin to "sense" and "feel" their clients without relying on their sight as the only way to perceive another human being.

All of you have experienced the power of healing long distance, whether you've sent a prayer to someone afar, given a get-well card to someone who's sick, sent flowers to show your appreciation, or mailed a care package hoping it might brighten someone's day. This energy exchange is full of meaning and emotion; it connects humans through the body's felt sense. The practice of healing from a distance is as ancient as a shaman sharing medicinal instructions with a family in a faraway village and as modern as a therapist seeing a client using remote technology during a pandemic. Whether it's through the telephone, letters, emails, or videoconferencing, it is possible, now more than ever, to provide healing to anyone, anywhere, anytime.

COVID-19 has changed the field of psychotherapy forever and these alterations will be an integral part of therapy for years to come. As I have faced my fears of learning how to teach across long distances, I've found that I am enjoying this way of teaching more than I could have ever imagined. When the pandemic is over, I know that I will continue to offer remote trainings because therapists have expressed that they like learning this way. To my surprise, the feedback I have consistently received from therapists is that because I teach from a grounded, connected, present place in my own body, they are sensing and feeling more in their bodies than they ever thought possible. Therapists working with me could identify what was blocking their ability to embrace remote therapy; it was their struggle to believe that connection is possible beyond a computer screen. What therapists need and long for is support, guidance, and practices that help them feel more empowered and capable of doing this work.

My friends who know me well are laughing as they see this book since I swore I would never write another book again. Writing is quite challenging for me because I have learning difficulties that impact my skills to put words on the page. When I was a young child, I struggled with my studies, and my mother would tell me, "You just aren't as smart as everyone else; you will have to work twice as hard to accomplish what others do to succeed." She had good intentions when she said this to me; however, I internalized the feeling of being stupid, different, and that something was inherently wrong with me. When I was growing up, the words "learning disorder" weren't in my vocabulary, and I believed I had to work harder than others to achieve what I wanted. My learning difficulties include flipping letters, words, numbers, and sentence structures when I write, making it difficult to communicate my ideas on paper.

During my graduate program, the number of papers I had to write was overwhelming. Every paper assignment took me at least four rewrites before I could hand it in to be reviewed by my instructors. I had to schedule when every paper was due and work backward to accomplish all the rewrites and still get the paper completed on time. The anxiety, worry, and shame I felt were exhausting. Many students made fun of me as a "goody-two-shoes, anal, uptight, kiss ass" because I always had my papers in on time. They did not know how much I was suffering to keep up the façade that writing came easy to me.

After graduate school, a friend of mine was conducting a research project for her Ph.D. program on learning and memory and asked me to volunteer. Once I completed the test, she took a long deep breath and looked me straight in the eye, and then asked, "Barb, do you know you have a learning disorder?" I was in shock; my body was vibrating from head to toe. I could finally make sense of my life. The revelation that I had a learning disorder was like discovering a jigsaw puzzle where all the pieces beautifully fit together. I could understand why I've struggled so hard over the years. Finally, I knew that my struggles had nothing to do with my intelligence, and now I could enter into writing with more compassion for myself and my process.

What compelled me to write again—*to write another book*—was realizing if I don't, I'll regret not sharing what I know with therapists who could benefit from my journey and discoveries over the years, especially given all we've experienced through the pandemic. Throughout this book, I will share some of my personal experiences to help illustrate the concepts of working somatically in remote therapy. I want you, *dear reader*, to know that I, too, have struggled and continue to find things that challenge me to grow. I will also share stories from therapists who have grappled with their remote therapy practices and together have taught me how to work remotely in successful and satisfying ways. My hope is that these stories are relatable so that you can see yourself in this book and find ways to tap into your own resiliency as you practice remotely. To protect therapists' and clients' confidentiality, the stories shared within this book are composites of several individuals I've seen in consultation. I have changed all identifying details to protect everyone's privacy and anonymity.

I am grateful that you've been brave enough to pick up this book to read and hope you embrace the value of offering remote therapy sessions. Working with therapists so closely, I have seen how their pain, fears, and struggles contribute to experiencing remote fatigue. As you read this book, I hope you begin to notice where you may feel blocked in offering remote sessions and see how to resource yourself around this block, which might be getting in your way of actually enjoying practicing remote therapy. By incorporating daily practices before, during, and after your sessions that connect, support, and nourish your bodymind, you'll find ways to help prevent remote fatigue, thus making your practice more sustainable. As you apply the practices I have outlined in this book, you'll feel less fatigued by the confines of working in front of a computer all day. You will also become more conscious of your traumas that may get activated during sessions and learn how to better care for yourself. As you develop a strong daily practice, you'll be able to guide, cultivate, and help your clients better regulate their nervous systems.

All of the practices in this book are for you to explore, experiment, and incorporate in ways that have meaning and purpose in your life. Allow your unique internal wisdom to shine through; this will guide you to what feels right for you and your clients. Consider this an invitation for you to find what helps nourish, support, and replenish your bodymind. I hope this book remains a guide for you in practicing remote therapy safely beyond the pandemic. As the future unfolds, "unknowns" continue to wait for therapists. By practicing the skills in this book, your nervous system will become more adaptive, flexible, and responsive to those challenges.

As you read this book, please take your time to sense, feel, and reflect on what resonates in your body. Let the stories wash over you so that you can discover things about yourself, such as where you may be holding back or feeling challenged or constricted in your remote therapy practice. Remember times when you have overcome adversity and how those strengths can help guide you in times of distress. See what practices in this book can help you feel more secure, connected, and present with yourself and your clients. Note the differences you feel as you incorporate these practices and watch any remote fatigue wash away. Remember that with remote therapy, the possibility of saving a life is just a click away. The more prepared you are to offer remote therapy, the better experience you and your clients will have for years to come. Through these practices you'll see that you're not alone in your journey and, though remote, you can find support, nourishment, and enjoyment in your remote therapy practice for years to come.

~ *Barb Maiberger*

MY JOURNEY TO REMOTE

....

Therapy requires a continual
exploration of the unknown.

....

MY RESISTANCE TO WORKING REMOTELY

Throughout my life, I have had a deep passion for learning and understanding the human psyche. I discovered this when I fell in love with movement and expressing my joys and pains through dance. Knowing that a simple gesture could make an audience lose their breath, feel their heart ache, or roar with laugher so hard they cried helped me grasp the power of nonverbal communication. After a severe injury early on in my dance career, I decided to leave the professional dance world to explore massage therapy. Through this exploration, I learned techniques to assess how people hold tension patterns in their posture, muscles, and cells. With my hands as finely tuned instruments, I could feel, sense, and explore how these patterns held muscular pain for the client as well as the psychological distress of unresolved traumas. Over time, I learned that unresolved traumas are stored in the body, impacting people physically, mentally, emotionally, and spiritually. This "need" to know more about my clients' underlying traumas then led me to study somatic psychology.

Through somatic psychology, I discovered that humans are incredibly complicated and that 60%–70% of all communication is nonverbal. That means that only working with the body, or only working with the mind, was an incomplete way of approaching trauma in therapy. Therefore, honoring the bodymind connection allows for a deeper, more profound healing so that clients can feel resolved with what has happened in their past, feel more present in the here and now, and find resiliency for their future. Through my studies, Bessel van der Kolk, a world-renowned expert in working with trauma, introduced me to EMDR therapy. He shared some of his experiences using this modality in one of his lectures, which excited me tremendously. As I explored this idea of learning EMDR therapy, I found the somatic psychology field was anti-EMDR therapy. Someone I trusted told me EMDR therapy was a fad, would retraumatize a client, and that it would drive trauma deeper into a client's organs, causing even more distress and pain. I vowed then that I would never learn EMDR therapy and gave it no more thought.

Yes, I kept hearing about EMDR therapy over the years. I ignored that it could be a viable form of therapy until a different colleague I trusted introduced me to it once again. She was so excited about what she was seeing in her practice that she piqued my curiosity—I just had to learn more. She offered me a practice session whereby the end of it, I was surprised as I felt my body, mind, and spirit shift on a deep and profound level. That session changed the course of my life in ways I would never have predicted. I had such a profound experience with EMDR therapy that I immediately sought out learning this modality to find a way to bring this gift to my clients. As I embraced EMDR therapy, I was fortunate enough to have a fantastic mentor, Molly Gierasch, who took me under her wings, helping me grow as a therapist, consultant, teacher, and human being. I eventually moved into becoming an EMDR trainer under her expert guidance. At that point, I devoted my life to teaching other therapists the power of EMDR therapy, integrating my somatic skills into this work.

As I stepped into becoming an EMDR trainer, I had no idea that I would also have to become an entrepreneur and learn how to be in my power as a businessperson. I just didn't understand the magnitude of running a business versus being a therapist in private practice. Without any business training, I quickly was in over my head. I was trying to balance teaching, consulting, and seeing clients while also being responsible for marketing, bookkeeping, scheduling, and so much more. I was a one-woman show of something I had no idea how to manage. The stress of wearing so many hats at one time was beginning to take its toll on me. After months of pushing to handle everything on my plate, I woke up early one morning, experiencing a full-on panic attack. My heart started racing, my breathing became rapid and shallow, and soon I thought I would die. Young sat by my side and gently stroked my back, just guiding me to slow down and breathe. As my breathing started to regulate and I became more oriented to the room, I began to sob deeply. I felt torn in so many directions; I couldn't see a clear path for myself. I had overextended myself energetically, and I couldn't get my footing on how to handle all that I had created. I loved my work, and yet I was overwhelmed by the magnitude of it. I was trying to be a superwoman without the skills to back it up. My life was totally out of balance, and I couldn't see a way out.

Through Young's gentle guidance, I began to see that my energy was too dispersed and that I would have to let something go in order to focus my energy. I had to figure out how I could best bring my gifts to the world without sacrificing myself. As I checked in with my body, I quickly assessed that my energy was flowing toward teaching and less toward working directly with therapy clients. I knew then that it was time to let go of my private practice, which was a heart-wrenching decision. I loved my clients and was honored to work with every one of them, and yet, something was pulling me in a different direction. This shift meant I could have a more significant impact by working with more people. The more therapists I trained to work with trauma safely, the bigger the ripple effect of healing I could create and hopefully make a significant impact on the world. As I started to speak my truth, my panic subsided, my breathing returned to normal, and I could see a path for what I needed to do next.

Making this decision was a massive relief in my bodymind; however, it did not resolve the issue of me not knowing how to run a business of this size. Even though I'd let go of my private practice, I remained overwhelmed and continued drowning in my need to be a superwoman. Young, who had a strong background in business and was in between jobs, saw my struggle and graciously stepped in temporarily to show me what I didn't know. I began to rely on him more and more, seeing his strengths and how much his expertise was helping support my business. After a couple of years of working together, the idea of temporary was no longer valid: he had become an integral part of the business, and we decided to partner.

Then the business grew faster than either of us had anticipated, leading us both to feel burdened because our jobs and workload grew beyond our capacities. The strain on our bodies and minds began to impact our business relationship and our marriage. We hit a breaking point. We knew deep inside ourselves that if we didn't hire more help, the business wouldn't survive, and it may even destroy our marriage. We agreed that the option of ruining our marriage for the sake of a business wasn't worth the price. But this agreement meant we had to take a considerable risk: trust other people. Young and I are both self-reliant and struggle with handing over projects to others to complete the way we want.

We had to transform our relationships to our business in order to thrive and find more balance as well as joy in our marriage. We made a list of our "wants" and what needed to happen to support our business. Young suggested I stop renting spaces just because they were cheap and, instead, invest in a work "home" by creating a training center. By renting other spaces, such as conference rooms in therapy agencies, co-working spaces, or spaces in community centers, I was at the mercy of other people's agendas; these interruptions made it challenging to develop safety in a somatic training. I found myself stressed and my energy drained after each three-day group training, just from dealing with what was happening in the physical training space. I wanted to focus my energy on the participants rather than waste it on handling unpredictable circum-stances beyond my control.

My fear of a space being "too expensive" was holding me back from having what I wanted. I was deathly afraid if we committed to our own training space, we would end up in debt, which would cause us to lose our personal home, and, thus, be homeless in a couple of months. Young kept assuring me that we could afford a space and that the training's quality would increase if I were less stressed. I had to trust, let go of my fears, and put in place something that would be good for me—and the business. Change is scary, and I had to find a way to work through it. I gave in and leaped forward, trusting that we would indeed be okay. We found a workable space that I could train and consult in, allowing me to ground my body, mind, and spirit. While I had found a new business "home," Young, on the other hand, decided that he needed the flexibility of working remotely so that he could work from home, a coffee shop, or a coworking space whenever he wanted. Working in separate spaces gave us autonomy and suited each of our personalities. I felt like I had more control of the trainings, and he felt free to work the way that best suited him.

ONE STEP AT A TIME

Now that both of us felt grounded in our workspaces, the challenge became automating our business, which meant becoming more remote so we could streamline our practices. Just the mention of automating and becoming more remote made my body cringe and I could barely tolerate the sensations, so I decided that this kind of change was a bad idea. I am a people person and kinesthetic, and I needed to touch and feel everything I was doing. I didn't want to change anything, and my stubbornness got in the way. Young gently broached the subject of transitioning parts of the business, and I quickly shut down the conversation, distracting him, and pushing to discuss how we could make the current system work more efficiently, which of course, was the problem.

Young felt that my reliance on my Day-Timer held me back and complicated my scheduling. If I didn't have my Day-Timer with me, I didn't know what was planned next. Young would gently bring up how my Day-Timer was heavy, took up a lot of space, and was not convenient for travel. I was complaining daily about how cumbersome my Day-Timer was to use, and at the same time, felt defensive because he was suggesting I use a digital format. He patiently explained the advantages of going digital: I could have my calendar with me at all times, makes changes quickly, and it would be much lighter to carry. My resistance was overwhelming! I'm a tactile person, so I loved the feel and smell of the leather cover, keeping my calendar available, and writing with a mechanical pencil to quickly make changes to my schedule as it continually changed. The act of writing in my Day-Timer gave each appointment weight and made each session feel important. I carried this bulky, heavy calendar system for years because it made me feel professional, like I had my life in control.

I truly felt how precious my Day-Timer was when I first moved to Boulder, Colorado, and someone stole it during a burglary. I had just arrived from New York City and never dreamed that something like this would happen. With my Day-Timer gone, I felt as if my life had ended. I was angry, confused, hurt, and deeply grieving, longing for the comfort of my old friend to reappear. I felt incapable of getting over the fact that my beautiful system was gone. The thought of finding a new Day-Timer was daunting. How could I ever replace the one I loved with another one? However, I had to push through this grief and find a replacement because I needed to have a system for scheduling my clients. I searched for a new Day-Timer, hoping to find the exact one I had owned. With each store I visited, my heart sank a little deeper into despair: my old Day-Timer just didn't exist anymore. I had to let go of this expectation and start my search all over again, opening myself to the idea I could find something that would please me just as much. The only way to do this was to stop comparing what was and embrace what was possible. By opening up to this process, I was able to find a new Day-Timer that had the right "feel" in weight as well as a color that soothed me and, of course, could hold my new mechanical pencil. I was back in business!

A few years later, as I started traveling more for work, I would carry my trusty Day-Timer, reading material, and training manuals in my backpack. As you probably guessed, my backpack was heavy! It made each trip feel cumbersome and hurt my body. Yet I refused to put any of my materials in my checked baggage out of fear that I would lose everything. After every trip, I complained about my weighty backpack, and Young grew more frustrated that I was unwilling to try something new that would make my life easier.

One day, Young surprised me with a Kindle to help lighten my load while traveling. Initially, I was upset that he gave me this gift but felt I had to use it so I wouldn't hurt his feelings. I reluctantly decided to give the Kindle a test run at home out of fear that I wouldn't like it when I was traveling. To my surprise, I fell in love with it. I was excited to carry it in my backpack instead of having a heavy book that weighed me down. Once I had adapted to and accepted the convenience of carrying a Kindle, Young once again broached the tender topic of giving up my precious Day-Timer. He pointed out that I could have my Kindle and my calendar on one device, lightening my load in the backpack even more. Young's reasoning was sound, so I gave in and took the risk to become more digital. The switch to an iPad was easier than I could have ever dreamed of, and I quickly said good-bye to my once-precious Day-Timer. I embraced this new technology with open arms and was grateful for Young's patience and that he did not give up despite me being so stubborn over the years.

As I started to use the new technology, I quickly discovered there was more for me to learn. I was accustomed to offering my consultations in-person or by phone and was afraid to switch to videoconferencing. Our business grew, so I worked with more therapists around the country, and I saw the demand for me to change my in-person and phone consultation sessions to video-conferencing. However, my resistance to change continued to be a challenge, an obstacle to advancing our business. Logically, I knew that videoconferencing would provide a more enriching communication method than phone sessions and would add a tremendous benefit to the participants. I would be able to see, hear, sense, and feel the therapists finding their way of learning new material. Still, I resisted this change every step of the way, dragging my feet, not allowing change to occur. I just couldn't get past doing things the way I had always done them, and this change was pushing me to my edge. I wasn't allowing for the trainings to evolve because of my deep-seated fear that things needed to stay the same so that *I* felt safe. After many conversations with Young, I finally agreed to try something new as an experiment over many months.

I quickly discovered that the benefits outweighed my outdated fear. To my surprise, once again, I embraced videoconferencing technology! I loved being able to see the participants and interact with them visually. Instead of just hearing a voice float through the air on phone sessions, I could feel and see the connection between us, which made the interaction more satisfying. I decided all the consultations from that point forward would be remote, making it easier and more convenient to work with a broader range of therapists around the country.

The next challenge of automating our business was to examine how we were conducting our marketing and then find a way to update our outdated system. I was "old school," using printed flyers and postcards that involved many laborious steps to make our marketing campaigns work. I was in charge of writing all the content, designing the postcards, having them printed at a copy shop, buying a mailing list, and driving to another city to have them mailed. I was attached to this process because this was how my predecessor did all her marketing. However, I had no control over the mailing lists, and stacks of postcards would be returned as "undeliverable," making me worried that I was wasting too much time, energy, and money. Young and I would spend countless hours arguing about this process because he saw how inefficient it was and how stressed it made me.

As Young made new suggestions that could streamline our process, my body would contract, my throat would constrict, and, again, I worried that we would spend more money than we could afford. One of his suggestions was to hire a graphic designer to create the postcards for a more professional, dynamic look. Then he wanted to find better ways to manage the mailing lists that we were buying as well as use an online service for printing and mailing. This would make our marketing more efficient. After months of going round and round with this problem, I was exhausted and finally agreed that we had to try something new. After only a few short months, we were both amazed at how much time, money, and energy we were saving. Our marketing became more practical, fewer postcards came back undelivered—and I had more energy for teaching and consulting. Each step we put in place paid off for both of us.

We weren't done. The next significant change to streamline the business was investing in a cloud-based system for sharing files. This system was a real game-changer for us because I could work on a document at my office, save it in the cloud-based system so that Young could immediately access it, and then work on it without any delay. Before the cloud, I had to print out what I was working on and bring it home for Young to look at, only to realize that he wouldn't have time to work on it until the following day. Then, the next day, I would come home tired after a long day, dreading that I would have to meet with Young to go over what he had accomplished that day. I was tired and wanted to end my day, resenting that I had to continue working when all I wanted was to be home, relaxing. I was less open to feedback, curt with my answers, and impatient with any delays created by his need for answers from me before he could complete the project. Our communication felt forced, challenging, and tense, full of resentment for how long each step of this process was taking. After we invested in the cloud-based sharing system, it was like a dream come true: we were able to communicate more effectively as well as get projects done quicker and easier *without* having to work after hours. By sharing documents effortlessly and in real-time, we could support each other's work and make things more efficient. Once we had this system in place, I was ready to become more remote because it made our lives so much better.

Automation, digitization, and the ability to work remote made our business processes more efficient. Our marketing campaigns were more cost-effective, and we ended up doubling our enrollment rate within the first year of making these changes. To handle the new workflow, we became acutely aware that we needed to hire more people. This would make our automatization even more effective and give us more time to spend as a married couple. We hired a virtual assistant, graphic designer, lawyer, accountant, personal assistant, and more consultants who lived and worked in different places than us. Their ability to get their jobs done remotely made our lives simpler, more efficient, and gave us more personal time to enjoy together. With this added support, I accepted that having a large portion of our business operate remotely allowed me to focus more on what was important: teaching and consulting.

REMOTE BLESSINGS

In 2013, we experienced the first test to our business regarding how remote workers could support us when we needed it, even when we weren't expecting it. I was teaching an EMDR training in Ambler, Pennsylvania, and at the end of the first day, Friday, I received a voice message that my mother was in the hospital due to unbearable back pain. She'd complained of this pain for a couple of months, seeing a chiropractor, changing her mattress and pillow, and adding some core strengthening exercises to her routine. None of these solutions helped reduce the pain. Once in the hospital, the doctors concluded that she would need surgery on her gallbladder, which was supposedly causing the pain. I wasn't overly concerned because it seemed like gallbladder surgery was pretty standard, and I was hopeful that her pain would finally resolve. At the end of the three-day EMDR training, Sunday, I checked my voicemail, finding a new message from one of my brothers, who said that during my mother's surgery, the doctors had discovered she had stomach cancer and that she had 2 to 18 months to live. When I heard this message, my head started to spin, my stomach dropped, and I began to cry. I was in disbelief. She was supposed to have gallbladder surgery, not have cancer! I struggled to process this information since my mom was a young 80-year-old woman, full of life and energy.

That night, as I rode to the airport for my flight from Ambler to my home in Boulder, I was exhausted from teaching, in need of food because my blood sugar level had dropped significantly, and I was still trying to absorb this distressing news. Yet, once I got on the plane, this strange calm came over my body. At that moment, I knew that my mother had a limited time to live on this earth, whether she lived 2 weeks, 2 months, or a year. Words came to me: this is what I would say at her eulogy. I immediately pulled out my laptop and started writing. It was late at night, so most passengers were sleeping, which gave me four glorious hours of uninterrupted time to gather my thoughts. I was surprised at how the words flowed, how I knew exactly what I wanted to say.

When I arrived home early Monday morning, Young and I started planning for my mother's imminent death. I had a training in Wichita, Kansas, the following weekend. We thought that I would be able to teach and then proceed to Ohio to be with my family. Since my mother had at least 2 months to live, Young and I seemed to have a good plan and felt comfortable with our decision. But by that Tuesday night, my mother's symptoms worsened, and the doctors ordered more tests. I began to doubt we were making the right decision to continue with the Kansas training. I found myself emotional, unable to decide whether I should pack a bag for teaching in Kansas or pack a bag to fly home for a funeral in Ohio. I couldn't settle my nervous system and worried all night long.

By Wednesday morning, I got a phone call from one of my brothers notifying me of a family meeting. The new tests showed that my mother did not have stomach cancer; instead, she had pancreatic cancer. My mind started racing. What?!!! I knew this was not good news. I felt my world begin to spin, making me nauseous and ungrounded, and unable to connect to my body. I tried to concentrate on what the doctor said. He laid out a logical plan that involved immediate surgery to relieve some of her current pain, and then she would receive chemotherapy and be released to go home. The doctor's plan sounded like it would require time, so I didn't need to rush to Ohio, and could go to Kansas as planned. I knew I could do nothing to help her at this point; instead, I could be more helpful once she was home.

Usually, when I have a plan in place and a decision feels right, my body settles with a resounding "yes." I can take a deep breath and feel grounded, which allows me to move forward with confidence. In this instance, my decision to continue with the Kansas training wasn't settling in my body. Something just didn't feel right. I was nauseous with a headache and I felt like I would crawl out of my skin. Why didn't this decision feel right to me? I called my oldest girlfriend, who knows me well, to see what advice she had. She asked me, "If your mom goes into surgery and doesn't wake up from it, how would you feel?" I immediately said that I would regret not being there. Once I said these words out loud, the choice I needed to make was clear. I had to reschedule the training, go home to Ohio, and see my mother for myself. That decision gave me a "yes" throughout my whole body.

Once I shared my decision with Young, he quickly took charge of the business, giving me the space to focus my energy on what was important: my mother. We decided he would stay in Colorado to handle rescheduling the training, then join me at a later date to provide support in whatever way I needed. The next flight to Ohio left the following day, Thursday, 6 days since the first voicemail that my mother was in the hospital. With Young's help, I could let go of thoughts about the business and focus on my mother. I was grateful that I listened to my body as it told me to drop everything to be with her. I found a strong compass inside of me, which helped me trust my intuition in every step of mother's journey.

Once my plane landed, I went straight to the hospital, not knowing how the surgery went. One of my brothers told me that she did survive the surgery, but she didn't look good and that I should prepare myself for what I was about to see. As I entered my mother's hospital room, she looked swollen, yellow, and in distress. I quickly went to her bedside and hugged her for a long time. The doctor eventually came into her room to give all of us an update on her surgery. He said that during the surgery, he discovered the cancer was too advanced for chemotherapy. Her next step would be to go home and spend the next 6 months with her family... until she died.

As the doctor spoke, my gut churned, bells rang in my ears, and blood rushed through my body. My gut was telling me that something was off in what the doctor said. After the doctor left the hospital room, I chased him down the hall. I told him that I lived out of state and wanted to know the truth of my mother's situation. He looked at me straight in the eye and said, "Get things in order because she has a week or two at the most." Then he turned his back on me and walked away.

I stood frozen, angry, and hurt that he had just lied to my

mother, to all of us. My mother, being a planner, would be thinking about the next 6 months rather than the next couple of days. She would not have time to prepare for her imminent death if no one told her the truth. A few minutes later, as the shock wore off on my body, I returned to my family and bravely told them the news while my mother slept. I knew in my heart that I had to tell her the truth as soon as possible to give her enough time to plan her final days.

The next morning, Friday, I was alone with her in her hospital room. I held her in my arms. Then I took a deep breath and told her that I had to tell her something—something that was the hardest thing I've ever had to tell anyone in my life. I said, "The doctor did not tell you the truth about how much time you have; you have only a week or two at the most before you die." She immediately said, "Thank you." I was shocked by her response, yet relieved that this was how she accepted the news. We spent the rest of our time that morning planning her remaining time so that I could make sure she had whatever she needed and wanted.

On Saturday, Young arrived to help support me through the next couple of weeks. I was so engrossed in what was happening at the hospital I forgot that my parents' home did not have an updated computer system or the internet. Young wasn't aware of this and didn't pack his laptop or iPad, assuming that my parents would have a computer he could use. That discovery left Young ill-prepared to deal with the unfinished business needing his attention. Luckily, my brother had an iPad that Young could borrow and then

Young found a nearby coffee shop where he could use the WiFi connection, allowing him to have a makeshift office. Here, he could orchestrate our business by engaging our remote workers to help him handle the situation. Everyone stepped up to help make the shifts necessary, giving me space and time to be present with my mother.

I am grateful that I listened to my body every step of the way through this formidable experience, from that first voicemail to the moment she took her last breath of life. My body gave me clear signals of what felt right and what felt wrong and guided me to be present, aware, and responsive to her needs, deepening our bond in a powerful way.

The process of recognizing that our business could still operate with having remote workers, helped provide me with the safety and space to have this remarkable experience with my mother. Through this process, Young and I felt closer, further showing us that we were a strong team and that we could survive and handle whatever came our way.

As Young and I embraced remote work as an integral part of our business, we learned that we were not alone. Millions of people were sharing live video feeds over social media. Families worldwide were chatting with each other over video using their mobile devices. Coaches were delivering workouts to athletes through apps; students were learning from teachers online; and even dating app users were using video chat features. The world was changing rapidly and working through my resistance was essential to embracing that technology was a gift, not a hindrance. I had to push myself to get out of my comfort zone and try new things. Changing how I worked challenged my way of being, opened me up to new ideas, and provided a gift in ways I couldn't have imagined. Little did I know that having all of this in place before the COVID-19 pandemic would be a blessing to help us handle the challenges created by a global disruption.

THE TRAUMA OF COVID-19

In March 2020, COVID-19 hit Boulder in full force. We were busy getting ready for a three-day intensive EMDR training, meaning twenty people were about to visit our center to learn this powerful modality. Young and I were watching the news trying to figure out whether we could hold the training safely or if we would have to cancel it. As we diligently gathered information from every source we could find, we were overwhelmed with the different ideas, theories, and realities of what was real news versus fake news. The unknowns were huge, and making any decision felt difficult, tedious, and scary. Here we were again, just like when my mother was dying, facing a crisis and having to make hard decisions very quickly that could impact our business on a profound level. We decided to trust our bodies again to help guide us and not rely too much on what we were thinking. If both of us got a resounding "yes" in our bodies, then we knew we could move forward with that decision, trusting that everything would be okay. If one of us got a "yes," and one of us got a "no," then we would wait, listen, and gather more information to get clarity. This system of listening to our bodies and minds over the years has kept us feeling like a team that supports and trusts each other to make the best decisions we can.

As we centered ourselves so that we could listen to our "yes" and "no," it required slowing down our conversations, grounding, and tuning out all the noise from the world to hear our bodies' wisdom. The only thing we knew for sure was that we were responsible for the well-being of twenty people, and we needed to make the best possible decision. With no real guidelines, and information changing day to day, hour to hour, minute by minute, we were swimming in fear, anxiety, and the unknowns. By slowing down and trusting our bodies to give us the answers, we were able to make our decision. We decided to hold the training and move forward, knowing that our plan could change at a moment's notice if necessary.

The training began early Friday morning. As therapists were checking in, I felt confident that we had made the right decision, and everything was going to be okay. I greeted each attendee as they arrived, but then an agitated therapist showed up, and it was clear he was distraught. I introduced myself to this man, wondering what had upset him so much on his way to the training. He raised his voice at me, stating no one at my institute was picking up the phone to talk to him. He said that he had been exposed to COVID-19 and shouldn't be in the training but was afraid he would lose all his money. Observing his distress level rise as he shared this information, my body froze. My mind raced, reviewing if I'd had any conversations with our customer support person about someone who was going to cancel from the training. I couldn't recall any and was sure that I would remember that conversation if we did. I was dumbfounded, confused, and wondering why this man chose to come here instead of leaving a message. I knew that this man's energy impacted me, and I needed to de-escalate the situation as quickly as possible. Safety came first above all else. I had to get myself grounded and get this man to leave as soon as possible. I assured him that he would get all his money back and insisted he needed to go. He continued to argue with me. I centered my voice, looked him straight in the eye, and said, "LEAVE NOW." He was surprised by my intensity, but it stopped him, and he left with no further words exchanged between us.

I now had a huge dilemma from this interaction: should I cancel the training due to *my* possible exposure to COVID-19 from this man who'd just left? My mind swirled with what to do next. I didn't have Young by my side to help me make this significant decision. I felt alone, ungrounded, and shaky. As I struggled with what to do next, I remembered that I work in a building where there's a medical team with whom I'm friendly. I rushed over to find a nurse who could give me some guidance on what to do. I found a nurse, and he was so kind to me and asked several questions to guide me in assessing the risks of COVID-19. He thought my exposure had been minimal and I felt reassured that I could go on with the training. I thanked him for his generosity and headed back to my training center.

But I could feel the adrenaline surging through my body. I knew I wasn't ready to walk into the training center, feeling so agitated. I decided to go to another floor in the building, to move this energy by shaking my body all over until the charge of energy released. I consciously changed my breathing by taking slow, deep belly breaths until I could feel grounded, centered, and ready to face the therapists who were anxiously waiting to start their training. Once I returned to the training, I became keenly aware of an underlying fear permeating throughout the room. Everyone was worried about the virus and their safety. We continued with the training with me trying to ground the entire space to make it as safe as possible, hoping that everyone could learn.

By Saturday morning, I noticed something different about the nurses who frequently walked past my office. They were now wearing masks and gloves, making me fearful that they knew something that I didn't. Some danger had escalated. When I got home after teaching that day, I shared with Young what I had observed watching the nurses. I turned to the news to confirm my suspicions that something significant had changed. Sure enough, the City of Boulder had just declared it was in a local disaster emergency response.

Young and I knew we had to stop the training immediately. We stayed up all night, walking through every contingency plan we could on the different ways to tell the therapists the news as well as options for how they could complete the training and what would happen if they couldn't make up that time as we had planned. Our exhaustion was palpable as we sent out the announcement early Sunday morning, informing the therapists we would not be meeting that day. To our relief, replies poured in thanking us for making this decision and gladly accepting our plans to complete the rest of the training. Young and I were finally able to breathe, let go, and trust, once again, we'd made the right decision.

As more information came to light about the virus, we not only had to stop this training, but we had to shut down *all* of our trainings for the next 3 months. I felt lost for the first time in years, wondering how our business would survive a mandatory stay-at-home order with no end in sight. Our training schedule is very complicated and finding new dates for each of these trainings was a logistical nightmare. Then we also had to inform all the therapists that their particular training would take place later in the year. We decided to give them a choice to either transfer their registration to a new date or cancel it and receive a full refund. Some therapists embraced this news with open hearts, yet others sent ugly emails accusing us of overreacting and denying them the training they expected. We were shocked by these responses. Still, we tried to remember that everyone was under severe distress and trying to survive the pandemic's unknowns. At least half of the registered therapists canceled on the spot, insisting that moving their training was unacceptable.

My fears increased, igniting my worries that we would lose our business at a moment's notice if more therapists cancelled. Trying to handle a global crisis, having my community on lockdown, and being unable to hold a training in-person safely scared me to my core. All the air blew out of my sails. I just couldn't see a future where we would be okay and thriving.

ADAPTING TO THE NEW ABNORMAL

With the stay-at-home orders in place, I needed to move my office into our home. As I walked into the building that housed my training center to pack up, I could feel the energy had changed. A heaviness hung in the air coupled with a pungent smell from the doctors' heavy use of sanitizers. My body immediately stiffened, knowing there was danger in a place where I used to feel safe. Feeling this uncertainty in my body made it easy for me to follow the mandated orders.

As I packed up everything from my office I would need to work from home, I was full of fear, trepidation, and apprehension of how I would "fit in" to Young's workspace. Like so many people, including the therapists we work with, we had to find places and ways to work—and do it safely. Although Young and I had run the business together for years, this was the first time that we would be sharing an office space. I had to set up my computer on the opposite side of Young's desk to make enough space for me to work. None of my things seemed to fit anywhere as I struggled to find a way to organize my new life. Young would walk in the room and just stare and say, "You take up so much room!" And he was right. My needs were much bigger than the available space. As I tried to condense, organize, and figure out how to make this work for both of us, Young and I struggled with each other's rhythm of moving and working throughout the day.

One of the biggest struggles we faced was where I could conduct consultations with therapists; it needed to be quiet and not distract Young from his work. Offering consultations at the same time Young was working in the same space was untenable. There was no other choice than to set up a second office for me in our dining room. When I consulted, I would move into my new second office, set up my laptop, change out my chair, bring my clipboard, paper, pens, books, and whiteboard to have everything I needed to conduct my sessions. I found myself moving between spaces daily, which was disorienting and made it difficult for me to physically, mentally, and emotionally ground myself.

Space has always been important to me, and I spend a lot of energy making sure that I feel grounded, peaceful, and safe wherever I am. Early in my career as a therapist I shared an office with someone. Every time I walked into the space, I could feel objects were moved and not put back the way I'd left them. I am so sensitive that I could sense if a chair, book, or crystal was in a different position. My body would tighten and brace as if there was danger lurking around the corner when actually, I was safe, and there was zero threat. I couldn't settle in the space until I had moved everything back the way I wanted, thus feeling more at ease in my body.

This sensitivity I have to different spaces added to my pandemic stress: now I had two home offices and I couldn't settle into either one. The result of this significant shift turned our home into our business 24/7. Now, everywhere I turned, I could see work that needed to be done, beckoning me. There was no time to rest. I felt as if I was drowning in this space to the point I could no longer feel rest in my body, mind, spirit, or relationship. There was no separation anymore between work and home life, making me angry, resentful, and moody. In this particular dance, I could not find a rhythm that made me happy to go to work anymore.

On top of this disorientation, Young, who is an Asian American, was experiencing overt racism. Before the pandemic, he would experience day-to-day micro-aggressions, but once the pandemic hit, something drastically shifted in our community. When I share this experience with people, they often express disbelief because our town is perceived as a safe, liberal "bubble." Sadly, it's a myth. People became bolder in their racism with threatening actions and words toward Young. He was filmed in the grocery store while simply shopping for food and then followed back to his car. He was also given the finger often or yelled at by people telling him to "go home to his own country." I watched his beautiful soul melt into a puddle of despair. Young felt threatened by a virus he couldn't see and by violence from people he didn't know, making his sense of safety in the world collapse. He felt trapped inside our home with no escape from the lockdown because the outside world had become way too dangerous for him to navigate. I felt helpless to make this better for him. I watched and listened as best I could.

We were drowning in trauma from the pandemic, from the racism, and the constrictions to our business, which took a toll on us physically, emotionally, mentally, and spiritually. Like so many people, there was no way to prepare ourselves for the changes that disrupted our lives on such a profound level. The pain felt insurmountable, as if we were being pulled underwater and drowning in a sea of despair. Some days, I thought I was losing everything: my job, home, and the love of my life.

This current situation played out as an ugly trauma that appeared to have no end. There were days when I found myself crumpled on the floor sobbing from the enormous grief and loss. Old memories haunted me, making it hard to distinguish what was now and what was then: memories of my mother dying unexpectedly; my first marriage ending in divorce; the time I felt like my soul was dying after years of living in New York City and losing my sense of purpose in the world. My trauma history raised its ugly head as the pandemic triggered me in so many unexpected ways. I felt irrational, out of control, and weak for falling apart. My ability to be rational was out the door, and I could see it, feel it, and recognize that I had to do something different, or I would lose my mind.

Fear was taking over my psyche in a way that wasn't healthy. I knew this trauma response was activating my limbic system and that my rational brain was offline. My sense of safety was lost to the point that even my most basic needs were hard to meet and trying to work from two home offices where I didn't feel grounded put me on edge. I was so full of fear I couldn't tell what real danger was anymore.

As I watched the news, I saw people in extreme states of fear, acting irrationally to the point of hoarding products or hurting other people. In stores where I needed to buy supplies, there was chaotic energy that made me feel unsafe. I could sense everyone was in a survival state, acting out of fear, terror, and scarcity. As I saw empty shelves in the stores, my body would contract, and I wondered if there would be enough for us. My world shrank in size as I felt the contraction, limitations, and control that made me feel small, unimportant, and afraid. Through this lockdown, as my social relationships became limited, I lost connections and my sense of belonging to a community. Phone calls and Zoom sessions became the norm to connect, to try feeling part of something larger than myself. Knowing that I couldn't fly to see my aging father, who felt isolated in a retirement center, was painful to endure. Hearing his loneliness seep through the phone line would leave me exhausted and fearful that he would become severely depressed, just as he had when my mother had died. For many, this isolation was horrific and debilitating. Humans need to be touched, connected, and socialized in ways that nurture and support the bodymind. And here I was, isolated from others, unable to do the work that fuels me and gives me a purpose to get up every day.

I found myself isolated in my fears and pains while also finding it difficult to tap into what makes me feel strong, capable, and able to handle stressful situations. I was grieving for the life I once had and praying that everything would just magically return to normal. I wanted to be like Dorothy in *The Wizard of Oz* (1939) and click my heels three times to find myself back in my normal life. Even though I knew many people shared this grief and depression, I was in an isolating fog that clouded my ability to make decisions, take care of myself, and handle hearing any more bad news. I had trouble concentrating and sleeping, plus I felt on edge, irritable, and angry. The things that usually please me or ground me were no longer working. I couldn't go to the yoga studio to practice, or take a walk without a mask, or find a safe place to meditate in my own home because work had taken over our space. These daily practices had been part of taking care of myself and I desperately needed them. Trying to engage in these grounding practices felt too hard, leaving me feeling empty inside.

I knew I had to find a way to tap into my strengths, but I felt hopeless, alone, and drowning in my pain. If I didn't get myself balanced, there was no way I could be available to consult with all the therapists who were turning to me for support as they too were struggling through the pandemic. I had to remember that I had a great support system of allies who have helped me through many difficult times in my life. They know how to help me ground, center, and find my truth. It was clear that I couldn't handle things on my own. I needed to reach out to my allies, to ask them to help me figure out how I could find my strengths once again.

MY ALLIES

After a week of feeling this despair, I reached out and set up a session with Robyn Outram, an intuitive healer who I've worked with for years. Our work is done remotely over the phone since I live in Colorado, and she lives in California. I am amazed at how I can sense and feel the work she does with me without us being in the same room. As she works with my energetic body long distance, it's like she is giving me a massage, only her hands are not involved in this process. I can tune into where the energy feels stuck in my body, and she helps me move that energy using my mind's eye. Sharp pains, aches, and fears can magically dissipate through this process. Once a session is complete, I can feel solid in my body, open in my heart, and feel more stable with my boundaries. This work has proven to me over the years that healing can take place from a distance, even if you aren't actually in the same room with someone.

As we began our first remote session during COVID-19, Robyn could feel I had lost my boundaries by taking on the pandemic's collective pain. I shared how lost I felt, the difficulty I was having sensing my body, and my struggles to make decisions. She quickly guided me to find and set new boundaries. My intuitive healer gently invited me to imagine an energetic bubble that would be big and strong enough to hold the collective pain and grief I felt from the pandemic. I imagined the pain as the color red as if it was a scene from a horror movie where an alien was taking over my body. In my mind's eye, I then created a transparent bubble that was strong enough to hold this alien away from me. As I felt the alien become contained, I saw the energetic bubble move farther away from me, moving into outer space until I could no longer see it. My body began to relax, I was able to take a deep breath, and the pain started to subside.

Next, Robyn guided me to imagine an energetic bubble around my entire body, helping me feel where I begin and where I end. As I thought about this direction, I instantly knew that this energetic bubble needed to be a layer of protection for me. This protective bubble was capable of keeping harmful things out and letting in only things that were nourishing. As soon as my protective bubble was in place, something shifted inside me. My heart expanded and opened, allowing me to feel compassion for others and myself. I was able to feel my body once again and become present in the room I sat in. From this grounded place, I was able to name my past losses that were being triggered and see how I overcame those pivotal moments. This allowed me once again to tap into my strengths. I no longer felt activated by those old memories, and they fell back into my history, just a part of my story. The pain was in the past where it belonged.

As I got in touch with my boundaries through imaging these energetic bubbles, I acknowledged that, by being a "highly sensitive" person, I would need to work with my boundaries more consciously. Practicing my boundaries every day helped them become more defined, letting me feel capable of making different choices, such as choosing when it felt safe to let myself feel the collective pain from the pandemic or not. Through this process, I could sense empathy and compassion for others who were also in pain without letting it overtake my entire body every time I thought about the pandemic. I also could feel my boundaries become clearer at home and work as well as with friends, family, and, of course, with my husband. My sense of self strengthened rapidly, helping me feel strong and capable of handling the challenges I faced.

By reestablishing my boundaries, I now had the strength to reach out to ask for help from more of my supportive allies. I contacted my eye doctor, who helped me mitigate the strain on my eyes from remote work. Then I set up an appointment with my business coach, who grounded me in making decisions about the business. I continued to make more appointments with other healers to keep my bodymind grounded and supported while reaching out to my friends, who let me moan, groan and laugh until we cried. By activating my team of allies, I was strong enough to start putting daily practices into place to take better care of myself. I needed this external support to help me turn inward to find what makes me feel safe, healthy, and capable of dancing with all the changes.

I then returned to my somatic psychology roots to help me establish these practices. I made time to slow down, settle in my body, and cultivate more self-awareness of how I was doing physically, mentally, emotionally, and spiritually. Connecting to my bodymind allowed me to be more available and present with the business, my marriage, and the therapists who reached out to me desperately needing more support. Through this process, I realized that I needed more time before my consultation sessions to ground, anchor, and support my nervous system. This time was crucial to help me be prepared to listen to what the therapists were struggling with while paying attention to my own body's responses as they were talking.

I would let my whole body perceive what was happening in the sessions to sense and feel a connection between us, even though we were in separate rooms. In these sessions, I would often need to regulate my own nervous system in order to find ways to regulate the therapist's nervous system. This dance was complicated, sensitive, and necessitated being present to sense and feel what was going on with each of us. This dance between our nervous systems required a lot of energy. By the end of the day, I found that I needed more time to rest my eyes, release any tension from my body, and find ways to let go of taking on too much responsibility for the therapist's pain and struggles.

As I put my somatic practices in place, my energy began to return; I felt more in control of my emotions, grounded in my body, and present in my interactions. I was able to make better decisions personally and professionally through honoring the wisdom my bodymind offered me. This whole process was like when you're on an airplane and the flight attendant says, "Put your oxygen mask on before assisting others." I had to put on my oxygen mask first, which meant taking better care of myself in order to be ready and available to help others. By tapping into my strengths and supporting my nervous system, I had more compassion for my husband and his struggles through the pandemic, along with the strength to open my heart to therapists who were desperately in need.

THERAPISTS IN DISTRESS

....

*Allowing fear to inform you when
something is wrong and then moving
through it is a part of resiliency.*

....

SOMETHING DIFFERENT

Therapists reached out to me for support with their remote
therapy practices and, as I began to work with them, I
noticed they were experiencing the same distress from the
pandemic personally and professionally as me. The biggest
challenge they shared was not knowing how to change their
practices from in-person to remote sessions. Many
therapists have had no training opportunities in their
master's programs, internships, or continuing education

courses to guide them through the steps necessary for safe remote therapy sessions. There was no manual or training therapists could turn to for the answers they desperately needed.

The pandemic's reality forced many therapists out of their offices and into their homes, creating new, unfamiliar stressors. They tried to "make do" in their homes in order to provide services for their clients, but many expressed that remote therapy felt too scary, mechanical, and potentially harmful to their clients. As a result, many of their clients expressed the same reluctance in doing remote therapy sessions, which created an energetic feedback loop between the therapist and the client. Therefore, many therapists and clients did not feel gung-ho about doing remote therapy. This transition from in-person to remote sessions was intimidating, and many therapists found themselves floundering. Questions arose around how to use the technology safely, how *not* to harm their clients, and how to connect with the clients when remote therapy felt cold, distant, and impersonal.

One of the most common phrases I kept hearing in consultations was, "Remote therapy is of lesser value and less effective; therefore, I should not offer it, and if I do offer it, I should charge less for my services." Seeing remote therapy as "less than" hurt therapists' self-esteem, making them feel that their work was not as valuable and was damaging the therapeutic process. As a result, many therapists shut down mentally and emotionally, grieving and longing for their in-person practices. These therapists were unconsciously signaling to their clients that remote therapy wasn't a viable option, and in return, clients would agree with the therapist and stop treatment. If a therapist saw remote therapy in a positive light, most of their clients would then see the value of continuing their sessions in this manner.

In the past, as a trainer, therapist, and consultant, I believed from a somatic perspective that therapists must be in the same room with a client to track their subtle nonverbal somatic cues. I thought if I were to offer remote sessions, I would lose the client's energetic connection and be ineffective as a therapist, wasting my client's time and money. This belief came from the tradition of learning through in-person trainings to model how to be an effective somatic therapist. Therefore, I believed in-person therapy sessions were the only viable method to offer effective treatment. Any other option for therapy would be less than and would be unacceptable to offer to my clients.

However, over the years, I have slowly come to accept the benefits of remote work by seeing technology as a gift rather than a hindrance. As I've moved out of my comfort zone and tried new things, I've found a whole new world, making my business more effective, efficient, and available to a broader range of therapists. Now in training and consulting with therapists, I find myself inviting them to explore their views on best practices for in-person sessions and helping them determine how to translate those best practices into remote therapy. Through my own challenges with embracing the fascinating world of technology, it's become clear therapists need to open their minds and hearts to see that remote therapy is here to stay.

RESISTANCE TO PRACTING REMOTE THERAPY

During the pandemic, as distressed therapists felt the trepidation of remote therapy, many were also haunted by feeling incompetent to set up and handle new technology. The feeling of being an imposter arose, impacting their ability to trust that connection through a computer screen *is* possible. Seeing themselves reflected in the computer screen also led to being self-conscious and feeling not good enough. Therapists felt alone, frightened, and overwhelmed, continuing to grieve for their pre-pandemic therapy practices. By continuing to insist remote therapy sessions were not as effective as in-person sessions, therapists were inhibiting their ability to embrace this new, valuable way of doing therapy.

Life Before Cellphones

In the early 1980s, while I was living in Pennsylvania, I was driving on a crowded four-lane highway, trying to make my way to Ohio for the holidays with my family. Suddenly smoke started billowing out of the hood of my car. My mind raced, my heart started beating out of my chest, and fear seized me. I was afraid my car was going to blow up, and I would instantly die. I was in the far-left lane of this four-lane highway, needing to get to the shoulder of the road as quickly as possible. As I slowly inched my way over, I was sweating profusely, feeling helpless that something terrible would happen, and there was nothing that I could do about it.

Once I got to the shoulder, I was able to take a deep breath, relieved I was safe. Then shock set in. I had no way to contact anyone for help; I was alone, isolated, surrounded by cars whizzing by. I paced by my car, wondering what I was going to do—and then, magically, a man pulled over and asked if I needed help. I gladly said, "Yes." He looked under my car's hood and said he knew what was wrong with my car and that he could fix it.

I was relieved until he said, "I'm happy to take you to get the part, and then we can come back and fix it; I just have a couple of errands to run on the way, do you mind?" Being in my early twenties, naive, and worried that I'd be stranded on the side of the highway with no help, I agreed without thinking about potential risks. I hopped into his car without any hesitation, happy that my problem was solved.

As we drove away, however, the shock and horror of what I had just agreed to started to set in. I had just gotten into a car with a stranger and had no idea where we were going. Was this a scam or a con? My mind sped a hundred miles per hour with images of this man raping me and leaving me dead in the woods. My heart felt like it was pounding out of my chest, and I feared that I would never see my family or friends again. Finally, after several stressful hours of running errands with this man, he took me to an auto shop, where he helped me find the part I needed. We then headed back to my car to fix it. I was still suspicious that this man actually knew what he was doing, and I was apprehensive that I had just wasted hours with him. After enduring all this fear, I worried that I would still end up on the side of the highway with no way to get home.

Once we got to my car, he went straight to work on it. He worked quickly without speaking a word and then said, "There you go, all fixed. You should be good for the rest of your trip." My mind started racing again, and I thought, Are you serious? You already fixed this, and it's going to be safe enough for me to drive? How am I supposed to trust you? Then a new fright took over my body. What did this man want in return for fixing my car? As I thanked him for his service, I reluctantly asked what he wanted in exchange for his help.

I was just a poor dancer with little cash to offer. He looked at me and said, "Do you have any pot?" What? Pot?! That's what he wants? I looked at him and said, "Sorry, but I don't smoke." He said, "No worries, have a good visit with your family," and off he drove. I stood there for a moment letting the shock wear off before getting back in my car to drive to Ohio, relieved nothing terrible had happened. I still wonder what made me trust this man in the first place because now I would *never* dream of getting in someone's car like that. Now, I would lock my doors, call for help on my cellphone, and let my family know where I was with little stress or worry, confident I could get trustworthy assistance with just a simple phone call.

How on earth did I ever survive without a cellphone? I am so dependent on my cellphone that whenever I'm not teaching or consulting, I have to look at it every 30 minutes to see what's going on. My life revolves around having my phone with me at all moments every day so I can stay in touch. That a cellphone hasn't been a part of my whole life seems impossible, and yet it's true. Now, technology keeps changing so rapidly that it's hard for me to keep up with it, and I have colleagues and friends who love it; they can't wait for the latest version to arrive. But I also know people who are like me, who want to hold onto their Day-timers and go back to a simpler time because technology seems to have taken over our lives. My 90-year-old father, who doesn't have a computer or the internet, is still mesmerized that we can talk over a cordless phone while living in different states. I must be getting old because I sound just like him!

Fear of Technology

Even as technology became an integral part of people's lives, there was still one area that didn't see its value: therapy. The pandemic was a huge wake-up call to therapists: they had to let go of the tradition of in-person sessions and find a new way of working that was safe for themselves and clients. Many therapists felt shocked by making such a significant transition without having time to prepare. It compounded their resistance to change, which impeded their confidence in offering remote therapy. The unknown elements of working with new technology and software as well as troubleshooting related issues were overwhelming and even impossible for many therapists. Their doubts and fears about remote therapy's efficacy provoked fear that the work would cause irreparable harm to their clients.

I naively thought therapists' fears and worries would dissipate if I shared information focused on the technical issues involved with setting up a remote therapy practice. I knew research had shown remote therapy can be effective and does not cause harm. Keeping those facts in the forefront of my mind guided me through advising therapists that remote therapy was doable and could be effective, just like their in-person sessions.

The first step in setting up a remote therapy practice was to find a HIPAA compliant platform to ensure security and confidentiality. Along with having a secure platform, therapists needed a high-speed internet connection for their computers to support live video. Once that was in place, therapists had to learn what steps to take if they lost their internet connection during a session. Creating simple guidelines for clients to use if they lost contact during a session would help therapists develop more safety throughout their sessions.

To my surprise, even with all this information, some therapists found the process of setting up remote therapy so overwhelming they decided to shut down their practices. Many of them wanted to wait out the virus, so they cancelled sessions, hoping that the pandemic would quickly end. What they did not realize they were doing was that they were resisting change and were not ready to face their fears of providing therapy in a new way. By holding onto the past, these therapists were denying their clients therapy, which was the opposite of their therapeutic oath, "do no harm," to their clients. Clients were in desperate need of therapy, and therapists needed to be available; it was as simple as that.

I took for granted that I had been working with this kind of technology for years and that the therapists who had already been consulting with me were also comfortable using it. Plus, I had the support from my husband, a "techie" at heart, who could help me troubleshoot when things went awry. I discovered that many therapists didn't have the luxury of this kind of support, leaving them feeling isolated and afraid. I found myself asking therapists more questions to see if they had reliable, high-speed internet as well as what kind of devices and software they were using. Many were unable to answer these questions, including how to trouble shoot when things go wrong. As I continued to probe, I learned some were not taking the time to set up a safe environment for themselves and their clients. They were doing the best they could without any guidance or support. I knew from experience that becoming familiar with problems that can arise during sessions was imperative to preparing for mishaps. By *not* preparing enough, therapists were swimming in worry of what *might* happen versus trusting that they could handle whatever came their way.

My years as a professional dancer taught me the solution to worrying about what might happen was to practice and rehearse all the steps before performing. This same discipline applied to using new technology for remote therapy and handling mishaps that can occur using technology. Therapists needed to recognize that mishaps are a part of using technology because *there will be glitches.* Becoming familiar with glitches such as power outages, routers not working, and/or connections dropping or becoming disrupted needs to be practiced by therapists on their own before proceeding with client sessions. Both parties need to be aware of the potential problems and how to handle them as smoothly as possible. These steps are unique to the technology being used for both the therapist and their clients; still, having a plan for how to solve them is essential. If therapists hyper-focus on what can go wrong without having any solutions, the fear can prevent them from embracing these glitches as just a part of the process. Knowing how to reach out to the tech support available for the platforms the therapists are using is essential in learning how to handle glitches when they do occur. Handling these mishaps in a calm and relaxed manner can help set the tone for your client to be okay with this aspect of remote therapy. If you're upset, the client will feel that they can't trust you, which can hurt the therapeutic relationship.

By practicing a sequence of what to do when any mishaps occur, therapists can act from a grounded, secure, and calm place rather than from a place of fear and panic. Properly preparing yourself and your clients for these moments allows for the therapeutic connection to remain even when disrupted. An example from my own experience is when the image freezes during a training. My body goes into a panic as I worry that I won't be able to continue, and my mind starts racing with thoughts such as, "I'm going to get horrible evaluations, everyone will think I'm incompetent, and they are all going to want their money refunded because they didn't get the perfect training." In that moment, I must slow down, and ask myself, "What would Young do?" I will then go through my checklist of what he would have me do. First, he would have me take a deep breath and center myself. Then, he'd suggest waiting for a moment to see if the glitch resolves on its own. If it doesn't then I need to shut down my Zoom session and see if I can access the internet at all before proceeding. If I can't access the internet, then I see if the internet is working on my phone. I may have to shut down my computer, shut down my router, and reboot everything. If I'm not calm throughout this process, my panic can take over and I can't think through the steps that would help resolve the issue. If I stay calm, this solution can be resolved in a short period of time, making it possible to reconnect with everyone in the training. When we reconnect, we can talk about what happened briefly, laugh about it, and then resume our training. This checklist will be different for every situation. For me, the question always starts the same way: "Take a deep breath, now, what would Young do?" Everyone needs that kind of support and sequence to feel grounded, prepared, and ready to act if glitches occur. Take time to develop your own checklist so that you can take a deep breath and remain ready and prepared for anything that comes your way. If it's helpful, you can ask yourself, "What would Barb do?" My answer, as you might guess, is "Take a deep breath..."

Whenever I'm teaching a new group of therapists EMDR therapy, I assure them in the beginning that learning something new can feel disorienting as well as bring up feelings of inadequacy. Letting oneself be a beginner, be in a place of curiosity, and then practice the sequence repeatedly creates the template for success. Trying to be an expert before you've even learned something is too high of an expectation for anyone. By practicing through repetition, neural pathways begin to lay down, making it easier to perform the sequence from the "felt" sense rather than relying on thinking. Through this practice, therapists' fears dissipate, which builds their confidence that everything will be okay. They are more ready to handle the unknown.

However, as the therapists I worked with gained more technical skills, their fears and worries lessened, but were not fully resolved. What I discovered was the technical issues were just a smokescreen. Layers of emotional issues surfaced as therapists tapped into grieving the loss of their "normal," feeling like imposters for not having any remote therapy training, which then made them feel inadequate as therapists. Many of these therapists expressed deep fears of harming their clients as well as not feeling good enough and needing to be perfect in whatever they did.

Loss of the Normal

As therapists switched their practices from in-person to remote therapy sessions due to the pandemic, many experienced a deep sense of loss on multiple levels. Many lost the security and familiarity that their offices provided, a safe refuge for their clients. This haven for in-person sessions offered a space for clients to explore their pains without any distractions from the outside world. When therapists moved their offices into their homes, their personal and professional lives co-mingled, causing confusion and disorientation. Therapists with children found that their children were also displaced, suddenly attending school from home. The added stress of worrying about their children's education while trying to work was distressing and problematic, impacting their entire family system. Families felt constricted within their bodies, restricted in their movement, and limited in their emotional tolerance. Many grieved for what once was that no longer existed.

Having to change the therapeutic container with therapists and clients in separate rooms connected by a computer screen was scary, unfamiliar, and, for many, not ideal. Some therapists felt they were abandoning their clients, causing undue harm. This shift from in-person to remote therapy sessions disoriented many therapists to the point that they felt a disconnection from their skills. It created a void in their identity as a therapist. Since their nervous systems were in overdrive as they tried to be superhumans for everyone, they were suffering internally with no safe place to express what was going on for themselves.

Many of these therapists were grieving and in extreme distress. As I consulted with them, I could easily track Elizabeth Kubler-Ross's Five Stages of Grief Model (1969) as therapists began to share their anguish from navigating the pandemic's fallout. The five stages of Kubler-Ross's model include anger, denial, bargaining, depression, and acceptance. Each of these stages was mercurial and could change from day to day, even from moment to moment, in our consultation sessions. My job was to help these therapists get in touch with what they were experiencing, create a haven for them to share unexpressed emotions, and guide them to find ways to move with and through the chaos that permeated their daily lives. As I began to track these different grief responses, I identified that *grieving* was impeding their abilities to keep them connected to their purpose and mission as therapists. Let's take a look at the different grief responses and how they were showing up in consultation.

Anger

During our consultation sessions, some therapists experienced high distress levels in switching their practices from in-person to remote sessions, making them feel angry and frustrated. They were irritated that they had to learn to work in a new way, overwhelmed with seeing their clients dysregulated from experiencing so much trauma, and exasperated by their family's life-changing demands. To feel safe, they would keep busy, never letting their nervous systems calm down from the demands being asked of them personally and professionally. They gave themselves little time to rest, forgot to use their skills of regulating their nervous systems, and became enraged that they had to do everything on their own. They tried to avoid anything that would connect them to their grief and pain. In return, many of these therapists experienced feeling ungrounded in their bodies; they were scared about what was happening in their lives and frightened for their clients' futures. Over time, some of these therapists felt depressed and even hopeless, wanting to shut down their remote therapy practice because they felt ineffective in their work.

Denial

Other therapists were in denial about how the pandemic impacted their work and minimized the severity of the loss they were experiencing. They showed very little emotion during our sessions. These therapists talked about unexplained somatic symptoms, such as headaches, nausea, fatigue, unidentified aches, and pains. For many of them, their symptoms were an expression of stuck energy held in the body from unexpressed grief and loss. They blamed their symptoms on sitting in front of a computer all day long rather than connecting the symptoms to unexpressed emotions. As a result, these therapists would become impatient with their clients who were experiencing difficulties handling the complexities of their lives due to the pandemic, racism, political unrest, and unresolved childhood traumas. They would often find ways to minimize the client's pain, distract the client by bringing up safer issues, and avoid helping clients address deeper unresolved traumas. To avoid their own feelings, the therapists would focus on "fixing" their clients, seeking the perfect intervention to instantaneously solve the client's issue. When I tried to slow the therapists down so they could become aware of their emotional pain, they would minimize, reject, and deflect their answers to avoid showing how vulnerable they really were.

Bargaining

Another aspect of therapists' loss was how they would bargain with themselves, trying to keep things the same rather than accept the new abnormal. Many felt that remote therapy was of lesser value than in-person sessions, which compounded their resistance to the changes, refusing to accept the loss, and avoiding embracing something new. Some of these therapists insisted on seeing their clients in-person even when they were mandated by their state not to, fearing that the clients would end therapy if they didn't do what the client wanted. If the transition felt too hard for these therapists to accept remote therapy, many would cancel appointments, bargaining with themselves to keep things the same, believing that the client would not benefit from remote sessions anyway. For many of these therapists, their lack of confidence would impede their ability to feel effective with their work, leading them to reason that the technology was the problem rather than acknowledging that they were grieving and needed support to provide remote therapy effectively.

Depression

The resistance and inability to let themselves grieve led many therapists to high levels of depression and burn-out. These therapists put their clients' needs before their own, losing their sense of self-worth as well as feeling like their identity as therapists was non-existent. Many of them tried to keep their lives in the status quo, not dealing with the fact that they were grieving the loss of their in-person sessions. Some of these therapists' healthy coping mechanisms broke down to the point that some turned to addictive behaviors to handle the emotions they were trying so hard not to feel. Addictive behaviors included overeating at night, drinking more alcohol at the end of the day, or losing sleep by binge-watching Netflix. These addictive behaviors, while effective in the short term, were not solutions for the uncomfortable feelings and body sensations due to the grief and loss they were experiencing.

Acceptance

As therapists began to accept that the pandemic was impacting their lives and their practices, they found more peace with the process of offering remote therapy sessions. They would identify what was in their control, put better safety plans in place, and learn how to dance with the unknowns of working with new technology. Through this process therapists started taking better care of themselves and set healthier boundaries with both their families and practices. By accepting the new reality, they allowed their emotions to be present and own what they were experiencing.

....

SPOTLIGHT: KEEPING IT TOGETHER

Let's take a look at a therapist who was experiencing grief and loss, making it difficult for her to show up for her remote therapy sessions. Like so many of us, she had to move her office into her home due to the pandemic's quarantine restrictions. In addition, she was a mother of three young children who were also at home needing a lot of attention. Her new office was located in her bedroom, which was the only space available to provide enough privacy for her remote therapy sessions. She brought a straight back chair into her bedroom, placed her laptop on a dresser, and tried to make do until she could get back into her office for in-person sessions. This makeshift office was awkward for her physically, emotionally, mentally, and spiritually. As she tried to cope with her new situation, she would minimize that it impacted her whatsoever. The only thing she would talk about was suffering from migraines at the end of the day, back pain from sitting in a straight chair, and that she found herself eating more sweets every night. Yet she was convinced that nothing was wrong with the way she was working.

In our first consultation session, she talked very fast, running through a checklist of all the things we needed to cover for the day. She urgently needed answers and solutions for complicated things her clients were experiencing, which actually required more time for me to help her find meaningful answers rather than just a quick fix. She presented herself as being in control, handling things just fine, as though she wasn't impacted by the pandemic at all. As I listened to her detailed checklist, the pressure in my body increased to where I felt like I would explode if I didn't take a breath. I had to slow myself down to tolerate the sensation I experienced in my body. I found it challenging to listen to what she was saying because I was so distracted by what I was feeling from her urgency. I knew that I had to get both of us breathing, or we would combust very quickly.

I gently interrupted her and invited her to take a breath, to slow down so that I could hear everything she needed to say. I assured her we had time to explore what she was feeling and find ways to help her clients. As she started to take a breath, she shared how frustrated she was with her clients. She found that most of them wanted to only work on how they were impacted by the pandemic, whereas she felt it was vital they work on childhood traumas to get to the core of what was happening for them. The more resistant the clients were to her plan, the angrier and frustrated she felt.

As she expressed her anger, the pressure in my body began to soften, but now I felt a sharp pain piercing through my heart. I could feel sadness coursing through my body as she talked, even though she expressed anger at her clients. As I tuned into this sadness in my body, I gently guided her to sense and feel her body as she expressed her anger. Her breath began to deepen, and immediately sadness flooded her body. She began to weep. She could sense and feel how much she needed to "keep it all together" when all she wanted to do was fall apart and cry. Once she named this, she deepened into her sadness, and tears arose *from the depths of her soul. In the safety of our session, she expressed what she was desperately trying not to feel: the grief and loss of her life before the pandemic. Our focus shifted from **fixing** her clients to sensing what was happening for **her**. She released her agenda for our sessions and gave into feeling these vulnerable emotions. Our session safely enabled her to lean how the pandemic was impacting her, providing her the space to experience her grief over trying to handle so much—including motherhood—all at one time without enough support. Both of our bodies began to soften, release, and be more open to whatever was arising in the moment. I could be with her, witness her pain, and provide safety so that she could be vulnerable without having to worry about what others were thinking of her.*

She then began to feel pain pierce through her heart, heat flooding her body as she began to tremble and shake. She was afraid to tell me she sometimes hated remote therapy. If a client refused, she would go into her office and see them in-person even though she was in an area mandated to work from home. Shame permeated through her whole body as she revealed this truth to me. Although she knew she wasn't comfortable with this solution, she overrode her needs to satisfy this client, which made her feel like a good, compassionate, caring therapist. She found herself rationalizing that her client was too alone, too isolated, and she was the only one keeping them alive. Taking on too much responsibility for her client's well-being led her to bargain with her own life, her family's life, and her profession. She felt wrong and shameful for not setting a clear boundary with her client.

As we worked together over the next couple of months, she began to accept that the pandemic was not going away soon. She needed to find different ways to interact with her family and clients as well as resolve her feelings about remote therapy. She grew more willing to ride her own waves of emotions of grief and loss, stay curious about the sensations in her body, and find ways that supported her through the pandemic-induced changes in her life. She was able to see what she was in control of, which included taking care of herself, setting healthy boundaries for her clients and family, and creating a home office that supported her physically, mentally, emotionally, and spiritually. As she put these pieces into place, she felt more relaxed in her body, secure in her skills as a therapist, and found her creativity returned in her work. She started accepting her new reality, thus allowing her emotions to be part of an improvisational dance where she could move, breathe, and interact in each moment with curiosity and kindness toward herself, her clients, and her family.

By acknowledging her grief and loss, she moved through ever-changing feelings by owning what was really happening. She allowed herself to feel the pain and process it. Now she could say that the pandemic had changed her practice and that when something didn't feel right, she could listen, honor, and respect the wisdom that her bodymind had to offer her. By providing safety for herself, her family, and her clients, she regained her energy, vitality, and desire to do remote therapy.

....

Imposter Syndrome

As therapists grieved fully for their pre-pandemic practices, many of them struggled with feeling inadequate because they had no training in providing remote therapy. Without any courses in their master's programs, internships, or continuing education, therapists were lost, feeling not good enough, powerless, and out of control. The need to be perfect took over, becoming so debilitating that many therapists would freeze and even forget that they had skills. The feelings of helplessness and self-doubt made therapists fearful their clients would "figure out that they were a fraud" and "shouldn't be paid for their services" at all. Shame permeated throughout their bodies, and they would lose the connection to their sense of worth. These feelings would tap into the therapists past unresolved traumas, which left many of them feeling young, stupid, and incapable.

I had to focus our work on helping the therapists get in touch with their bodies, their unresolved traumas, and this deep sense of being an imposter. My job was to help them remember that the skills they already embodied while working with their clients in-person would be the same skills they would need to conduct remote therapy. Although I helped these therapists get in touch with feeling like an imposter, many of them grew angry with me, feeling that I was holding back by not giving them the perfect interventions for their clients. Many of these therapists were quick to blame their clients for being resistant to remote therapy, rather than looking deeper inside themselves to identify what was really blocking their sessions: their feelings of being an imposter.

As the therapists shared their insecurities, I could sense they were disconnecting from the wisdom in their bodies. Many of them would start our sessions by speaking so rapidly about their clients' pandemic-related troubles that my body contracted, my breath became labored, and my mind swirled. In these moments, I found it challenging to make sense of what the therapists were communicating. I had to slow myself down, ground in my body to sense and feel what was happening for the therapists. They focused so intently on their clients' distress that they disconnected from their bodies, which became a barrier to their therapists' skills, fueling the sense of being an imposter.

Before we could address interventions for their clients, it was apparent that they needed to find ways to center, ground, and feel safe in their bodies, to once again connect to their skills. I trusted that when therapists connect to their bodies, they will stay curious about what they are sensing and feeling as well as find more resources to feel more capable, confident, and able to help their clients. My job was to go beyond the therapist's agenda and notice what was happening between our nervous systems. This dance between our nervous systems informed me almost immediately that these therapists were in crisis both personally and professionally from the effects of the pandemic's impact.

Through my consultations with more therapists, I saw repeatedly the pandemic's devastating effects on them. Many of them were spiraling into despair, over-concerned about their clients and their own family's well-being, leaving themselves last on their "to-do" lists. I had to help these therapists see that they were also in crisis and needed some tender loving care. Because I was able to be present with them, many therapists would start crying from the relief of someone seeing their pain, fears, and vulnerabilities. As I gently guided them to feel and sense their bodies, they slowly began to express how hard their lives were and how they felt out of control. They shared their deep concerns, such as: *Who am I to offer remote sessions without any training*; *I don't want to harm any of my clients working this way when I don't know what I'm doing*; *How can I help my clients when I'm barely holding it together*; and *I can't possibly charge my full fee for something that is of lesser value.* These thoughts therapists were grappling with led to feelings of being incompetent and imperfect to a fault, so much so they felt like they were imposters.

By slowing down our process and making it safe for therapists to reveal their vulnerabilities, I allowed them to have the space to let go of "having to be perfect" and having it all together. Many of these therapists felt a huge relief when they could share these feelings in a safe place. Their bodies began to soften, their breath deepened, and they started to communicate more coherently. The therapists discovered that they were trying to be superheroes carrying the weight of the world on their shoulders, feeling over-responsible for everyone else's well-being—except their own. This challenging burden contributed to many of them experiencing exhaustion physically, mentally, emotionally, and spiritually.

As they allowed the support I gave them to move through

their bodies, their truth came forward, enabling their wisdom to guide them on what choices they needed to make in their personal life and which skills to use professionally. Their emotions began to regulate, which automatically helped them feel more in control. As their connection to their bodies increased, they were able to feel more self-compassion; tolerate uncomfortable emotions and body sensations more gently; and feel more grounded in their abilities to handle the challenges they faced. Feelings of being an imposter dissipated, helping them feel more empowered and capable of sitting with their client's distress without having to shut down, run away, or fix what they were feeling.

....

SPOTLIGHT: REVVING UP

An example of the effects of imposter syndrome was a therapist who was stressed by the pandemic's impacts on their family and work life. Setting up a remote therapy practice from their home while being quarantined with their family was overwhelming and scary. As we began our remote consultation session, they rapidly told me how hard it was to balance family and work. Their mind was racing all the time, interrupting their sleep, and causing them to fall behind in everything. They described doing remote therapy as crippling to their sense of self as a therapist because they felt inadequate to help their clients, who were in a constant state of crisis.

As I listened to this therapist, I could hardly track what they were saying because they were incoherent, jumping around from story to story, with little focus on what they wanted from our session. Similar to my experiences with other therapists, my muscles contracted, my body wanted to retreat, and my mind swirled in circles, making me dizzy and uncomfortable. As I sensed my nervous system becoming dysregulated, I adjusted my breathing, slowing it, and feeling my feet on the ground so that I could be centered before I spoke. With my body's reaction slowed down, I encouraged them to pause talking and just begin to breathe. I had them take several exhales with me to help discharge the energy that was building like a pressure cooker ready to explode inside their body. Through this breathing practice, they became aware of their shoulders' tension, their upper back's pain, and their neck and jaws' rigidity. They shared with me that they felt out of control, helpless to change anything, and that they felt like an imposter on the verge of clients finding out they're an incompetent therapist.

As they deepened into being vulnerable with what they were truly feeling, their body began to soften and relax. Their breathing slowed down, and they recognized how fast their thoughts were racing, not allowing themself to feel and sense what was going on inside their body. They were so busy trying to make everyone else feel okay that they forgot to connect to their own needs. The therapist was able to name this feeling of "revving up" like an engine as a pattern that was very familiar; it had caused a lot of *pain for them over the years. By recognizing this pattern, they began to have more compassion for themselves, using kinder self-talk.*

I helped them identify what changes they needed to put in place with their family; how to shift ways they were working with their clients; and steps take better care of themself before, during, and after conducting their remote therapy sessions. In our next session, they happily reported that they felt connected to their family, no longer resenting others for having needs, and their feelings of being an imposter melted away. They felt competent, confident, and capable of offering remote therapy sessions and started enjoying their work again. Their energy level also increased so that they felt more available to their family at the end of the day.

....

Loss of Connection

As therapists shared how vulnerable they were feeling, I often heard them say they couldn't work with their clients' trauma because it was impossible to feel and sense their clients through a computer screen. Many described remote therapy as working with a computer rather than connecting with a real, live human being. Some therapists said remote therapy "dehumanizes" the client by being too impersonal and that it's not a viable, effective therapy. What became apparent to me is that therapists believed if they couldn't "see" their client's entire body, they assumed that they were missing too many of the client's somatic nonverbal cues, ultimately leading to the harm of their client. Therapists needed to learn how to trust that an energetic exchange between people *does* exist, whether they interact in-person, over the phone, or through a computer screen. Their inability to believe and trust in this energetic exchange was a huge roadblock, one many therapists considered unsurmountable.

In working with therapists to address this roadblock, I recalled trying to talk to my father over the phone for the first time in my adult life after my mother had died. When my mother was alive, she was the voice for both of them. If my father picked up the phone, he'd say, "Hello," I would reply, "Hi Dad," and then he would hand the phone over to my mother saying, "Here's your mother." She was the only one who would talk, and I had no idea what my father was thinking or feeling. After her death, my father and I had to find a new way to communicate; our *go-between* was no longer able to translate our conversations for us. When we were on the phone and he'd begin talking, I felt the heaviness in his body; his voice changed to sounding tired and sluggish; and his thoughts jumped around like a ping pong ball, seeming like they did not know where to land. Any mention of my mother triggered his grief, and he would begin to cry, tremble, and shake. His whole world had just fallen apart. But he would shut down those feelings faster than I could recognize what was happening. The shock of this change in my father was challenging for me to navigate. I would feel my body become heavy, trembling, and shaky. I would feel his unbearable pain, the pain he was afraid to express, in my body. Once our conversation ended, I had to take time to let these powerful emotions run through my body until they no longer had a hold on me. I had to let his grief run its course and allow my feelings to find expression as well. I didn't need to "see" him to sense and feel how much he was missing his wife of 48 years. Our energetic connection was palpable, real, and powerful. If I could feel this energetic exchange with my grieving father over the phone, then the potential for a therapist to feel a client energetically through a computer screen is also possible.

Recently, I was teaching a remote EMDR training and some therapists shared that they were experiencing some apprehension about whether connection is available through remote therapy. Throughout the training, I instructed the therapists to become aware of their bodies as they observed me doing live therapeutic demonstrations. I wanted them to increase their awareness to see if they could sense and feel an energetic connection between myself and the volunteer on the other side of the computer screen. Following these demonstrations, therapists have been consistently surprised that they can sense and feel this energetic connection between us. Having this experience during the training began to open up the possibility for these therapists to believe an energetic connection is real, powerful, and possible even while being in separate rooms. The therapists' resistance began to shift as they saw remote therapy can be effective, meaningful, and dynamic, a way in which clients can still heal and safely grow from their pains. Therapists had to open their minds and believe that connection is possible through a computer screen. Then they had to open their bodies to sense this powerful energetic exchange that can occur through remote therapy.

Energetic Exchange

I first started exploring the concept of energy when I was a dancer. We would spend hours sensing and feeling our bodies with different intentions behind each movement. Did we need to move quicker or slower? Lighter or heavier? Softer or harder? The dynamics were endless, and how we used our energy directly influenced how the dance unfolded. Through the changes in each movement's dynamics, the audience would experience different emotional responses. Would it make the audience feel sad, angry, afraid, or giddy with joy? The energy behind each moment was the key in expressing the nuances that engaged the audience in different ways. Without this sensitivity, all dances would look and feel the same as well as be robotic and void of any intention.

After choosing to leave the professional dance world, I became a bodyworker. Here I started working with energy on a whole new level. My hands were like finely tuned instruments able to sense areas in the body that had too much energy, causing tension and rigidity. In contrast, my hands could also sense other areas that lacked enough energy for the muscles even to engage. As I started learning more about feeling energy in the body, there were times the client's energy would begin to flow through my hands up into my arms. Initially, this feeling was scary because I didn't understand what was happening to me. If I wasn't careful during the sessions, this energy would stick to me, and I would feel nauseous and sometimes develop headaches after sessions. I was taking on my client's energy, which was ultimately hurting me. I had to learn how to sense with my hands without absorbing my client's energy, which meant having a clear boundary to take care of myself while massaging my clients.

The more skilled I became at sensing energy with my hands while keeping my boundary, the more clients would get in touch with unresolved traumas stored in their bodies. Their body tissues had accumulated the felt sense from the terror, hurt, and pain that was not digested and processed from being sexually, physically, or verbally abused either in their childhood or adulthood. As clients started tapping into these unresolved traumas, I found myself questioning how I could better help them. My job as a bodyworker wasn't to be their therapist, and I found myself frustrated that I didn't have the skills to navigate these traumas.

My encounters with these unresolved traumas held in the body led me to study somatic psychology to deepen my understanding of the bodymind connection. I had to learn how to translate my skills as a bodyworker into sensing my clients' emotional, physical, and mental energy *without* using touch. Through my studies, I started sensing and feeling an energy exchange between the client and myself. As my therapy clients expressed their pains, fears, and joy, my body would begin to vibrate and resonate with the client's energetic body. In response, I had to learn to track and sense the energy moving in my body as information to help me tune into my clients' experience as well as my own.

Just as I had practiced as a dancer, repeating distinct sequences to embody the dance, I had to apply this same discipline to being a therapist. By practicing daily, I trained myself to be highly attuned to my body so I could sense what was my energy versus what was my clients' energy. I had to develop clear boundaries to remain open energetically without enmeshing with my client's experience. Without these boundaries, I would take on my client's energy and sometimes feel ungrounded, disoriented, and headachy after sessions. Setting these boundaries was a new challenge because I wasn't using my hands to inform me of what I was sensing; instead, I had to use my whole body to sense, feel, and be present, tapping into my intuition more fully.

Through opening up to the idea that there's an energy exchange during in-person sessions, therapists can now apply these same principles to remote therapy. By attuning to the client's bodymind connection, therapists can sense and feel their clients even if they can't see their entire body. As therapists bring more awareness to their own bodies, they will begin to sense what's happening for their clients. Therapists need to develop these skills so that their bodies become tuned instruments capable of sensing and feeling energy. The energetic exchange creates a dance that provides the conduit for connection with the client even when the therapist and client are in separate rooms brought together by a computer screen. As therapists practice this energetic exchange, their bonds with clients will increase, helping build the therapeutic rapport. When therapists tap into the wisdom, creativity, and spontaneity of the bodymind connection, more flow will come into their sessions.

Fear of Dissociation

As therapists contemplate remote therapy's efficacy, fears often arise regarding the possibility of the client experiencing dissociation. Therapists worry that if dissociation occurs, it will cause more harm to the client rather than healing. If therapists are afraid of their clients' dissociation, they will hold back in remote therapy trying to avoid, deflect, or distract the client from working on more challenging material. Therapists need to remember that dissociation is an everyday occurrence that helps clients disconnect from their thoughts, feelings, and body sensations for survival. The process of dissociation is a mechanism that allows humans to protect themselves from feeling too much pain. Dissociation is a normal, natural process and therapists must understand it is *not* something to be afraid of, but rather a process to get familiar with intimately.

Dissociation therefore occurs when the client's nervous system is overloaded and can't process what's happening in the moment because they don't feel safe. It is common if the client experienced physical, emotional, mental, sexual, or spiritual abuse in their childhood that their nervous systems will go into a dissociative process for survival. This dissociative process can become a habitual response whenever the brainbody interprets something is not safe in the here and now.

An example of this would be an adult client working on a childhood memory of being sexually abused by their uncle. The uncle wore a particular aftershave that smelled sweet and musty. The client would smell this aftershave with each violation, during which the client would freeze, lose their voice, feel nauseous, and dissociate from their body because the pain was so overwhelming. As the client grew into adulthood, this dissociative pattern became imprinted in their bodymind. Now, as an adult, whenever the client smells something sweet and musty, their nervous system activates into the dissociative pattern. The client experiences the same feelings of not being safe as they did as a child, even if they are safe in the here and now. This dissociative pattern was protective in their childhood but no longer serves them as an adult. As a result, the client feels isolated, alone, and disconnected from themselves and others, while longing to feel safe, grounded, and connected in the present.

Therapists must learn and then trust their skills in working with dissociation, whether the sessions are conducted in-person or remotely. If a therapist does not know how to track when a client is dissociating, the client may experience harm since the therapist is not equipped to regulate the client's nervous system. Successfully working with dissociation requires therapists to learn about the "window of tolerance," a term developed by Daniel Stern (Siegel, 1999). The window of tolerance describes the client's ability to feel their feelings and stay present in their body while also remaining present in the room without dissociating. Helping a client keep one foot in the present so they know they're safe in the here and now while visiting painful and challenging material in their past is part of working safely in the window of tolerance. As the client finds an ideal range to feel their feelings and body sensations, the client will process and work through old unresolved traumas without retraumatizing themselves. This ideal range helps the client tolerate uncomfortable emotions and body sensations without the client having to run away, shut down, or completely disconnect from their emotions and body sensations to protect themselves. When the client feels safe in the here and now, a repatterning in the nervous system occurs. The client will find a new understanding of what happened in the past and how dissociation protected them then but is not helping them feel present now. When clients appreciate that their nervous system was wise to dissociate in the past while the danger was real, this awareness will help them have more compassion for themselves. By developing this awareness, the client learns they can respond in the present moment differently because they now have a choice that's different from their past response. The dissociation pattern begins to unwind, and the client will begin to feel more present, connected, and embodied in what's happening in the here and now. Understanding that clients' nervous systems dissociated for survival and that this process occurs in stages can help therapists learn to work consciously with this process to keep their clients safe during remote therapy.

Shape Shifters

I recently watched a documentary on Netflix titled *My Octopus Teacher* (Ehrlich & Reed, 2020) about an octopus and its ability to shapeshift, demonstrating the stages of dissociation. The narrator of the documentary, Craig Foster, intimately observed an octopus every day for almost a year, developing a deep bond with her. This relationship evolved through a delicate balance of Foster patiently waiting, pausing, and listening for when the octopus was ready to connect, just like a therapist must do in therapy to connect with their client. When the right moment presented itself to Foster, he simply reached out his hand as an invitation for the relationship to begin. Through their intimate dance, Foster observed the octopus in her natural habitat, seeing things that no other human being on this earth had ever witnessed. Foster learned that the octopus was a living, breathing, and responsive animal that was highly intelligent and capable of learning, feeling, and bonding. This animal's complex responses to various situations were fascinating, and Foster learned that around two-thirds of the animal's brain lives in its tentacles. The octopus's living, responsive, intelligent brain would have different reactions to whether it felt safe or in danger.

If the octopus felt safe, she would be playful, curious, and responsive to other fish as well as to Foster. There was freedom in the octopus's movement: she would spin, turn, and flow effortlessly through the water. If she sensed danger from a hungry shark, she would immediately flee to escape the threat, lengthening her body so that she could propel herself swiftly through space to find safety. If necessary, she would even leave the water and thrust herself onto land, running to escape, only to return to the water, hoping that the danger had disappeared. If the shark were still there, she would begin to change her body's shape into various distinct shapes, hoping not to be detected. She would use colorful forms to camouflage her body in a way that would match her environment, making her a skillful shapeshifter. This camouflaging process involved changing her shape, texture, color in ways that seem magical and impossible. She would often make herself into a small ball and wrap green kelp around her with only her eyes peeking out to see if the danger was still present. Other times, she would pull shells up by her tentacles, creating a protective shield around her entire body, making her look like a completely different creature at the bottom of the ocean.

One day, she couldn't fool the shark with her shapeshifting magic, and the shark detected her scent through the wall of shells. He quickly dug his teeth into her tightly wound body, twisting and turning, hoping that he had scored a big dinner for the day. The two animals were now in a full-on battle, one ready for a meal and the other trying to survive. The octopus, being an amazing shapeshifter, mysteriously found a way to get out of the sharks' gripping teeth. She landed on the shark's back, confusing him because he didn't know where she went. The octopus stayed on the shark's back as he continued to search for her, until she found a safe cavern in which she could gently glide off his back and out of harm's way. The graceful movement seemed like a dance involving flexibility, adaptability, and quick thinking to outsmart her persistent opponent.

On most days this unique dance would help keep the octopus alive; but on one occasion, the octopus was not as quick as she would have liked. The shark took hold of one of her tentacles, twisting and turning it until the tentacle broke off. She was wounded and bleeding and needed to find safety. As Foster watched this scene in horror, he desperately wanted to intervene and rescue the octopus. She now felt like a part of his family, and he didn't want to see her suffer. He was relieved to see her escape from the grip of the shark as she propelled herself away from the danger. Knowing she was injured, Foster worried for her well-being and searched for her, hoping that she found somewhere to hide that was safe. He eventually found her tucked away in her tiny home pale, lifeless, and not eating.

Day after day, Foster felt helpless watching his friend the octopus become lifeless. After many days of feeling despondent that she would not survive, a miracle seemed to occur. A small new tentacle began to grow, the color in her body started to revive, and the octopus seemed to come back to life. Her wounded appendage was more than just an appendage; it was a part of her brain and nervous system that carried wisdom from generations that came before her. This tentacle, a large part of the octopus's brain, was regenerating and, after 100 days, was entirely back to its full size and function. The brain's ability to heal was evident, and the octopus was able to continue with her life until it mated, gave birth, and then died, as was its destiny.

Sensing Safety and Danger

Just like the octopus, your brain and nervous system sense and react to your environment when you feel safe or threatened. Dr. Stephen Porges's (2011) Polyvagal theory looks at the autonomic nervous system (ANS) importance and the vital role it plays when you feel safe or threatened. When there is danger, just like when you sense the shark is on the hunt, the (ANS) will activate without conscious awareness, allowing you to take action for survival. When there is no threat, the (ANS) signals safety; therefore, you can relax, digest your food, bond, and be playful.

Porges (2011) calls this process of assessing safety or danger "neuroception." Neuroception is not always accurate because it occurs through how your brainbody perceive a situation or your environment. This process of perception is filtered through your historical experiences. In times when you felt safe and secure, your nervous system would respond in ways where you could laugh, play, bond, and experience intimacy. If you experienced situations and environments that were *not* safe physically, emotionally, sexually, or spiritually, your nervous system responded in ways to keep you alive. When these experiences of danger to your safety are not fully processed, they become unresolved traumas, thus creating a template in your brainbody where you are in survival mode. This template becomes a filter in which you perceive situations and your environment based on your past. Therefore, perception is not always accurate to the current situation since it filters information through your past experiences.

Part of sensing danger and safety involves the vagus nerve, which runs through the entire body and becomes active when you feel safe or under threat. The vagus nerve connects to many areas in the body, including the primitive part of the brain, stomach, gut, heart, lungs, throat, and facial muscles. This nerve is multifaceted in purpose and very sensitive to the environment, helping to keep you functioning without conscious awareness. Since the vagus nerve connects to the gut, it can let you know when something feels right and when something feels wrong.

The gut is often referred to as the gut-brain (Mayer, 2018) because it has over 100 million nerve cells. The gut-brain does not have conscious thoughts like your rational brain; instead, it is connected to emotions, helping you sense and feel your experiences. When your gut-brain signals something is wrong, you may experience feeling anxious, nauseous, or even the sensation of "butterflies." Hans Solo's character from *Star Wars IV: A New Hope* (1977) is a perfect example of someone who connects to his gut-brain for information in assessing the danger or safety in his environment. Viewers often hear him say, "I have a bad feeling about this," and, sure enough, a moment later in the movie, danger is upon him. Rationally, everything in his environment looks safe and sound, but his gut-brain gives him a warning signal to prepare for what is about to come: danger.

As danger arises, the sympathetic nervous system (SNS) activates throughout the body in an energetic, alive, and dynamic way. If there is danger, the (SNS) mobilizes into action, elevating cortisol to get the body to move as quickly as possible to escape for survival. This process happens without conscious thought. At first, the body will freeze just like a deer in the headlights to promptly assess the level of danger. All your senses are heightened, preparing you to take action so that you can run away as quickly as possible. If fleeing is not possible, your body will try and fight your opponent to defend and eliminate the danger. When fighting is not working or isn't even an option, reality sets in that you cannot escape the current situation. Dissociation then starts to set in, causing feelings of panic, dizziness, nausea, lightheadedness, tingling, or numbing, collapsing into the dorsal part of the vagus nerve. Here the body system begins to shut down, decreasing cortisol and lowering blood pressure, causing paleness in the skin as well as disconnection from painful feelings and body sensations. A sense of paralysis and immobilization take over, eventually leading to a fainting response for pure survival.

In contrast, when you feel safe, the social nervous system will be at play, activating the myelinated ventral part of the vagus nerve. Here both the mobilization of play and the immobilization of relaxation, bonding, and loving behaviors can take place. Feeling safe, secure, and at ease with situations and environments is critical for the social nervous system to put the brake on the activation for survival when there is no danger present. That's why in therapy safety is critical and can be established in remote therapy with awareness on the therapist's part. Repatterning the response to danger when there is no danger in the present moment can start to change clients' abilities to present, aware, and responsive to different situations appropriately.

Let's return to *My Octopus Teacher* to see how the octopus's (ANS) responded throughout interacting with the shark. When the octopus detected the shark was circling her, she sensed the danger and immediately mobilized her (SNS). She quickly went into action by extending her body like a jet propeller so that she could flee from the threat. When she couldn't escape the danger by fleeing, she fiercely fought against the shark, trying to defeat the threat. When the shark won the battle by severing off one of her tentacles, the octopus's response sent her into a dorsal vagal shut down, and she became immobilized. In this state, she retreated to safety in her home, becoming pale, lifeless, and motionless because her life depended on it. Within the safety of her cave, her tentacle regenerated, bringing her back to life. Once again, she was able to play and interact with other fish and continue with her life, assessing when she felt safe or in danger.

Matching Traumas

Like the octopus threatened by the shark, many therapists experienced their (ANS) in high gear due to the pandemic. Therapists felt that their world was no longer safe due to being away from their offices, working with new technology, and feeling out of control, concerned that danger lurked for their clients because they weren't together in the same space. On top of this, as therapists were professionally dealing with the pandemic's devastation, their personal experiences matched that of their clients. Matching traumas can occur when therapists and clients are both going through a divorce, grieving for a loved one, or grappling with things like floods in their communities, terrorist bombings, school shootings, and, of course, going through a pandemic. During these times, therapists can enmesh with the client emotionally, mentally, and physically too much, making it harder for them to stay therapeutic in the relationship. When this happens, it can feel like there is no one guiding the ship, and both therapist and client are left wandering in the session, sinking into the pain with no end in sight. As the therapist taps into their own pain, it can fuel the client's nervous system response and vice versa, creating a feedback loop of dysregulated nervous systems.

Somatic Resonance

Through the experience of matching traumas, therapists may encounter what Stanley Keleman (1987) calls "somatic resonance." Somatic resonance is when therapists experience sensations in their bodies at the same time as their clients. An energetic and vibrational dance occurs between both therapist and client where the therapist feels sensations in their body that match what the client is feeling. Einstein's synchronization theory is another way of looking at somatic resonance. If you put several grandfather clocks in a room and set them at different times, they will automatically begin synchronizing with each other time. This same process happens between therapists and clients. Their nervous systems will synchronize with each other, where the powerful nervous system state will take over the weaker nervous state to synchronize in rhythm in order to connect.

When therapists have a healthy boundary with their clients, this energetic exchange helps the therapist experience empathy, mirror the client emotionally, and attune to the client's experience. It also allows therapists to connect to their intuition. During times therapists experience matching traumas, they must be aware of this energetic exchange to maintain a healthy boundary, distinguish the clients' experience from their own, and not get lost in both nervous systems becoming dysregulated.

Somatic resonance is the key to feeling any connection with a client. This energy exchange can be powerful, but if therapists are not working with it consciously, it can leave them experiencing somatic residue from their clients after sessions. Over time this accumulated residue can lead to compassion fatigue, remote fatigue, or even burn-out. By staying awake to this energetic exchange, therapists will begin to trust what they are sensing and feeling in their own bodies as information that can help them get to know what their clients are experiencing. Clients will report feeling heard and seen in ways they have never experienced before, which can deepen the trust and rapport between therapist and client. By being aware of somatic resonance, therapists will remain more active and present in the dance between each other's nervous systems, leading to a more profound sense of connection in each session.

....

SPOTLIGHT: FEEDBACK LOOP OF FEAR

Let's look at an example of somatic resonance in a remote therapy session. A therapist shared with me how difficult it was for her to feel solid in her body whenever her clients expressed fear around the unknown due to the pandemic. At the end of each day, after multiple sessions of clients sharing their fears, she felt drained and exhausted. Several of her clients were worried about how dangerous the virus was, how long the pandemic was going to last, and how hard it was to be quarantined with their families. These clients were experiencing the same fears as the therapist. However, the therapist blamed her exhaustion on sitting in front of a computer screen for long periods rather than looking at her matching traumas. Without an awareness of somatic resonance, the therapist struggled to maintain a healthy boundary, contributing to her sense of fatigue at the end of the day.

During times when her clients talked about their fears, the therapist's anxiety would escalate to the point she could hardly ground herself during her remote sessions. Her mind would go blank; she could feel her body tremble as her heart started to race. She found it challenging to remain present in each session. When one session finished, she found herself dreading the next one, worried that all her clients were in crisis just like herself. At night, she found it difficult to sleep, feeling energy surge throughout her body, denying her an opportunity to rest and rejuvenate.

Both the therapist's and clients' fears created a feedback loop fueling each other's nervous systems and increasing their sense of being out of control. Fear escalated between them so that the therapist was not grounded in her body, losing her sense of self. Both therapist and client were collapsing into fear with no one leading the way.

This feedback loop was exhausting her, which contributed to her feeling that remote therapy was too hard. It was easier to blame remote therapy than to see that her own fears around the pandemic were matching her clients. My job was to help her recognize that she had matching traumas with her clients and give her more tools to assist her in taking better care of herself while working with her clients. Through helping her slow down and connect to her body, the therapist became aware of her matching traumas, recognizing that part of her exhaustion was from the enmeshment that was happening with her clients' experiences. We discussed her working on a plan on what to do before, during, and after her sessions to better regulate her nervous system.

Before sessions, she took time to contain her own concerns about COVID-19 spreading, how it was impacting her family, and her feeling incapable of doing effective remote therapy with her clients. After she contained this distress, she focused on grounding her bodymind, allowing her to be more present to face her day of remote therapy sessions. During sessions, she started tracking the energetic exchange between herself and her clients, learning how to dance with the energy in a conscious way that made her feel more in control of what she was experiencing. To put a deliberate end to her workday, she made time to clear any somatic residue she had picked up from her clients, allowing herself to connect with her own energetic body. Through these practices, she set healthier boundaries around her personal life, which allowed her to settle her nervous system while working with clients. She found that she felt more solid, in control, and able to empathize with her clients better without enmeshing with their somatic processes. When she felt somatic resonance with her client, she was more aware, present, and capable of dancing with this energy to remain therapeutic in her remote sessions.

....

Do No Harm

As some therapists struggled with their matching traumas and somatic resonance, many expressed that remote therapy brought up a deep-seated fear that they would harm their clients. These therapists felt that if they couldn't see the client's entire body, they would miss nonverbal somatic cues, leading clients to dissociate. As therapists bumped up against this particular fear, their bodies would go into a freeze response. In the freeze response, therapists would lose their focus to the point of forgetting they had skills that could help their clients regulate their nervous systems, enabling them to remain safe in the therapeutic process.

Many of these therapists felt that if they couldn't see a

person's whole body, they would refuse to engage in trauma therapy because it was too risky and dangerous. By not trusting that they *did* have skills to handle dissociation, therapists would find themselves in avoidance of working with traumas clients desperately needed to address. The fear of harm became a debilitating barrier that prevented therapists from fully engaging in remote therapy.

As I reflected on how to help with this barrier, I recalled recently training a blind therapist on how to do remote EMDR therapy. This therapist embraced what he was learning and was not afraid of what he couldn't see. Rather than relying on his eyes to see his clients' nonverbal somatic cues, he relied on his body to sense and feel the somatic resonance that was happening between them. His curiosity and openness to use his whole body as his guide gave him information about what was happening in his own body as well as in his clients' bodies. This therapist remained grounded, connected, and centered in his body, trusting his intuition to lead the way. Having observed this in my training, I remained curious about the sighted therapists who were fearful that something terrible would happen if they didn't see the client's whole body. This apprehension was exhausting them so much that they longed for the world to go back to normal so they could retreat into the safety of their therapy office to do in-person sessions once again. These therapists were missing a deep understanding of what nonverbal communication entails. By not trusting what their bodies were sensing and feeling, therapists lost access to information about their clients.

What most therapists tend to pay attention to in their

sessions is what the client is verbally expressing. Only 30%–40% of how humans communicate is through verbal language. The other 60%–70% occurs through nonverbal communication. This nonverbal communication influences how we respond, react, and interact with each other. In somatic psychology, when therapists track nonverbal somatic cues in sessions, they are getting to know their clients on a deeper level through the client's attitudes, emotions, verbal communications, and nonverbal communications. Paying attention to nonverbal cues can help a therapist track if what the client is saying is congruent with their nonverbal communications. Just as much as therapists track their client's nonverbal communications, clients are watching to see if the therapist's verbal communication is congruent with their nonverbal communications. When therapists' nonverbal communication matches what they're saying, clients feel their therapist is better prepared, better understands the client's experience, and has more sincere empathy for the client.

Let's take a more in-depth look at the different kinds of nonverbal communications and how they can impact remote therapy. There are three primary categories of nonverbal communications: kinesics, paralanguage, and proxemics.

Kinesics

Kinesics is the use of body language, including the study of posture, gestures, facial expression, and eye contact. Often in therapy, the therapist and client will simultaneously be in a dance where they mirror each other's movements, such as crossing their legs, scratching their heads, or taking a sip of water. This perfect dance in unison helps build the bond and trust between the therapist and client. When this dance is out of sync, the client may be doing something that makes the therapist uncomfortable, such as biting their nails, twirling their hair, or pursing their lips repetitively. In these moments, the therapist may unconsciously distance themselves from the client nonverbally by crossing their arms, avoiding eye contact, distracting themselves by taking notes, and/or checking emails or text messages during remote therapy sessions. Falling out of sync with the client nonverbally can occur without being aware it's even happening. It takes conscious awareness on the therapist's part to find ways to stay present with the client.

Once therapists recognize they're having difficulty tolerating their clients' nonverbal communications, therapists can take a deep breath, ground their feet into the floor, or gently look around the room to refocus their energy. Therapists must consciously work with what's happening in their own bodies in order to remain therapeutic in their interventions. They will find it easier to witness their client's nonverbal communications when they regulate their own experiences throughout the session. Remembering that the client's nonverbal communications may signal that something deeper is trying to arise in the sessions can help therapists lean into the discomfort rather than run away from it. If therapists continue struggling to stay present with the client, they may want to take this information to explore in their consultation, supervision, or their own therapy.

Paralanguage

Paralanguage refers to the nonlinguistic part of speech related to verbal communication. Listening for the subtleties in the client's tempo, pitch, volume, and timing as well as how they pause when speaking can reflect different emotional tones. Take, for example, the words "I'm fine." How a person says these words can express something completely different, such as giving the impression of being nonchalant, questioning, definitive, defensive, or happy. These simple words can have many different meanings, so paying attention to *how* a client is saying something rather than just paying attention to the words is essential. A client may be stating they are fine, but their body may be slumped over, heavy with no eye contact, and their tone of voice may not match what they're saying. In this case, when the client's verbal and nonverbal communication is incongruent, therapists need to remain curious and pay attention to what the client's nonverbal communication is trying to express. Words may be covering up what the client is truly conveying. Spending time developing enough trust in the therapeutic relationship will help support the client in being able to share how they are genuinely feeling. Be careful not to bring the client's awareness to the incongruency between their verbal and nonverbal communications too soon because the client may feel too vulnerable and shut down even more. Slowing down the process and building rapport is essential to deepen the therapeutic alliance.

As therapists listen on a deeper level to what the client's saying, another vital part of paralanguage is allowing room for silence to exist in the remote therapy sessions. Many therapists experience silence as a problem that needs to be solved. When clients get quiet, therapists often quickly fill the space with more words that can interrupt the client's ability to slow down, sense, and feel what is happening in their bodies. The therapist may become anxious in the silence and rush the client's pacing to calm their own anxiety. By not allowing the silence to be a part of the sessions, clients may feel defensive and block what they are experiencing or rush to please the therapist and be a "good" client.

In observing the client's paralanguage, therapists need to be aware that cultural differences may exist. Being careful not to interpret, put meaning, or judge the client too quickly can help avoid misinterpreting the client's paralanguage. For example, in some cultures, talking swiftly and loudly is an expression of excitement and passion, while other cultures might interpret this as anger and aggression. When I first moved to New York City, I was confused by many of my new friends' paralanguage. It seemed like they were talking so loud and fast that they were shouting at me the entire time. My nervous system would tremble, shake, and I would retreat, believing they were angry with me. Over time, I was able to realize this way of communicating was a part of their culture and had nothing to do with me. I was misinterpreting their nonverbal communication through my cultural lens, which was completely different. I learned that they were more expressive than my family; when my family got loud that meant I was in trouble. Once I became aware of our differences, my nervous system calmed down, and I enjoyed our interactions.

Just like I didn't know how to interpret my new New York friends' expressions, therapists must be careful not to interpret a client's paralanguage as "wrong" and needing to be fixed. Slowing down and remaining curious without judgment or assigning meaning too hastily to the client's paralanguage is essential to keep the trust in the therapeutic relationship. Therapists need to stay open, curious, and respectful with how their clients are expressing themselves by tracking when the client's verbal and nonverbal communications are congruent or incongruent. Congruency will let therapists know that the client is speaking their truth, whereas incongruency signals that their nonverbal communication needs more room to express.

Proxemics

Proxemics is the perception of a space and how much space you take up personally and socially. Since the pandemic, everyone has gotten very familiar with proxemics and "social distancing," the distance needed to remain safe from contracting a deadly virus. Typically, families, cities, states, even countries have different kinds of proxemics as a part of their culture. When I was living in New York City, my personal space was limited. Often when I rode on a subway, people were pushed up against me, and I had little wiggle room to maneuver. In the beginning, this kind of contact was unfamiliar and quite frightening to me. When I felt invaded in my personal space, my body became rigid, fearful, and on guard. Eventually, after years of living in

New York City, my body grew more comfortable being in such tight quarters with people. I knew how to be in this constricted space, remain alert to potential danger, focused on my surroundings while breathing and staying grounded. Then, years later, when I moved to Boulder, my sense of personal space changed dramatically. Wide walking trails at the mountains' foothills felt expansive, open, and inviting. I could take up more personal space because there was more room to expand my body, mind, and energy without ever bumping into another person. In the beginning, I felt a sense of freedom that was confusing, disorienting, and hard to trust, but I eventually grew comfortable with this as the new normal of proxemics for the Boulder culture.

The proxemics for in-person therapy, can impact the therapeutic relationship without the therapist even being aware of it. It is quite common for the therapist to dictate how much space a client can take up in the therapist's office. The therapist has placed the furniture in a way that's comfortable for them. The client walks into the office and sits where the therapist has determined they will sit. How close or far away they are from each other has been pre-determined. For some clients, this arrangement is acceptable and they never question it, but for other clients, this may feel wrong, uncomfortable, and not safe.

In somatic psychology, therapists work with the proxemics in the space by consciously setting up experiments to allow clients to explore proxemics until safety in the body occurs. By having the client consciously experiment with how close or far away they want to be in a relationship to the therapist, the client gets to connect to their felt sense in the body, empowering them to feel at ease, and relaxing their nervous system.

In remote therapy, therapists can apply this same concept even though the therapist and client are not in the same room. By experimenting with how close or far away both the therapist and client are from their computer's camera, safety will develop, allowing the therapeutic relationship to build trust and rapport. In many of my consultation sessions, therapists tend to sit too close or far away from the camera. When the therapists sit too close to the camera, it feels like they're invading my space, and I want to pull back to find more distance between us. When a therapist is sitting too far away, I find it harder to track their nonverbal communications. Taking time to set up an experiment so that both therapist and client spatially find positions that feel comfortable to each other's nervous systems can go a long way in building the safety needed to do remote therapy.

Using this knowledge about nonverbal communications can help therapists track the kinesics, paralanguage, and proxemics in remote therapy even while being in separate rooms and not seeing the client's whole body. As a somatic resonance dance forms between the therapist and client, the therapist can track the client's nonverbal communications. Therapists can then rely on the nonverbal communications they are sensing to inform, guide, and connect them with their client's somatic experiences. As therapists fine-tune their ability to feel and sense this information, clients often report that their therapist sees them on a level that no one in their life has ever done before. Let's not forget—all of this is happening in separate rooms connected energetically through a computer screen.

Building Safety

As therapists learn to accept they're not going to "see" the client's full body and begin to trust the energetic exchange of nonverbal communications, they can then add safety factors to make remote therapy feel safer for both the therapist and client. Taking time to educate clients on what dissociation is, looks like, feels like in the bodymind can be normalizing and empowering for the client. As the client becomes savvy at describing their somatic experience, this can help the therapist trust that the client knows what is happening in their body. This information can then guide therapists to respond appropriately with different grounding practices to help keep the client feeling safe in the window of tolerance. To assist in this process, therapists can give the client a list of somatic vocabulary words to help them develop a language to express what they are sensing in their body. These descriptive words can include cold, hot, tingling, prickly, sharp, dull, numb, open, or closed. These somatic words create a bridge for the client to communicate in ways they have never done before. Both therapists and clients will become familiar with the client's dissociative patterns by tracking the somatic cues that signal they no longer feel safe. With this information, helping clients learn how to ground in their bodies can support the client's nervous system to heal and repattern habituated nervous systems responses by bringing more safety into therapy.

....

SPOTLIGHT: NONVERBAL MISSTEPS

Let's look at an example of a therapist struggling with a client's nonverbal communications and how she had to become aware of this process to shift how she felt in her sessions. The client would sit extremely close to their computer camera, which distorted their facial expressions. This felt frightening to the therapist. The client's voice was loud, with bursts of energy and then long pauses where the client would stare off into space, making the therapist anxious, afraid, and frozen in her body. The therapist felt she was on high alert, fueling her sense of being incompetent, an imposter, and incapable of doing remote therapy with this client.

*First, I had to help this therapist ground in her own body before she could ever help her client in the way she wanted. She needed to see that her bodymind responded to her client's nonverbal communications without her even recognizing it, which was ungrounding to her sense of being. The first step was for the therapist to practice grounding **before** working with this client so she felt prepared to be present with the client's nonverbal communications. In her next session with this client, she needed to set up an experiment to see how close or far away each of them was sitting in relationship to their cameras to help create a sense of ease in their bodies. Both therapist and client willingly participated.*

Once the proxemics were in place, the therapist needed

to recognize that the long pauses the client was experiencing might be a form of dissociation. The therapist needed to help her client learn about the window of tolerance and dissociation in order to become familiar with what was actually happening in the long pauses. As the client learned about the process of dissociation, they struggled to describe what they were sensing in their body. The therapist provided the client with a list of somatic words to help give the client a vocabulary of what they were sensing and feeling. With this new language, the client was able to verbalize the first signs they experienced when dissociating: ringing in their ears, blurriness in their sight, nauseousness, and then a desire to hide or runway. As both therapist and client became familiar with this dissociative pattern, the therapist was able to teach the client grounding practices, which created more safety for the client.

By building more safety for the client through proxemics as well as providing grounding practices, the therapist no longer felt frightened by this client's paralanguage. The client's nonverbal communications became useful information in the sessions, guiding the therapist rather than terrifying her. Now the therapist could ground in her own body easier, allowing her to be more present with this client and their experiences. Through this process, the therapist began to trust that she didn't need to see her client's entire body to track and respond to her client in remote therapy. By consciously working with nonverbal communications as key information, the therapist built more safety for her clients without being in the same room.

WRAPPING UP

With the pandemic impacting therapists' practices on such a deep level, they had to face the reality that there was a new abnormal—and, potentially, a new normal in the future. Many therapists were in distress, needing more support and skills to handle all the changes. During consultations, I found myself serving as a steady guide, a beacon of light, where darkness was taking over. Part of this process helped therapists recognize that they were grieving for how things once were and then helping them find new ways to embrace remote therapy. Therapists had to face their fears of technology to get comfortable with not being in the same room as their clients. By accepting that technology was a gift for continuing their sessions with clients, therapists could come from a place of acceptance, compassion, and gratitude that this opportunity was even available. Therefore, this technology provided a beautiful way to continue working with their clients through this crisis, which has changed the field of psychotherapy forever.

Even with the therapist and client in separate rooms, therapists began to sense that connection *is* possible by tuning into the powerful energetic exchange that can occur in remote therapy. By seeing the computer as a conduit for connection rather than a barrier, therapists can facilitate real, powerful, and transformational sessions for their clients. In addition, developing awareness around non-verbal communications as information about how grounded or dysregulated the client is during sessions can guide therapists in building more safety throughout the process. By teaching their clients grounding practices to help them feel more in control of their emotions as well as educating them on how to regulate their nervous systems, the clients will feel more secure in the process of remote therapy, also allowing therapists to trust the process more fully.

Therapists taking more time to prepare for sessions, especially when clients' traumas match their own, is essential to the therapeutic process. This is a must to help therapists feel more grounded, present, and capable of handling what's happening in each session. As the therapist builds safety in their own body, it will provide more safety for their clients, and, thus, develop a solid foundation for remote therapy. As therapists ground themselves into their competent, capable, and skillful selves, they will realize that remote therapy is just therapy, and their sense of being an imposter can melt away.

REMOTE FATIGUE

....

*You can see with your whole body, not
just your eyes.*

....

DYNAMIC FACTORS

While learning how to take better care of myself before,
during, and after remote sessions, I realized that I could
help therapists navigate the transition from in-person to
remote sessions due to the pandemic. In making this
transition therapists now sat in front of a computer all day
long, which strained them emotionally, physically, mentally,
and spiritually. For many therapists, the isolation from not
being in their offices was becoming unbearable. Many of
them felt distracted by their home life, emails, and texts,

leading to difficulties concentrating or feelings of boredom in their sessions. Some therapists found they forgot what their clients were sharing. Some avoided having their clients work on unresolved childhood traumas out of fear that they would create harm. In almost every consultation session with therapists, I heard complaints about somatic symptoms of tension in necks and shoulders, migraines, and eye strain. These therapists unconsciously disconnected from their bodies, which caused exhaustion, fatigue, and loss of interest in their work. All of these symptoms were contributing to what I call "remote fatigue."

As I started working with therapists who were experiencing remote fatigue, I identified patterns of over-scheduling clients and losing boundaries; fears preventing therapists from working with trauma; and ongoing somatic complaints. Many of these therapists were suffering from remote traumatization and matching traumas. In addition, as we explored in the previous chapter, therapists' own unresolved traumas were apparent. Each of these issues by themselves can lead to symptoms of exhaustion and compassion fatigue but experienced together can lead to complete depletion and burn-out of the bodymind. And it was. Many of the therapists who reached out to me were feeling overwhelmed, out of control, and incapable of showing up for their remote sessions.

Let's take a look at each of these issues and how they contribute to remote fatigue.

Lack of Movement

As therapists began to offer remote therapy, many of them kept their schedules the same as seeing their clients in-person, not realizing how this impacted them physically, mentally, and emotionally. Logically, seeing clients back-to-back while sitting in front of a computer screen all day seemed like it would be the same as seeing their clients in-person. However, by not taking any breaks between sessions, therapists felt rushed and unable to relax in their bodies from sitting for long periods. Many therapists were overriding their bodies' signals, sacrificing their own needs so they could see the same number of clients in the same amount of time.

As I helped therapists become aware of what they were sensing from sitting in front of the computer screen without any breaks, many expressed that they wanted more time between sessions to get up and move away from the computer. Some therapists found they needed 15 to 30 minutes between sessions to bring movement back into their bodies, rest their eyes, and clear their minds. Although the therapists acknowledged they wanted more time to rejuvenate between sessions, many struggled to put this change into action. I encouraged them to prioritize their breaks as essential to their well-being so they could be more present with their clients throughout the day. It took reminders and repeated encouragement, but, over time, many of these therapists adjusted their schedules, allowing movement and breath to come into their practices. They turned to activities such as yoga, qigong, tai chi, and stretching or even playing a piece of music and letting their bodies dance for a while. As an increasing number of these therapists embraced this idea of scheduling a more extended break between sessions, it became clear that many of them had been longing for a sense of freedom in their bodies.

As these therapists started feeling more of this freedom in their bodies between sessions, I also invited them to find more movement *within* their sessions. From a somatic perspective, movement is the key to life and can be vital for both client and therapist to keep the energy flowing throughout the session. While offering remote therapy, many of these therapists felt that they would freeze, become static, and make themselves energetically smaller due to the edges the computer screen created. This screen formed a false boundary that was small, shrinking the therapist's energetic field. It's as if the therapists were trying to fit their entire bodies into a small box, becoming frozen like a block of ice: tight, constricted, and contracted. This contracted state left many therapists feeling aches, pains, headaches, and extreme exhaustion by the end of the day. Therapists needed to let go, expand their energy into a larger space in their room, and let the computer screen be a conduit for connection rather than a barrier. Having therapists imagine sitting in the same room with their client allowed the computer screen edges to melt away, naturally bringing more ease and movement to their bodies.

....

SPOTLIGHT: FINDING MOVEMENT

A therapist shared with me that their client complained of shoulder pain. The therapist said they would know how to work with this client in an in-person session but felt frozen and helpless in the remote sessions. I knew that this therapist was a yoga instructor, and I was curious why it was so easy for them to bring yoga into their in-person sessions but not into their remote ones. The therapist felt it would be impossible to add movement while being in separate rooms because they felt the computer created an artificial boundary themselves and their client. I said, "If I were your client and we were together in the same room, what would you have me do right now?" They quickly went into action, guiding me into a yoga pose to support the pain in my body. Their eyes widened as they said, "You did it!" That's all it took to remind this therapist they could follow their instincts and incorporate the skills they already had by letting go of the false sense of constriction from sitting in front of a computer. The idea that the computer screen was no longer a limitation opened up possibilities for this therapist to embrace remote therapy.

See if you can bring more consciousness to the kinds of movement you can incorporate into all aspects of your remote therapy sessions. Both you and your clients can stand, stretch, walk around the room, or you can even just become more aware of how the client is breathing. Removing the barrier that the computer screen limits the space you and your clients can use allows for more breath, movement, and aliveness in each session. Your computer screen becomes a beautiful conduit for connection, helping you remain active, alert, and awake during each therapy session. As you bring more movement into every aspect of your day, you can begin to find the right pacing for scheduling your remote therapy sessions. By honoring a schedule that feels good physically, mentally, and emotionally, remote fatigue will dissipate, making your remote therapy practice more sustainable.

....

Suspended

As overscheduling clients for remote sessions became an issue for therapists, many also lost their boundaries between their work and family life due to the pandemic's impact, which added to their sense of remote fatigue. Boundaries that were once in place seemed to be suspended in time once the pandemic hit, making it difficult for therapists to feel effective in their remote sessions. Many therapists struggled to end their sessions on time; find value in their work; and felt enmeshed with their family's energy because they were quarantined at home. These lost boundaries impacted therapists during their sessions, contributing to extreme stress and pure exhaustion by the end of the day. Emotionally, these therapists were struggling with feeling incompetent, inadequate, and incapable of helping their clients.

....

SPOTLIGHT: TIME & VALUE

Let's look at a couple of examples where therapists lost their boundaries when they switched to remote therapy sessions.

As a therapist shared how distressing it was for him to do remote sessions, his words flew around, disjointed, and vague, making it difficult for me to track what he was saying. Usually, I can easily follow this therapist's train of thought, but this time I felt confused and frustrated and I wanted to pull my body away from my computer screen to create more distance between us. As I tracked this reaction in my body, I invited the therapist to slow down and feel his feet on the ground, take a deep breath, and focus. As he settled his nervous system, he revealed he was afraid to share how much he hated remote therapy, fearing I would judge him as an incompetent therapist. I assured him that I wouldn't judge him, and this was a safe place to share how he was feeling. He said that when he does remote therapy sessions, he loses track of time, space, and orientation to himself and his client. It's as if he gets sucked into the tiny, confined space of the computer screen with no escape. When he finally peels himself away to look at the clock, he has gone over time, which he never does in his in-person sessions. He then anxiously tries to end his session only to find himself starting his next session late. As the pattern continues throughout the day, he feels guilt, shame, and fear that he is an incompetent therapist.

We explored the difference between in-person and remote sessions with his boundary around time. He told me that in his in-person sessions he had a clock, which was large and easy to read, situated by the client, and now with the computer, he didn't have any way to track what time it was. Without a clock, he lost his orientation to the here and now, becoming absorbed in his client's emotions and pain. Once he was able to see that a clock orients him in the here and now, he decided to try the same thing in his remote sessions by placing a clock by his computer. He was excited to put this plan into place and see if he could quit losing track of time. In our next session, he reported that having a clock by his computer worked well in reestablishing his boundary. He felt more grounded in his body and less anxious with his thoughts. Plus, he'd started and ended all of his sessions on time. By incorporating this simple solution to reset his boundary, he began to regain his sense of confidence as a therapist in his remote sessions.

However, his hatred for remoted therapy lingered. As we continued to explore this, he shared his feelings that remote therapy was of lesser value and less effective, and also disclosed it would be unethical to charge his clients his full rate. I pointed out that this belief was undervaluing his skills as a therapist and that he was still doing therapy; it was just in a different format. Therefore, charging his usual rate was professional and ethical—and showed his clients that he values remote therapy as an effective treatment.

I could feel the therapist's resistance to what I was saying and decided to explore with him more deeply why he held onto this belief. I invited this therapist to get curious about his negative belief about himself when he thought about charging his full rate for remote sessions. He immediately said, "I'm bad." As he got in touch with this belief, I asked him the earliest time he had ever felt this way. He stated, "When I was 8 years old, I broke one of my toys and blamed it on my brother. My brother got punished for this lie, and my parents never knew the truth." As he tapped into this childhood memory, he felt shame, guilt, and nauseous for doing such a bad thing. Once he got in touch with the emotions in his body, I asked him if he could find forgiveness for that little boy. He was able to feel this forgiveness, and the shame dissipated from his body.

Next, I had him think about charging his full rate for remote therapy sessions. This time he could see that feeling bad about himself for stealing and lying as a child had nothing to do with his current situation as a therapist. He could see that switching to remote therapy was not trying to deceive his clients by getting away with something of lesser value; instead, he offered the same services just in a different way. He was able to see that this change in his practice had triggered him and that he was acting from earlier unresolved childhood trauma. With this knowledge, he was able to get back in touch with his value as a therapist and saw that not charging his full rate was undervaluing his services. Once he named this underlying trauma, he quickly realized that he needed to let his clients know remote therapy sessions billed at his full rate. By reestablishing his boundary around what he charged for therapy, he felt better about engaging in the work with his clients, valued what he had to offer, and appreciated his clients' progress once again.

While this therapist struggled with timing issues and valuing his work, I witnessed other therapists losing their boundaries by enmeshing with their family's energy, which was then spilling over into how they felt about their clients. As therapists worked from home with their children who were trying to do distance learning, the strain of attempting to establish boundaries was significant. These therapists often felt as if they had to give more to their families and be available at all times, making it challenging to show up for their clients. Many of these therapists found they had no transition time between their roles of therapist and parent. Having to be "on" 24/7 was too much to ask of anyone, and these therapists felt overextended: they had no time for themselves and were resentful that they had to see their clients. As a result, some of these therapists felt their clients were too needy, too demanding, and wanting too much attention.

. . . .

SPOTLIGHT: BOUNDARIES

One therapist shared that their children would be standing by the door anxiously waiting for them to finish their remote sessions. This therapist could feel their children's energy pushing, clawing, and demanding their attention. Sensing this needy energy behind the door while working with a client caused the therapist to feel annoyed, impatient, and resentful, thus making it very difficult to focus on their client's session. The client, unconsciously sensing this anxious energy from the therapist, would become even needier in their session. Both therapist and client were spiraling into a feedback loop of neediness and resentment that was not nourishing, therapeutic, or satisfying for either of them. Once the therapy session ended, the therapist opened the door and become inundated by their children's demanding energy. There was no transition time between work and home life for this therapist, leaving them drained, burdened, and feeling incapable of meeting everyone's needs.

As I helped this therapist get in touch with the loss of their boundaries, they could sense their exhaustion from trying to be available to everyone at all times. The therapist stated they used to have a 30-minute drive to transition from work to home. Without that commute buffer, they felt guilty, believing they would be a bad parent if they didn't immediately respond to their children. By not having this transition time, there was no boundary, leaving the therapist drained, exhausted, and impatient with their client as well as their children. Once the therapist understood the connection of not having clear boundaries between work and family, they could see how much it impacted them mentally, emotionally, and physically.

We first explored what kind of boundary they needed after their remote therapy sessions in order to transition from therapist to their parental role. As the therapist heard the word "boundary," they began to cry, naming that they felt there was no "me" time anymore since having to *quarantine with their family. I gently encouraged them to explore how much time they needed to put work away and transition before being with their children. They felt 10 minutes would be enough and that they wanted to take a "time out" before engaging with their children. As I asked the therapist to imagine giving this time to themselves after sessions, they felt this weight lift from their shoulders, their body relax, and they were able to breathe once again. Then the therapist came up with a plan to display a "work time" sign on their door and give their children a clear boundary that if the sign is up, it means "do not disturb," which includes waiting by the door.*

The therapist put this new plan into action. At the end of the day, they sat in their chair for 10 minutes, closing their eyes, breathing away stress and tension from their bodymind before reengaging with their children. The therapist was grateful to have this plan and felt their boundary had become reestablished. Their children respected this new boundary by not waiting at the door, making it easier for the therapist to be fully present with their clients before reengaging with their children. Allowing 10 minutes to transition between work and home gave the therapist time to reset their nervous system, enabling them to be prepared and present throughout their day. The therapist began to feel more vital, energetic, and present both personally and professionally.

By having clear boundaries, you can ground yourself in a stronger sense of self, tapping into feeling competent and capable of offering help to your clients. Taking time to set clear boundaries around timing issues, separating work from family, and seeing the value in remote therapy is essential. It's also important to take time throughout the day to notice when and where you feel drained as it can help you identify any indicators that you may need to set stronger boundaries. Establishing and maintaining clear boundaries can help you can stay in integrity with your work and find value in being a therapist while connecting to a greater sense of worth. Clear boundaries can help you keep your energy fluid, vibrant, and dynamic, ultimately preventing remote fatigue.

....

Pushing

Another contributing factor to remote fatigue was therapists fearing that their clients would dissociate because they weren't in the same room. By not seeing the client's entire body, therapists feared they would miss too many nonverbal somatic cues. In response to feeling afraid, many therapists pushed with their eyes to see, fixating their gaze on their clients and staring intently, worried that something terrible would happen if they weren't on hyper-alert, ready for danger to arise. As I consulted with therapists regarding remote therapy, many would lean closer to their computer, pushing their eyes forward to make contact with me. It was as if they were trying to teleport themselves into my room out of fear they'd lose control at any moment. Many of them were on guard, behaving as though they must push for this contact or something awful would happen and they would be responsible for causing harm. Some of these therapists would stare with such intensity that I found my back, jaws, and hands tighten so much I wanted to back away from my computer just to feel more space between us. Here we were in separate rooms, and I felt the impulse to run away as fast as possible. I could sense and feel the therapist's anxiety, worry, and fears through our energetic connection. As I tuned into this strong somatic response in my own body, I wondered: if this is what I was experiencing with these therapists in consultation, what must their clients feel in their remote therapy sessions?

I knew I had to help these therapists ground their fears in a supported way that allowed their nervous systems to relax into safety. As I felt the therapists' fear come into my space, I invited them to notice how they felt in their bodies and minds as they tried to connect. Many therapists described that they felt a chasm between us and, due to the limitations of sitting in front of a computer, there was no way to bridge this distance and make it feel safe. They became frozen, rigid, and fearful because they couldn't see the client's whole body, and, therefore, they might miss vital information about what was happening to the client. Because they could only see the upper half of the client's body, the therapists acted as if the rest of the client's body disappeared and there was no way to sense it. Many of these therapists were trying so hard to "see" the entire client's body that they would push their eyes forward and lean their torso closer to the computer screen, reaching out to protect and rescue their clients from the dangers of the unknown.

This pushing and reaching for contact narrowed the therapist's visual field rather than expanding it, causing tremendous strain on them physically, mentally, and emotionally. Through pushing, straining, and contracting, these therapists experienced remote fatigue, impacting their ability to show up for their clients in a grounded, supported, and safe way.

My job was to get them reconnected in their own body so they could find a gentler way to see and perceive their clients. I invited these therapists to sit back in their chairs, take a deep breath, and see what happened when they found more support from the earth. These therapists immediately reported that their gaze would soften, the tension would release through their bodies, and anxiety would start to melt away. Their nervous systems began to regulate by letting go of being on guard, and then therapists described a shift to feeling a sense of yield, support, and relaxation in their bodies. From this grounded place, therapists could begin to "see" with their whole body versus over-relying on their eyes. Remembering that humans are real, live, breathing, dynamic organisms can help therapists sense, feel, and respond to the vibrational energies available through remote therapy. Trusting that this energy is real can soften the bodymind to be more receptive to sensing and feeling without forcing it to happen. As therapists begin to tap into their own nonverbal somatic cues for information regarding what's happening as their clients express their experiences, they can begin trusting the wisdom in their bodymind even though they're not in the same room.

If you struggle with believing in this concept that you can

sense and connect with your clients while doing remote sessions, try remembering a time in your past when you were on the phone and someone told you some bad news. As you connect to this memory, see if you notice any disturbing images, thoughts, feelings, or body sensations. Remember, you experienced a powerful energetic exchange that let you connect to the other person even though you were on the phone. From this exercise, now see if you can suspend your doubt that you need to see your whole client's body to keep them safe. Just like your experience over the phone, see if you can acknowledge that connection *is* possible even though you aren't in the same room. When you start to "see" with your whole being, a beautiful dance can emerge between you and your client. Through this dance, you can begin to track nonverbal somatic cues in your clients—even though you can't see their whole body—by sensing somatic cues in your own body.

By tuning into this attentional dance, you can track nonverbal somatic cues in your clients while remaining grounded, centered, and embodied throughout the process. These nonverbal somatic cues include the nonlinguistic components of the client's speech patterns, such as voice volume, tempo, pitch, intensity, emphasis, timing, and pauses. Along with the nonlinguistic components, therapists can track micro-movements that are easy to see, such as the twitch of an eye, pursing the lips, breathing shifts, or changing skin color. These somatic cues help you assess if the client is tapping into challenging emotions and body sensations. Some of these somatic cues are obvious and easy to see, while others are more subtle and harder to perceive. When you become aware of your client's nonverbal cues, you can begin to track when your client's nervous system becomes dysregulated and can immediately stop and ground them to help build safety in the session.

As you begin to track nonverbal somatic cues with your clients, the next step of the attentional dance is for you to track what is happening in *your own body* during remote therapy sessions. Through becoming aware of your nonverbal somatic cues that can arise during sessions, you can then notice whether you are experiencing transference, countertransference, or somatic resonance. You may experience transference when the client projects their feelings onto you as the cause of what they're feeling. On the other hand, countertransference is when your own unresolved trauma gets activated because of what the client's sharing. Somatic resonance is when you may sense what the client is experiencing in their body at the same time. Any of these situations can bring up intense sensations in your body, such as constriction in your throat, heat rising in your spine, or throbbing pain in your head. These sensations in the body are cues an energetic exchange is happening, and they become useful information to help guide you to stay grounded, aware, and present with the client. Through becoming aware of the energetic somatic exchange, you can work with the energy in your own body by moving, containing any trauma, or guiding the client to become more aware of their body. Your body's cues can inform you when the client is stuck, emotionally dysregulated, or needs more help to ground into safety. As you become more finely attuned to opening up your body to sense the energetic exchange, you'll feel more present, alive, and active in your sessions. Your perceptions will expand, sensing your whole body as an instrument rather than overusing, straining, and constricting your eyes to see.

As you become more familiar with sensing your body, you can begin to move your attention back and forth freely between your client and yourself without fearing you'll miss any nonverbal somatic cues. If you focus too intently on the client, forgetting about your own body, the client may experience you as invading their personal space. This hyper-focus may cause the client to shut down their process, protect themselves, and disconnect from their body. On the other hand, if you get distracted and overly focused on your own nonverbal somatic cues, the client may experience you as abandoning them energetically. The client may misinterpret your somatic cues as not being emotionally available, not caring, or being bored with them.

In either case, it's your job to be aware of when they may get stuck through balancing your attention out toward the client or inward toward yourself. If you get stuck too long in one attentional state, you may feel exhausted at the end of the day, adding to your sense of remote fatigue. The key is to allow your attention to move back and forth freely between the client and yourself to stay aware, present, and active throughout your remote session. If you do get stuck in one attentional state, you'll need to regroup by shifting your focus, adding movement, breath, and grounding. It's vital you allow the attentional dance to be fluid, graceful, and flowing so that you can perceive with your entire body versus overusing your eyes. As you wake up your body to support what you're seeing, you will feel more connected with your clients, and your clients will feel more connected with you.

············

SPOTLIGHT: ATTENTIONAL DANCE

A therapist struggled with her attentional flow staying fluid as she worked with one particular client during remote therapy. After each session with this client, she would feel utterly depleted, exhausted, and drained. This client expressed anger with such intensity the therapist felt her life was threatened even though the client was not in the same room as her. The therapist was hyper-aware of her client's agitation, pressured speech, and the intensity in their tone of voice. She found herself gasping for breath with heat rising through her spine and stabbing pain in her back. The therapist would lean forward with her body, pushing with her eyes to ensure she could see all the danger that the client was presenting.

This therapist was hyper-focused on what was happening with her client, thus making her lose connection with the grounding, support, and awareness in her own body. As I helped guide this therapist to gain insight into what was happening as she worked with this particular client, she immediately remembered a childhood memory where her mother got angry, yelled, and screamed with such force she feared for her life. As a child, she felt alone, afraid, and helpless to handle the intensity of her mother's rage.

As the therapist got in touch with this childhood memory, she could see that working with this client who was expressing anger was also triggering her own trauma from her childhood. By getting in touch with this unresolved childhood trauma, the therapist became aware that her fear was not proportional to what the client had expressed. Once she made this connection, she found ways to resource herself in the present moment to remain aware that her childhood trauma needed healing in her own therapy. Through this awareness, she learned to soften her gaze, remembering to shift her attention between herself and her client in order to sense, feel, and stay connected in her own body.

The therapist also discovered she needed to move farther away from her computer screen to distance herself from the client and remain grounded in her own body. She permitted herself to look away from her client if she started to stare too long. By shifting her attention away from the client, she could slow down, breathe, and reset her nervous system. Allowing her attention to move between this client and herself, she felt more freedom in her body; less fixated on her client's anger; and became more effective with her interventions to help this client. Her awareness of her own body became more fluid, active, and supportive, which allowed her to sense this client in a new way. From this grounded place in her body, she could sense this client's anger while remaining solid in her own body without getting triggered into her past. By shifting her attention *more often, the therapist found she felt more engaged in the therapeutic process and less exhausted at the end of each day.*

When you consciously give the attentional dance a role in remote therapy, a sense of freedom helps nourish your bodymind throughout every session. Your own body becomes a vital resource that can help guide and sense what's happening for the client and inform you of how present you are as well as facilitate movement and breath throughout the session. The therapeutic relationship strengthens throughout this process, which allows the client to get in touch with their more vulnerable feelings. By practicing this attentional dance regularly, remote fatigue begins to melt away, helping you sustain your remote therapy practice more fully.

....

Straining

Another significant issue many therapists experience when doing remote therapy is strain on their bodies and eyes. When I first switched my practice to remote work, I found that I was exhausted at the end of the day due to all the brainpower required to learn how to work with the technology. Once I got familiar enough with the technology, I thought my fatigue would go away. Unfortunately, the opposite was true, and my symptoms increased. My shoulders hurt, my lower back ached, my right arm felt heavy and disconnected from my body, and my legs and feet would go numb. I found myself scheduling more sessions with the chiropractor and massage therapist to mitigate the strain my body felt from sitting so long. These appointments helped—but I was frustrated that the symptoms would return the next day.

The worst of all my symptoms was the pain in my eyes. My eyes felt dry as well as burned, itched, and stung like I had sandpaper in them. My sight was fuzzy, blurry, and cloudy, no matter what I did. I struggled to see what was on my computer screen, read my training material while teaching, or drive at night. As the pain in my eyes increased, I gave up wearing contacts, and switched to glasses, hoping the change would soothe my eyes. Unfortunately, the symptoms continued to worsen, and so I attributed all of this to the aging process.

When I finally went to the eye doctor, I discovered my prescription was just fine. What wasn't okay was that my eyes were too dry and not producing enough tears to keep my eyes lubricated throughout the day. The doctor gave me a diagnosis called chronic dry eye, which was causing inflammation. This diagnosis is common among people aging and working long hours in front of a computer, and if left untreated, the dryness could cause severe and permanent damage to the eyes. This news scared me since there's a history of eye conditions in my family, and I didn't want this diagnosis to be a path toward blindness.

The eye doctor recommended using costly eye drops for 18 months to reduce the inflammation, hoping that, eventually, I could ween off this medication. I had to visit the eye doctor every 3 months to evaluate if this medication was working correctly. After three long years of visiting the eye doctor regularly, the medication was still not working as promised. I felt defeated, like a failure, like something was wrong with me because my eyes weren't improving at all.

When I shared this information with my massage therapist, she recommended I consider a holistic eye doctor, Dr. Sam Berne, in Santa Fe, New Mexico. I started listening to his podcasts and was very excited to hear him talking about the eyes as an organ that can heal through the bodymind connection. Here was an eye doctor who spoke my language, using somatic terms, and suggesting the possibility to heal my eyes was attainable. He explained that chronic dry eye is common and is treatable through using natural remedies and eye exercises. I got excited about what he was saying, and I immediately set up an appointment to see what he had to say about my specific eye condition.

During our in-person session before the pandemic, Dr. Berne took one look at me and saw the distress in my eyes, face, and body. He somatically guided me to slow down and become aware of what I was experiencing at that moment. His presence made me feel safe, secure, and held in a way that allowed me to believe healing my eyes could be possible. As I tuned into my eyes, I started to connect to my body more fully. I immediately began to cry, tremble, and shake, allowing all the pain that I had been holding in my eyes to release. My eyes were communicating with me that I was too stressed, didn't know how to take care of myself while working on a computer for long hours, and still had some unresolved childhood traumas impacting how I see and interact with the world.

From this session, Dr. Berne recommended I go off the expensive medication I was using because it wasn't working. Instead, he said I could find more natural ways to heal my eyes by aligning with my bodymind. He gave me daily practices to soothe, bathe, and calm my eyes, releasing the strain they were experiencing. I also committed to working more consistently in therapy on my childhood unresolved traumas so that I could feel more safety in my body as I interacted with the world.

As I have incorporated these simple practices into my daily life, I'm happy to report my eyes no longer burn, itch, or feel irritated. The other remarkable benefit from these practices I still use today is that my prescription for my glasses *decreases* every year even though I'm aging. As I continue to release stuck energy that doesn't serve me anymore, my world has changed: I feel safer and more in control, all with less strain in my eyes. I'm grateful to my massage therapist for guiding me to this holistic eye doctor who has become a powerful healing force in my life. Both of these healers have become an essential part of my team of allies who support, guide, and keep me on track, feeling vital, healthy, and dynamic as I continue to teach and consult in my remote practice.

Now I'm happy to share my experience to help therapists protect their eyes and support their bodies while working in front of a computer. If therapists ignore the signs and symptoms that naturally result from doing remote therapy, they'll feel undue strain and fatigue at the end of the day. Overtime, remote fatigue will burn out therapists and cause them more severe health problems down the road.

The following five practices—protecting, blinking, palming, aligning, hearing—are some simple ideas you can easily incorporate into a daily routine to help take care of yourself when doing remote therapy. Since I am not a doctor, these are just ideas and not guidelines. If your symptoms of remote fatigue increase, consult with a professional to prevent any health problems from developing. These simple practices may help counterbalance the effects of remote fatigue. I encourage you to listen to your body, adjust, adapt, and make these practices your own so that you feel nourished, refreshed, and supported in order to sustain your remote therapy practice.

Protecting

As your eyes become tired, sore, and burning from looking at a computer screen during remote therapy sessions, it can be helpful to wear "blue blocker" glasses to protect your eyes. I've found that wearing these glasses has significantly decreased my eyes' strain at the end of the day. Research has shown the blue light that emanates from the computer screen can lead to digital eye strain and eventually cause more severe vision problems over time, such as chronic dry eyes. (Sheppard & Wolffschon, 2018). This research is controversial, and not all eye doctors believe blue blockers are helpful or necessary.

As therapists struggled with headaches and their eyes burning at the end of the day from doing remote sessions, I suggested they try using blue blocker glasses to help mitigate their eyes' strain. Many of them found that wearing the glasses significantly decreased the strain on their eyes and eliminated their headaches. Be careful when you purchase a pair of blue blocker glasses over the counter because these can create a glare on the lens, making it harder for clients to see your eyes. Talk to your eye doctor about having a professional pair of blue blockers made with high-quality non-glare lenses that will eliminate this issue so you can connect easier with your clients.

Blinking

Another byproduct of remote fatigue is therapists blinking *less* than usual due to looking at a computer screen all day. Studies have shown that people normally blink 15 – 20 times per minute, which moistens and lubricates the eyes. When looking at a computer screen, phones, and iPads, blink time reduces almost in half. (Cardona, Garcia, Seres, Vilaseca, Gispets, 2011). The simple act of remembering to blink is not easy but can make a big difference in preventing dryness, irritation, and achiness. Try to remember that blinking more often during sessions while looking at a computer screen helps take care of your eyes and can prevent them from hurting at the end of the day.

Palming

One of my favorite practices to help soothe the eyes from the strain of looking at a computer screen is an adaptation of Marc Grossman's (2004) "Palming." This practice merely involves rubbing your hands together to create some heat. Once the heat builds, you can gently place your warm palms over your eyes. You can then focus on breathing, relaxing, and letting go of any stress or tension accumulated during sessions. Doing this practice every day will help support your eyes' health, thus preventing the damages from remote fatigue.

Aligning

Another component of therapists experiencing remote fatigue is aches and pains in the body. Many therapists complained about pain in their necks, shoulders, and back; strain in their fingers and wrists; numbness in their legs and feet; headaches and extreme exhaustion. Poor posture can contribute to these kinds of pains in the body because it can cause the computer screen to be positioned incorrectly. Taking time to align your computer camera at eye level will help bring more support to your body. When using a laptop computer, purchase a stand to raise the laptop's camera to the appropriate height.

You also need to consider finding a chair that can support your spine, neck, and head, in order to prevent straining when looking into the camera. Make sure that the chair is at a height where your feet can touch the ground for support. Since I'm five feet tall, most furniture does not fit me, making it difficult for me to support my body. I've found that placing a stool under my feet helps ground my body so I'm not straining all day. Many of my friends have made fun of my stool, but it saves my body from going numb.

Hearing

Another contributor to fatigue when doing remote sessions is wearing earbuds. Wearing earbuds for extended periods may irritate the ears once removed. Some therapists have said they feel like the earbuds are still in their ears even though they're not. My husband likes to call this phenomenon "phantom ear syndrome." Phantom ear syndrome can cause feelings of dizziness, spatial disorientation, and feeling ungrounded. After removing your earbuds, take time to orient in the present moment by looking around the room, feeling your feet on the ground, and breathing to calm the nervous system before moving onto your next activity.

STRESS OF TRAUMA

What intrigues me even more than therapists' physical symptoms as they switched their practices from in-person to remote was how they experienced different kinds of traumas during the pandemic. Through experiencing matching traumas, being triggered with their own unresolved childhood traumas, and being exposed to remote traumatization, many therapists reported feeling depressed, angry, resentful, anxious, panicky, and physically ill. Many of them were overwhelmed by their pain personally and professionally. These therapists were feeling alone, frustrated, and depleted from working with their clients, who were also traumatized.

As therapists struggled to handle the effects of experiencing these kinds of traumas, many were also suffering from compassion fatigue. Compassion fatigue is common for people in the helping fields, such as doctors, nurses, emergency medical technicians, firefighters, police, and therapists. These people may see or hear their clients' traumas daily, which can be traumatizing for them physically, mentally, and emotionally. Therapists, in particular, can develop compassion fatigue from listening to their clients' stories of pain and suffering. Over time, if therapists do not acknowledge or deal with this buildup of stress that can accumulate from listening to traumatic stories, it can lead to extreme fatigue, exhaustion, and even burn-out, eventually making it difficult for therapists to show up for their sessions.

Let's look closer at the different kinds of traumas and how they impact therapists through the pandemic.

Remote Traumatization

Technological devices can be excellent tools that help people connect as well as feel validated and supported when they may otherwise feel alone, isolated, and abandoned. Using technology can have beautiful benefits, such as connecting with people; however, it can also create trauma on a personal and global level, such as seeing horrific images or words transmitted through social media, emails, texts, or the news. This use of technology can create secondary trauma, which I call "remote traumatization." On a personal level, remote traumatization occurs when one person targets another through bullying, manipulating, harassing, or terrorizing. Examples of this harm include cyberbullying, cyberstalking, revenge porn, S.W.A.T.-ting, ransomware, trolling, and catfishing.

Global remote traumatization happens on a massive level, when violent images and words are spread across the world instantaneously, hurting people of different races, genders, and cultures. The process of sharing violent content is instantaneous, persistent, and available 24 hours a day. When I was growing up, there were only three news channels and one newspaper in my town. We had to wait to find out what was happening in our community and our nation. Now, we no longer have to wait to find out what is going on around the globe. Everyone is creating the news, making news, and impacting the news, whether it's "real" or "fake," which can profoundly affect a nation's people with just a single swipe of a finger, traumatizing them for years to come.

During the pandemic, remote traumatization was rampant with violent images and words bombarding people every day. Images of elders separated and isolated from their families. Empty store shelves from people hoarding products out of fear there wouldn't be enough for them. Death tolls rising from COVID-19 with no vaccine in sight. Devastating videos of racism showing people being injured, shot, and killed in plain sight. Images of children being held in overcrowded facilities, separated from their parents while trying to enter the United States. People storming the Capital and threatening to overtake the election. These examples are merely a snapshot of what was spreading worldwide, just like a deadly virus. These powerful images tap into the fear and anxiety that destabilize people's nervous systems and cause debilitating post-traumatic stress disorder (PTSD) symptoms, including nightmares, flashbacks, sleep issues, disorientation, hyper-vigilance, social isolation, and even suicide.

As I dealt with adjusting to the new abnormal during the pandemic, my husband, Young, experienced remote traumatization firsthand. Images were posted on social media of Asians around the world being spit on, yelled at, bullied, harassed, violently beaten, and killed. As he watched these horrific images, his body responded by becoming stiff and rigid, he lost his ability to speak, and he has feared for his own life since. Young had been experiencing similar events himself since the pandemic began, which also made him recall his own pre-pandemic trauma. He watched these shared videos to validate that what he was experiencing was real and not imagined. Unfortunately, this also traumatized him at the same time, triggering his own debilitating and exhausting experiences with anti-Asian racism throughout his life. As a result, Young developed PTSD symptoms of terrifying nightmares and intrusive thoughts that made it difficult for him to concentrate. He avoided everyday activities that he felt were dangerous, which included going to the grocery store or even taking a walk with me in our neighborhood. His unresolved childhood traumas began to surface, mixing and matching with the cultural context of what he was experiencing in the present, making it hard for him to feel safe, grounded, and able to make good decisions in the present moment.

As I watched my husband suffer, feeling alone, isolated, and helpless, I struggled with how I could help him through such pain. White privilege allows me to move about my community without fearing for my life, feeling relatively safe even while wearing a mask. On the other hand, Young has experienced people accusing him of being responsible for the spread of COVID-19 and yelling at him out of disgust and hatred to "go back to your own country." People in our own community recorded him, following him around in stores or to his car while he minded his own business. Young felt afraid, anxious, and fearful that something terrible would happen to him, so he isolated himself in our home. He was lost, trying to make sense of something that he couldn't comprehend. Were these people trying to make a viral moment to become famous, or trying to incite a racial incident so that the police would come and arrest him, or were they hoping that they could be a hero and protect others from this "dangerous foreigner?" These questions haunted him and fueled his fear, making it difficult for him to trust the world—and our own block—as being safe enough for him to move freely. Even though we're married and living under the same roof, our experiences in our community, nation, and the world are entirely different every moment, every day of every year.

As Young sought validation that he was not alone in his encounters, he turned to social media to see if others were experiencing the same thing. His therapist suggested we watch these videos together so that Young had more support through this process and so that I could better understand what he was going through as an Asian American living in a predominantly non-Asian community. While I love supporting my husband in the ways he needs, this request to watch videos of violence against other human beings was (and continues to be) challenging for me. It was (and is) traumatizing for me to watch these kinds of videos with my husband, especially since I listen to therapists sharing cases of trauma every day, which can take a toll on me mentally, emotionally, and spiritually. As I see these painful images, I feel the bile rise in my throat, have the urge to throw the phone across the room, and want to scream out loud for the injustice I witnessed. I feel the pain so deeply that it hurts my soul, interrupts my sleep, and makes me cynical about the human race.

While I have the privilege of choosing when and how I watch these videos to protect myself, Young does not have that kind of privilege. His body holds the pain of racism 24 hours a day, which sometimes exhausts his nervous system beyond his capacity. Young has no escape. He has the challenge of living in a reality where his world is not safe, and he must find ways to empower himself even when the world tries to take that power away. Our sense of the world is quite different: intolerable for him to experience and impossible for me to comprehend.

As we both try to navigate how we interact with these images in order to process what we see, there is no good answer on the best way to handle this situation. Our dilemma: How do we watch this kind of violence to be conscious of what's happening in our community and nation and still know how to take care of ourselves? Without witnessing this material, it's easy to be ignorant of others' pain and suffering, remain unaware of biases, and avoid seeing the truth of what's happening. On the other hand, without creating safety to view this material, we both become traumatized in the process, exhausting our nervous systems and adding to our senses of remote fatigue.

One thing that has helped us through this process is to set a boundary between when and how we view these videos. We try to set up time in the middle of the day to watch, which allows us to digest, discuss, and process the violence we've just witnessed. We have found that when we keep this boundary, we can connect more fully, have time to process the despair in our hearts and souls, and provide each other the space to let our love be the guiding force. Providing a clear boundary gives us the safety we both need to share in this process by providing consent and context for what we're witnessing.

Although this is only one example of someone experiencing remote traumatization, there are billions of people interacting on social media, sending/receiving emails, and watching the news every second of every day. If you find yourself saying, "I don't want to look at my phone or watch TV anymore," that may be a clear sign you're experiencing remote traumatization. It's a signal to yourself that you're trying to avoid the pain from the violence you witness through technology. The potential for you to experience trauma from using phones, tablets, computers, and televisions is very high, especially if you're already suffering from unresolved trauma. As you see violence on social media, in emails, and in the news, it's necessary to have a safe place to discuss, explore, and process what you are witnessing. While it's essential to be aware of what's happening in your community, country, and the world, be mindful of how it impacts you. Don't ignore the signs of distress in your bodymind.

Without conscious attention given to this material and a safe avenue to express how it impacts you, remote traumatization can begin to undermine your sense of seeing the "good" in people, thus making it difficult to hold a positive light when working with your clients. Over time, you may start to feel cynical, hatred, and even disgust for other human beings, ultimately impacting your ability to hold a safe place for your clients to express what they're experiencing. If you try to handle all of this on your own, you may take on too much responsibility for your clients, potentially trying to rescue them from their pain, or sacrificing your own needs by making your clients' traumas more significant than your own. All of this may lead you to feel inadequate and helpless, impacting your self-esteem as a therapist and exhausting your nervous system. Remote traumatization is real and may explain why there can be resistance from both therapists and clients to do therapy remotely. Just the act of turning on a device can trigger the association of trauma unconsciously. The key is that we have to be careful using technology safely and begin seeing positive associations with technology. Remote therapy can counterbalance the harmful effects of remote trauma-tization by offering hope, healing, and transformation.

If you find yourself over-giving, challenged to remain

centered, and unable to ground in your body due to remote traumatization, you may end up extremely exhausted, tapped out with nothing left to give to yourself or your clients. Seeking support in consultation, supervision, or your own therapy can help you navigate the damaging effects of experiencing remote traumatization.

Be aware that as much exposure you experience with social media, emails, texts, and the news, your clients are going through the same thing. Take time to ask your clients questions about this topic and see how it impacts them mentally, emotionally, physically, and spiritually. You might be surprised how much they are being traumatized and they may not have the words to share it with you. Look for signs of PTSD and help your clients find safety in how they view traumatizing material and help them find better ways to take care of themselves.

Matching Traumas

Another type of trauma that therapists had to become aware of during the pandemic was matching traumas with their clients. Matching traumas can occur when both therapists and clients are simultaneously experiencing the same traumatic event. On a personal level, both therapists and clients may be going through a breakup, divorce, grieving for a loved one or pet, or having similar cultural or childhood traumas that resonate with each other at the same time. On a community level, therapists' and clients' personal and professional lives may be disrupted by experiencing disasters, terrorism, shootings, and even a pandemic.

As I consulted with therapists through the pandemic, I discovered many of those I was working with lacked the awareness that they were experiencing matching traumas with their clients. They were so focused on their client's distress that they were in denial that the pandemic also affected them personally and professionally. By overly focusing on their clients' problems and forgetting about their own bodies, many of the therapists' nervous systems were enmeshing with their clients' energetic bodies unconsciously. This nervous system dance was awkward, uncoordinated, and unsteady at times. Both the therapist and client became lost in feeling overwhelmed, anxious, and fearful without anyone leading the way, making it difficult for therapists to stay in the therapeutic process with their clients.

Without knowing this energy exchange was happening, many therapists felt as though they were failing or, at the very least, confused and incompetent. By ignoring the signs that their own traumas matched their clients, many of these therapists lost their boundaries, became ungrounded, and felt unable to lead the therapy session. By dismissing, minimizing, and negating their own somatic resonance, therapists felt exhausted, depleted, and dreaded showing up for their remote therapy sessions.

When I pointed out to these therapists that they were experiencing matching traumas with their clients, their facial expressions were pure shock and surprise. It seemed like I was bursting their bubbles of denial. The reality came crashing in: they were struggling just as much as their clients. For some of the therapists, this information was difficult to digest, and they would put up a wall of resistance, insisting I was wrong in my observation, and that they were just fine. Other therapists felt so relieved, crying with huge smiles on their faces because someone could see and name what they were going through. These relieved therapists began to see the somatic resonance as a feedback loop of feelings, and body sensations exchanged between themselves and their clients, resonating through their matching traumas. Without therapists consciously acknowledging their own trauma, they found it challenging to stay present in their clients' sessions.

....

SPOTLIGHT: DISTRACTIONS

Let's look at an example of a struggling therapist during the pandemic who was quarantined with her family while doing remote therapy sessions from home. Her biggest complaint in the consultation was that she was having trouble concentrating while doing remote sessions because she felt guilty for not giving her children her full attention when she was home. Work, therefore, felt like a burden, a distraction, pulling her in different directions and depleting her every day. She longed to get her therapy practice back to "normal" by seeing clients in-person so that she could have more separation from work and home.

In response to my inquiry about how she starts her day, the therapist quickly said she has to prepare her children for their long-distance learning, helping them focus and concentrate on their lessons. Then she would take a quick shower while having no time to eat anything for breakfast and neglecting her meditation practice before seeing clients. When it was time for her first session, she would hurriedly find a place to set up her computer, hoping and praying the internet would work, and try to make do with her new makeshift office.

As the therapist continued to share, she talked about one particular client she couldn't stop thinking about where she experienced her mind wandering; she got bored and sleepy, hoping that the session would end soon. I wondered what was happening with this therapist during these sessions. She said her client felt trapped being quarantined at home with his family. He felt distracted by his children and their needs while still trying to find time to work. His work was no longer bringing him joy because he felt alone, depressed, and resented the pandemic for changing his life so drastically. With no separation from his home life and work life, he felt burdened by his responsibilities and longed for the day when things would go back to normal. As this client shared his struggles, he would become sleepy in each session, blaming not getting enough sleep as the problem.

The therapist was in denial that her client's traumas from the pandemic matched her own. When I gently pointed this out, her heart started to race, her breath began to quicken, and she became full of rage. Her body felt heavy and like it was on fire. The therapist started to weep, feeling overloaded by too much responsibility for her family and this client. She found that she was exhausted beyond her capacity to give freely to this client in her sessions. By denying that she had matching trauma with her client, she tried to distance herself from feeling what was happening in her own body. She cut herself off from her body's wisdom, preventing her from connecting, sensing, and feeling what was happening in the session.

This lack of awareness kept her from understanding the somatic resonance that was taking place during each session. The client's nervous system dropped into a hypo-arousal nervous system state whenever he was getting too close to his true feelings. When this occurred, he would become sleepy, disconnecting from his feelings and body sensations. This sensation of sleepiness was a protective mechanism that came into play to protect him from feeling the pain. Once the client's nervous system changed, the therapist's nervous system unconsciously started to match his. The therapist began to feel sleepy, bored, and longed for their sessions to end just like the client. This dance happened instantaneously, with neither the therapist nor the client realizing what was occurring between them. It was easy for the client to blame lack of sleep for feeling this way, and the therapist accepted this as his truth without observing this nervous system dance.

Once the therapist recognized that matching traumas with this client were making it difficult for her to stay present, aware, and awake during sessions, she prioritized her mornings by setting healthier boundaries. She organized her children's things the night before; created a remote therapy office in her home that was consistent and reliable; and woke up 30 minutes earlier to make sure she had time to eat and meditate. This new routine helped her set healthier boundaries with herself and her clients in order to be more present, track somatic resonance, and work with it consciously throughout her sessions. She no longer dreaded working with this client; instead, she could focus, concentrate, and enjoy the therapeutic process.

Through her naming that she had matching traumas, the therapist could recognize when she was shutting down, over-emphasizing, or taking on too much responsibility for the client's healing process. By shifting her attention to bring more breath, movement, and support to her body, she could then facilitate helping her client ground in his nervous system in order to stay more present, aware, and awake to what he was feeling and experiencing. This dance allowed the therapist to have more energy throughout the day, and her resentment toward this client dissipated. She also found that she could enjoy her children again without them being a distraction.

If you become aware that you have matching traumas with your clients, you'll need to find ways to stay separate in your experiences while still being open to sense, perceive, and feel what's happening for your clients. Remembering that somatic resonance is a powerful energetic exchange can be informative to the therapeutic process. Consciously practicing how to be aware, awake, and active during times of somatic resonance will help you learn how to regulate your nervous system in the therapeutic dance.

Part of this therapeutic dance is to make sure to ground yourself before sessions; stay flexible and adaptable during them; and clear any stuck energy once you complete your day. Consciously being aware of how your traumas are similar to your clients while remembering that your experiences are unique and different can deepen your sense of empathy, compassion, and support for a client's process. If you have difficulty working with clients who have matching traumas to you, get support in consultation, supervision, or your own therapy to help deepen your understanding of what's happening in your bodymind during these sessions. Take care to develop a plan on how to better take care of yourself during these times, which will help dissipate the effects of experiencing remote fatigue. Through deepening your awareness, you may also uncover unresolved childhood traumas that may need to be explored and resourced in order to help you stay more solid with your client's experience.

....

Unresolved Childhood Trauma

The last kind of trauma that contributes to remote fatigue can occur when the client's stories or nonverbal communications trigger the therapist to experience their own unresolved childhood traumas. Therapists may experience flashbacks, overwhelming emotions, and strong body sensations that make it challenging to stay present with their clients. When this powerful exchange between client and therapist occurs, therapists must regulate their nervous system activation by finding ways to contain the distress, ground their bodies, and center their minds in the present moment. Once the session is complete, therapists may need to take the unresolved traumas to consultation, supervision, or their own therapy to explore more fully. By working more consciously with their own traumas outside of sessions, therapists will become less triggered during sessions, stretch their affect tolerance, and support more fluidity in staying in the dance with their clients.

As an EMDR trainer, I often do live demonstrations to help therapists see this powerful healing modality in action. During one of my remote demonstrations, the volunteer "client" wanted to work on the first time they failed taking the LPC exam. When we began the EMDR session, I felt grounded, secure, and at ease as the client talked about the trauma they wanted to process. As the session progressed, the client remembered a time in middle school where they struggled in math class and received a "C" on their report card. Their father was angry, disappointed, and shamed the client for not working hard enough. Midway through the demonstration, I felt tremendous heat surge through my body. It was so hot that I wanted to rip my clothes off and jump in some cool water. As I became aware of this uncomfortable sensation in my body, my mind started to race, reviewing a checklist of questions to identify what was happening. I wondered if the room was too warm, or if I was having a hot flash or experiencing somatic resonance with the client, or if any of my own unresolved trauma was getting activated. As I started asking these questions in my mind, I thought of an old memory when I struggled in math class, where the teacher called on me for the answer. I felt so hot, anxious, and afraid to give the wrong answer that I froze, losing my voice, unable to speak out loud. With my inability to answer the teacher's question, he belittled, shamed, and mocked me in front of my peers. I was frozen at my desk, with nowhere to run, having to endure the torture from this teacher with tears welling up in my eyes. Shame permeated throughout my body. As I saw the flash of this memory in my mind's eye, the answer became apparent: my client's experience was triggering with my own unresolved trauma.

I had to quickly decide how to handle this information while remaining present with the client. I knew I needed to find a way to contain this trauma in order to be more grounded, centered, and present with what was happening so that my own experience didn't hijack the session. In my mind's eye, I invited this old trauma to move into a transparent, energetic bubble, letting the bubble hold the memory until I could review it at a later time in my own therapy. Once I could contain this trauma, the heat released swiftly, relaxation returned to my body, and I could focus once again on the client. All of this happened instantly and internally, and I did not reveal it to the client. My responsibility at that moment was to regulate my nervous system so that I could stay active in the attentional dance between us.

This same process can occur when I'm consulting with therapists around their client's cases. I can energetically sense when the therapist's own unresolved childhood traumas are getting activated during sessions with their clients. I can feel the therapist's presence shift in how they share their cases, what kind of struggles they're experiencing in their sessions, and what kind of interventions they seek in order to resolve the issue for their client. Sometimes, these therapists will appear smaller, younger, helpless, and share that they feel out of control, shameful, and unworthy of being therapists. In these moments, I am witnessing an unconscious "part" of the therapist who experienced trauma in their childhood. This part still holds some aspect of the experience that hasn't fully sequenced, causing the therapist to feel uncomfortable emotions and body sensations. As I saw this happening with many therapists during the pandemic, I knew that I had to help them identify the part connected to their unresolved childhood trauma in order to become more conscious of staying grounded in their competent therapist self. Both the young part who experienced the trauma and the competent therapist part needed attention, regulation, and grounding.

There are many theories on how to work with parts, such as Ego State Therapy developed by Watkins & Watkins (1997), Internal Family Systems created by Richard Schwartz (1997), and Structural Dissociation by van der Hart, Nijenhuis, & Steel (2006). For this book's purpose, I want to explore parts work from the lens that when therapists become triggered by their clients' stories or nonverbal communications, they may experience a young, wounded part that needs attention. Without conscious awareness, the therapist may feel incompetent and unable of remaining present in remote therapy sessions. This can lead to extreme emotional distress, physical symptoms, and a sense of hopelessness that can contribute to remote fatigue.

Parts work is not typically a part of therapists' training, so it's not always easy for them to understand it when I first bring it up. But once they get the concept, it can change how they feel about themselves and how they work with their clients. Imagine for a moment a baby that is helpless and utterly dependent on you. You have to feed the baby, change their diapers, give them clothing, provide emotional nurturance, and interact in an attuned way, listening and responding appropriately to the baby's needs. This baby is entirely dependent on you for their survival. Your interactions help the baby develop into an integrated, intelligent, and emotionally stable person. By being consistent in your interactions, congruent with your verbal and nonverbal communications, you help the baby bond so that they grow up feeling safe, secure, and provided for in this world.

You are considered the psychobiological regulator of this baby's nervous system (Schore, 2012). You provide the external regulation to help shape the baby's physiological responses by interacting with your baby. As the baby signals to you what they need, you can begin to regulate the baby's physiological and emotional states through how you touch, move, and use your gaze to interact with them. These signals are both verbal and nonverbal, bonding you and your baby by letting your baby know that they are wanted, loved, and that they matter.

When this psychobiological dance is interrupted, a *lack* of bonding occurs, and your baby may develop defensive reactions and patterns in order to adapt to becoming compliant with your needs. By ignoring or rejecting them, you, the caretaker, mis-attune to the baby's needs. This means the baby may grow up into an adult feeling misunderstood, struggling in relationships, and finding it challenging to regulate their nervous system responses. When these moments of mis-attunement occur, a part of the baby is traumatized and can get stuck emotionally, mentally, and physically in that trauma state. The baby grows up into an adult physically; however, emotionally, a part of them still carries that trauma.

As an adult, this trauma is like a sore spot that takes very little stimulation to activate the old trauma without your conscious awareness. The brain and body may perceive whatever is happening in the present moment and trigger a trauma response. You will then act, behave, and feel the same emotions as you did in the past. You may want to run away from the situation; fight with someone who feels threatening; become frozen and unable to act; collapse into depression, feeling hopeless, helpless, and paralyzed all over your body. This trauma response can be disorienting, confusing, and ungrounding, leaving you feeling vulnerable, frightened, and out of control without consciously knowing why you feel that way.

Two Sides of a Coin

I have spent years getting to know my wounded parts intimately in my own therapy. I grew up in an era when doctors taught parents to let a baby cry it out so that the baby didn't control the parent. My mother used a timetable of when to feed me, when it was time to go to the bathroom, when it was time to sleep, and when it was time to be held. If I had a need that didn't meet this timetable, my mother waited until it was the correct time to respond to my needs. I would be left crying, screaming all alone, fighting to get my needs met until my nervous system would collapse into a complete sense of exhaustion. This sequence happened daily, repeating over and over, causing tremendous distress to my nervous system. I learned early that my needs were not important and that the schedule was the deciding factor that determined what was best for me.

Through this repeated interaction with my mother, I developed two parts that act in very different ways emotionally, mentally, and physically. They are like two sides of a coin. One part of me is "needy," while the other part is highly "self-reliant." The needy part holds the early trauma of not having my needs met through controlling me via a timetable. I learned from this experience that I had to do what others wanted me to do in order to meet my needs. As an adult, when the needy part activates, I can collapse into despair, hopelessly crying to be heard and seen, feeling that I am all alone in this big, scary world. It has caused me a lot of pain over the years and can arise when I get triggered by someone crossing my boundaries physically, being aggressive and controlling with their words, or accusing me of wrongdoing. I can drop into a state of overwhelm, despair, and fear that things are out of control. Once this occurs, it's difficult for me to hold my boundaries, have my voice, and stand up for myself in what I believe is my truth.

While the needy part feels weak, vulnerable, and lonely, the self-reliant part feels strong, competent, and in control. This part developed from being left alone so much, forcing me to learn to take care of things myself because no one else would be there. This part of me believes I just have to put on my "big girl pants" and do whatever it takes to succeed, leading me to be an over-achiever and highly successful in whatever I chose to do. When I over-rely on this part, I can push too hard, override my needs, and collapse back into the needy part who feels alone, afraid, and unable to take care of herself.

As an adult, I have had to heal this early childhood wounding in therapy. I've had to learn that I do have needs and that my body gives me signals when I'm hungry, when I need to go to the bathroom, and when I need to sleep. By becoming familiar with the two sides of the coin inside me, I have learned to resource both of these parts to be more resilient. When the needy part feels safe, she can relax, bond, and receive love, trusting that support is available. When the self-reliant part feels safe, she can let others support her, allowing her to relax in her bodymind, knowing she doesn't have to do everything on her own.

As I respect my needs and become more resilient, I've found that taking more time to prepare myself for teaching and consulting helps me be less triggered when working. I can stay in my competent, self-assured, adult self that allows support to guide me. As I continue to discover, create, and change my dance in my bodymind, nothing is ever static, perfect, or status quo. I have devoted my life to this dance of stretching and building my resiliency. There are still times that I can feel myself get triggered, such as when the pandemic impacted my life and I collapsed into my "needy" part who felt all alone. But through listening, practicing, and respecting myself, my ability to reconnect to my higher resourced self is more available, easier to connect to, and I trust that I will survive whatever comes my way.

Strengthening Parts

Just as I have had to explore my wounded parts and continue to heal them, many therapists need to become aware of their own parts as they continue to work with clients in remote therapy. In many of my consultation sessions during the pandemic, I observed therapists' somatic cues signaling to me that a younger part of them was taking over as they talked about their clients. The therapist's posture would collapse or become more rigid. Their voice tone would become softer or louder. Their words would become disjointed and choppy, or they would repeat a gesture that was hard for me to tolerate observing, such as picking at their nails, or playing with their hair repetitively. These cues let me know that the therapist needed to slow down and become more curious about what was happening in their own bodymind rather than me just giving them an intervention to use with their client. I had to help these therapists move into their pain and discomfort as their nervous systems became dysregulated so I could determine if a younger wounded part was activated.

As therapists get in touch with their younger parts, they will need to resource these parts to help them feel more organized in their bodymind. Part of this resourcing process for me is to become the therapist's psychobiological regulator by providing support, warmth, and genuine interactions. Through this gentle guidance, therapists got in touch with unresolved childhood trauma that was activated and impacting them in the present moment. With me providing safety, the therapist could explore what their missing experience was in the past traumatic event. Missing experiences can include not being nurtured, protected, or receiving the guidance that they needed when they were younger.

As the therapist discovers their missing experience, I like to help them find resources to strengthen and begin to repair this trauma. As their resources strengthen, the therapist will feel more relaxed in their body and feel relief from the emotional distress. The therapist can then begin to trust that they are repatterning the missing experience and strengthening their sense of self. Once the therapist feels strong enough to move on, they can begin to contact their competent therapist self in the here and now. By orienting back into the present moment, the therapist can begin to feel more solid in their body, focus their thoughts, and regulate their nervous systems. With safety in place, the therapist can talk about their client without becoming dysregulated from their past trauma.

....

SPOTLIGHT: STENGTHENING PARTS

An example of this is a therapist who hated remote therapy ever since her in-person sessions switched to remote sessions due to the pandemic. She stated that she was too exhausted to pay attention to someone else; she felt sad, lonely, and full of grief. All she wanted to do was sit on the couch, drink hot tea, and shut out the world. As she talked to me, her voice sounded like a young child and softened to where I could barely hear her. She started looking away from the computer screen, staring off into the distance as if she was far away from me. The therapist's breathing started to slow down and her body curled in on itself. All I could "see" was a little girl curled up on a sofa holding a teddy bear.

From all of the somatic cues I observed, it was clear that a younger part of the therapist felt activated. I knew that I was no longer talking to the competent therapist; I was engaging with a wounded little girl who was traumatized by something from her past. I asked the therapist how old she felt at this moment so we could both orient to the age range in which this trauma had occurred. She quickly responded that she felt like she was 7 years old. The therapist said her parents were going through a divorce when she was seven and that neither parent had time to pay attention to her. She felt alone, overwhelmed, and not safe. This wounded little 7-year-old was feeling abandoned and desperately needed support.

Once the therapist remembered this memory, she had an ah-ha moment. She stated that she felt the same intense feelings from losing her therapy office because of the pandemic. Switching to remote work was overwhelming, disorienting, and frightening to her. By leaving her therapy office to work from home, she became triggered by her unresolved childhood trauma of her parents divorcing, where she felt abandoned, alone with no support.

As the therapist connected to what she was feeling, this insight brought tremendous relief to her whole nervous system. She was able to take a deep breath for the first time in weeks. I gently asked her 7-year-old part what she needed that she didn't receive from her parents at that time: nurturing, protection, or guidance. She said she needed someone to nurture her so she wouldn't feel so alone. I asked her to find an ally, which could be real or imaginary in her mind's eye and could provide the nurturance she was missing. The ally must be predictable, dependable, and able to support her in the way she desired. The therapist quickly chose a polar bear because it was large, soft, and nurturing while still protecting her from danger. Once she found this nurturing ally, I asked her to imagine where she needed the polar bear to be so that it would feel supportive. She could have it in front, side, back, above, below, or holding her, whatever her heart desired. The therapist decided it would feel good to have the polar bear holding her young part and rocking her. As she imagined her 7-year-old part being rocked and supported by the polar bear, her body began to relax, and she was able to give in to the support. Her breathing started to become more even between her inhales and exhales, bringing more ease, comfort, and safety to her body.

I then proceeded to ask this therapist if she wanted any other allies to help her handle all of her feelings. She said she needed more support and imagined being at the foot of a mountain that felt grounding in her body, along with an angel hovering above her shining light all around. Then she decided to include two of her trusted friends, placing one on each side of her. The last piece she wanted to add was a pack of wolves in front of her to keep her safe and protected. As the therapist gathered her allies, creating an incredible team of support, her 7-year-old part was relieved and able to take in the nurturing, protection, and safety that the team of allies provided for her.

Once the therapist's wounded part felt this support, I asked her if she could orient back to the present moment and get in touch with her competent therapist self. The therapist said yes, and as she connected to this part of herself, she reported feeling calm, grounded, and present with me. Her nervous system was more regulated, and I helped her understand that the pandemic triggered her 7-year-old part that didn't feel safe from her parents abandoning her while they were divorcing. Trying to show up and be a therapist when the therapist felt like an abandoned 7-year-old was too hard on her psyche, making her feel overwhelmed, exhausted, and depleted of vital energy. With this new knowledge, the therapist had a giant grin on her face knowing her little 7-year-old was being cared for by a supportive team of allies. She realized this part of her did not need to be running her remote therapy sessions; instead, her competent therapist self knew what to do. By reconnecting to this part, this therapist felt more grounded, secure, and capable of showing up for her clients.

We ended this session by creating a plan that would help this therapist feel more in control, confident, and capable of doing remote therapy. She decided to check in with her 7-year-old part before seeing clients, ensuring that the team of allies was taking care of this part. She also wanted to take time to ground, center, and focus her energy, to connect to her competent therapist self before engaging in remote therapy sessions. At our next consultation, the therapist happily reported that her clients no longer triggered her; she felt energized to see her clients; and enjoyed doing remote therapy for the first time.

....

SELF-REFLECTION

As you've done remote therapy sessions with your clients, you may have experienced some remote fatigue from various factors: over-scheduling clients, losing your boundaries, worrying that your clients will get harmed, or experiencing trauma. If you feel strain in your bodymind, exhausted at the end of the day from seeing clients, or have a lack of desire to do remote therapy, you may want to do this next practice to see if you are experiencing remote fatigue.

The following Reflective Questions are a way to explore what factors may be contributing to your remote fatigue so that you can find ways to mitigate its damaging effects. Start this practice by taking some quiet time to reflect on what might be contributing to your sense of exhaustion, apathy, or lack of desire to do remote therapy sessions. Find a quiet, calm, and peaceful space where you have time to let your answers flow freely without any editing, judging, or controlling how you feel. Ask yourself one question at a time, giving yourself space to explore, expand, and uncover your truth. Take a moment to sense and feel your body after each answer, allowing your bodymind to guide you in where you may be struggling. Through this practice, you're getting to know yourself better in order to find ways to ground yourself and prevent remote fatigue. You may want to write down your answers and spend time examining what issues you may be experiencing. Later in the book, you'll find practices that can help you mitigate the damaging effects of remote therapy. As you go through this practice, be gentle and pace yourself; it can be tender to become aware of what might be causing your remote fatigue.

....

PRACTICE: REFLECTIVE QUESTIONS

- How has the pandemic impacted me *personally*, mentally, emotionally, physically, and spiritually?

- How has the pandemic impacted me *professionally*, mentally, emotionally, physically, and spiritually?

- How do I feel about seeing my clients doing remote therapy sessions?

- How many clients do I see in a day? Do I have enough time between sessions to move, breathe, and rejuvenate?

- How many clients do I see in a week? Do I feel overwhelmed, exhausted, drained when I think about this?

- Do I feel it's okay to charge my full rate when seeing clients for remote therapy? If not, why?

- Do I have clear boundaries around my time in remote sessions?

- Do I feel any eye strain at the end of the day? What is the impact this is having on my remote sessions?

- Am I pushing with my eyes and body to see my clients during sessions? If so, what is the impact on my clients and myself in my remote sessions?

- Is there anything that I'm longing for that I am missing right now: more rest, more movement, or more connection with other therapists for support?

- Do I have energy throughout the day that sustains my remote therapy practice? If not, what do I think is making me feel this way?

- Am I doing things that feel nourishing and rejuvenating throughout the day?

- Is there anything I've done in the past that helped me feel grounded that I'm not using right now?

- Is there anything I'm doing that isn't good for me? If so, why do I keep doing this activity?

- Is there anything blocking me from taking care of myself? If yes, what is this block?

- Am I feeling burdened by my client's traumas and struggling to show up for work?

- Am I feeling traumatized by images or words that I see on social media, the news, or in emails?

- Am I experiencing any lingering images, thoughts, feelings, or body sensations after my sessions with clients?

- Am I experiencing any matching traumas with my clients? If so, what are they?

- Is any of my unresolved trauma getting activated during sessions as I listen and watch my clients? If so, what do I need to take care of this part of me?

- Are there any parts of me needing attention, safety, protection, or guidance?

....

WRAPPING UP

The more I consulted with therapists throughout the tragedy of the pandemic, the more I saw therapists challenged by switching from in-person to remote sessions. As a result, therapists felt the effects of offering remote therapy, which can cause fatigue, exhaustion, and apathy, making it difficult to show up for their clients. Many of these therapists were overwhelmed, complaining that they felt drained from too much on their plates. Things that once worked for them to manage their stress were no longer helping them handle the new stressors from dealing with the pandemic's impact on their lives personally and professionally. Many therapists felt like they were losing their sense of self and purpose in the world by working in a way that felt unnatural.

With therapists losing their boundaries by over-scheduling their clients, many struggled to handle remote therapy. Their fears of harming their clients by not tracking nonverbal somatic cues took a toll on their nervous systems. All of this contributed to a sense of remote fatigue. By dealing with the reality that the pandemic was not going to end quickly, therapists had to lean in, accept, and shift how they worked. Without support, many therapists felt helpless, inadequate, and incapable of doing the work leading to feeling over-burdened and burned-out.

By becoming aware of remote fatigue as a real phenom-enon, you can mitigate the impact on your bodymind by changing how you approach practicing remote therapy sessions. Finding a schedule that gives you time to breathe while inviting conscious movement into, between, and after remote sessions you will feel freer, more open, and alive throughout the day. Setting up healthy boundaries around time, money, and energy will help you feel your worth and value in the world. Practicing the attentional dance to create fluidity between yourself and your clients' nervous systems will keep sessions feeling dynamic and will help your eyes feel less strained at the end of the day.

Finally, pay attention to whether you are experiencing remote traumatization from social media, matching traumas with your clients, or your own unresolved childhood traumas that can arise during remote therapy sessions. By trusting your body as an instrument that needs to be taken care of emotionally, mentally, and physically, you can learn ways to better take care of yourself to prevent experiencing remote fatigue. As you become aware of how to take better care of yourself, you'll increase your capacity for being resilient; connect to feeling competent; and find value in your work that is so important to help the world heal. If you are struggling, you may need to get more support through consultation, supervision, or therapy. By reaching out and getting support, you'll see that you are not alone in your struggles and that there are ways to mitigate the damaging effects of remote fatigue.

CONNECTION

....

*Practice makes you flexible and
adaptable to handle the unknown.*

....

SELF-CARE IS A DIRTY WORD

Over my many years of teaching and consulting, I consistently heard therapists struggling mentally, emotionally,
physically, and spiritually in their practices. I could see they
needed better self-care before, during, and after their
sessions, only to have them insist they were fine. I found that
the therapists' focus was solely on their clients, hoping to
find the magic intervention to solve all their client's
problems with the wave of a magic wand. When I asked in a
training how many therapists were doing self-care, many of

them had no practice in place and didn't feel it was necessary even though I could sense they were struggling.

Before the pandemic, I created workshops addressing this issue of self-care for therapists, only to be disappointed that they would not fill. I couldn't find a way to market these workshops so that therapists would see self-care as worth their time, energy, and money. I tried changing the workshop's name to "self-care for therapists, preventing burn-out, preventing vicarious traumatization, or building resiliency," and, again, the workshops received very little interest. I heard over and over that therapists were more interested in helping their clients heal rather than learning how to take better care of themselves. Self-care is essential for therapists to fuel their bodymind, which is essential to sustaining their practices for years to come. I knew something they didn't from my practices as a somatic psychotherapist: the bodymind needs attention daily to center, ground, and focus so their energy can be more present and available for their clients. Without practice, therapists can easily burn-out and leave the field of psychotherapy forever.

Although I struggled with helping therapists see that self-care is one of the essential pieces of being a therapist, I now see that the word "self" is a part of the problem. The word "self" can be a dirty word that brings up the feeling of being "selfish," which is counter-intuitive to what therapists are all about: being of service. As I reflected on the word selfish, what came to mind was when I first told my mother I wanted to receive massages regularly as a part of taking better care of myself. She responded that I was narcissistic, selfish, and full of myself for feeling entitled to spend money in such a frivolous manner. The concept of massage as a regular, essential way to increase one's physical and mental well-being was beyond her comprehension; massages were a luxury for wealthy people—not for anyone else. Listening to her words, I had to remind myself that she grew up in a time where she had to sacrifice her own needs for the good of her family. Taking care of herself just wasn't a reality because she was constantly trying to make ends meet and ensure her family's needs were met.

As therapists struggled with the concept of taking time for themselves so that they could be more available to their clients, the pandemic made it even more difficult for them to see the importance of self-care. I saw firsthand that many therapists were struggling from the trauma of switching their practices to remote therapy and dealing with the strain of taking care of their families. As a result, many therapists were hyper-focused on their clients' needs and not recognizing they were also in distress and needed to take better care of themselves. When I broached the subject of taking more time for self-care, I could feel these therapists' resistance, adding to their sense of being too selfish, too narcissistic—and that there just wasn't enough time in their day to make this happen. Many expressed that self-care was optional, not necessary.

Without recognizing their self-care was essential to their remote therapy practices, many of these therapists would take on too much responsibility for their clients' pain and drain themselves of vital energy, leaving them feeling incapable of being therapists. I had to help these therapists move through their resistance to the word "self-care" by changing the language to "daily practices." I would define daily practices as what you do daily to take care of yourself, like washing your body, brushing your teeth, and eating nourishing food.

Repetition

When I was a professional modern dancer, I had to take technique classes every day to develop skills that would strengthen and lengthen my muscles in order to perform steps that were quite difficult while making them look easy. This practice involved going to the studio and warming up my bodymind by performing foundational steps to prevent injuries as well as to support more complicated movements later on in practice. The repetition of these foundational steps laid down a neural pathway in my brain and body to perform the choreography from an embodied place rather than "thinking" about what would happen next. Tremendous care went into every step and how it sequenced through my body. These warm-ups were essential in focusing my energy to articulate my body in complex ways.

Just like a dancer practices every day, therapists need the same kind of practice to build support for the bodymind to feel alive, responsive, and rejuvenated. Daily practices involve using techniques to ground, stay flexible, and consciously support energy through the body. As the pandemic took hold, I found that many therapists did not have enough support to handle the strain on their bodymind from everything they were trying to navigate. Their self-care practices of exercising, eating healthy, and sleeping just weren't enough to sustain them. As therapists worked with me for support, they began to see that they needed ways to handle their distress better before, during, and after their remote therapy sessions. They were experiencing remote fatigue, a new phenomenon they'd never experienced before the pandemic. Some of these therapists were so exhausted from working in a new way, having matching traumas with their clients, and juggling their personal and professional lives, that many of them wanted to shut their doors for good and never practice therapy again.

Recently, in one of my remote consultation groups, a therapist took the risk of sharing that he struggled to stay present with his clients while working remotely. Since he was exercising regularly, eating healthy, and getting enough sleep, he couldn't understand why he felt so exhausted all the time. His usual self-care just didn't feel as good to him as it used to before the pandemic. As I asked more questions about his practice, he shared that he had more responsibility taking care of his family, was worried about getting COVID, and didn't feel remote therapy sessions were good enough for his clients. He also shared that he was distracted by his surroundings at home, constantly thought about his "to-do" list, and found that he was checking emails and texts during sessions because he was bored. Admitting that he was struggling on such a profound level brought up feelings of shame, guilt, and fear that there was something wrong with him.

As he shared such vulnerable information, the rest of the group chimed in that they, too, were struggling and didn't know how to deal with the extreme exhaustion they were experiencing. Many of them thought if they could just get back into their therapy offices, everything would get back to normal, and they would be okay. As they expressed how they were feeling, the truth came forward, revealing how ill-equipped many of them felt to handle what they were dealing with in their personal and professional lives. Shame permeated through the group that, somehow, none of them were good enough to handle all the pressure they'd been under since the pandemic hit.

In all my years of being a trainer and consultant, I have never seen therapists overloaded personally and professionally on such a massive level. I assured all of them that their anxieties, worries, and fears were real as well as challenging to navigate because their workload had changed dramatically. Everything these therapists were dealing with was out of the ordinary: having to work from home, learning new technology, and somehow being superhumans who were not being impacted personally and professionally by a worldwide pandemic. Therapists thought they were supposed to remain steady, even, and capable of helping their clients without the proper training to support themselves in the magnitude of what was happening around the world. Many of these therapists felt burdened by the enormity of fulfilling this new expectation and were losing their ability to take care of themselves on any level. Their usual self-care practices were not enough to help them navigate the complexity of what they were experiencing.

I found myself sensing how anxious and fearful these therapists were to share how vulnerable they were feeling.

At the same time, their feelings tapped into my history of anxiety, which has played a significant role in how I think about myself and how I handle situations. I could see therapists were struggling with their self-care because I, too, felt my usual practices of taking care of myself were inadequate to deal with all the pandemic-related challenges I was facing. When the pandemic shut down my training business, and I collapsed into the anxiety of despair, my ability to take care of myself did not feel adequate to soothe my tender nervous system.

Anxiety is not a new feeling for me; instead, it is an old familiar pattern that causes me pain and hurt. I grew up in a household where anxiety was normal since my parents are both highly anxious. I recently had a conversation with my father, in which he said, "I have nothing to worry about, but I'm going to sit here and think of something to worry about before we hang up." I was stunned by this statement and found myself holding my breath, not knowing what to say to him. Here was a man who *didn't* want to feel calm: anxiety and worry were his best friends. My father's statement put into context my lifelong struggle with anxiety and how strong the template has been for me to repattern in my life.

Over the years, I have tried many different techniques to overcome the challenges I face from my dear old friend, anxiety. As I was sharing this struggle with a colleague, she suggested I try a yoga practice designed to create rest in the bodymind. Some of her clients have used this practice daily which has transformed their anxiety into a calmer state. I had practiced yoga for years and had moments of relief from the anxiety, so I embraced the idea there was something even better that could help me on a deeper level. I immediately bought a book and recording and began this practice. There were times when I could feel my body begin to relax and soften into the floor. More often, though, I found it hard to get up off the floor, stay awake, or function throughout the day after this practice. I found this confusing since, in the literature, I read that you "should" feel rested and rejuvenated, yet here I was feeling heavy and drained, with little desire to participate in my life.

Within one short week of beginning this practice, I started to feel depressed, apathetic, and even had suicidal thoughts like, "The world would be a better place if I weren't in it." Even though I was experiencing something that felt wrong, I convinced myself that this was "good" for me. The reality was, the more I did this practice, the more I sank deeper into a quagmire of despair. I wanted this practice to rewire my nervous system so much that I was overriding my wisdom in my bodymind, and it screamed STOP!

Luckily, something deep inside guided me to wake up and see what was happening: this practice hurt me rather than helping me. It took a couple of months for my nervous system to recover from this experiment, and I'm grateful I started listening to my truth. I learned from this process that listening, honoring, and respecting your bodymind and what feels nourishing to your soul is individual. Pay attention to what your bodymind is telling you and develop practices that help you, not hinder you. You will only find this out if you try, explore, and honor your process.

Developing daily practices involves taking time to see what you need to support your anxiety, fears, and worries, noticing what makes you feel solid, strong, and capable. *You are the creator of your dance!* If something doesn't bring you a sense of wellness, then it's time to adjust, be flexible, and try something new. Checking in to "feel" your experience—rather than staying in your logical brain and doing what you "think" is good for you—is essential in this practice. It's like how I thought the restful yoga practice was the solution to my anxiety, yet I had to honor that it made me feel alone, unsupported, and incapable of interacting in the world. I am constantly creating a dance that supports my nervous system by letting go of what doesn't serve me and finding ways that refresh, rejuvenate, and connect me to my truth.

As I share my struggles with finding practices that support my anxiety, fears, and worries, I want you to know you're not alone. There is no shame in owning that you're having a hard time handling being a therapist. By checking in and observing what practices support your nervous system before, during, and after your remote therapy sessions, you'll learn how to take better care of yourself. As you design and develop your daily practices, it will create a dance that helps build resiliency in your nervous systems, supporting you when life is spinning and twirling out of control. Your nervous system will be able to rebound more quickly, making life's challenges more manageable to handle. Just like when I had collapsed on the floor, lost in my anxiety, fears, and worries because of the pandemic, I was able to pick myself off the floor and adjust my daily practices so that I could be more supportive of others who were struggling and couldn't find their way through the muck. As much as you want to help your clients, you must turn your attention inward and listen to the wisdom that will balance you physically, mentally, emotionally, and spiritually. There is no shame refueling the bodymind because it is essential—not an option to ignore.

As you develop the skills to listen to your inner wisdom, you'll begin to feel your value and self-worth modeling to your clients during remote therapy sessions how to handle powerful emotional states. Daily practices are not an option for you; rather, they are *essential* for sustaining the bodymind and remaining vital, aware, and awake. By practicing, you can build resiliency in your nervous systems that support your work to be grounded, centered, and present in ways that invigorate your energy rather than drain it to the point of experiencing remote fatigue. This resiliency is like an emotional muscle that develops overtime so you can tolerate your client's distress without being thrown off-balance. Finding daily practices to warm up your bodymind before sessions, attaining flow during your sessions, and incorporating ways to cool down after your sessions is essential to make your practice more sustainable.

BEFORE SESSIONS: WARMING UP

Preparation

Before you start your day of remote therapy sessions, it is essential to warm up your bodymind. Warming up before remote therapy sessions consists of being quiet and reflective about how you're doing personally and professionally. Just like a dancer must warm up their muscles to become embodied with the choreography, you have to take the time to do a similar practice to become embodied before your sessions. Many therapists fill their lives with things to do right up to the moment before they begin their sessions, giving no thought or preparation to what's about to occur in their sessions. When therapists push the time clock, they usually feel rushed, ungrounded, and unfocused during their sessions. One of the significant advantages of having a remote therapy practice is that many therapists no longer have to commute to their offices, which gives them extra time to create a ritual of warming up the bodymind before working with clients.

Taking time to find your baseline of how you're doing mentally, physically, emotionally, and spiritually can help you become more embodied in your practice. Once you have your baseline, it's easier to track when your personal issues are distracting you, identify if you are experiencing remote traumatization or matching traumas with your clients, and/or see that your unresolved childhood trauma is making you feel small, overwhelmed, and afraid of doing the work. Becoming familiar with your baseline will help you see what kind of resourcing you may need before working with your clients. Often, clients show up for remote therapy with a heightened sympathetic or parasympathetic shutdown, which can instantaneously overtake *your* nervous system and become overwhelming. Since you are the psycho-biological regulator in therapy, you need to be aware that working with your energetic presence can significantly impact the client's nervous system and change your therapeutic interventions. Supporting your baseline to feel solid, strong, and secure before interacting with your clients will help you track the physiological, energetic exchange that can occur during remote sessions. Taking time to resource yourself by consciously putting away things that distract you, setting healthy boundaries between yourself and your clients' traumas, and finding allies for the wounded parts of you that need more support will strengthen your ability to stay strong in your competent therapist self. Adding breath, movement, and sound to this warm-up can help your nervous system feel more grounded, centered, and focused on being ready and prepared to sit with your client's pain and suffering.

Let's take a look at a therapist overwhelmed in her remote therapy sessions and who needed help with her warm-up before seeing her clients.

....

SPOTLIGHT: WARMING UP BEFORE A SESSION

During a consultation, as the therapist shared that she felt she had no time before her sessions, she became fidgety in her chair and kept repeating phrases over and over, stumbling to find her words. I could feel a collapse in my chest, a tightening in my jaws, and I was growing sweaty through my core as she continued to speak. I invited her to focus for a moment and just feel her body. As her breathing started to slow down and deepen, her posture began to collapse forward, and her voice sounded younger and very tender. She said she felt overwhelmed by her clients' emotional dysregulation due to being isolated from the pandemic, which left her feeling incompetent to help them and incapable of doing remote work. Her body began to tremble as she shared this vulnerable moment with me. As she got in touch with this younger wounded part, she was able to name that her brother had cancer when she was nine, and her family was trying to protect her by pretending that he wasn't sick. She felt alone, afraid, and overwhelmed by her experience, with no one to guide her in making sense of what she was feeling.

I asked her to find allies that would feel supportive at this moment for the 9-year-old part of her. She imagined an angel behind her spreading its wings for support and comfort. Then she added an image of Wonder Woman in front of her to provide safety and protection. Next, she imagined her childhood dog by her side to bring warmth and guidance. As she brought in the support for this younger part by finding her allies, her fear lessened, her heart rate began to slow down, and she gradually felt tension dissipate throughout her body. She expressed that she felt more in control of her emotions, and she started straightening her spine as well as making eye contact with me.

As this young part found her resources, I invited her allies to take this young part to a safe place where she could rest, play, and relax with no concerns about being in charge of the therapy sessions. The child part was relieved as she imagined her allies taking her to a castle where she had friends, toys, and art supplies that provided support, nurturing, and playfulness all day long. Sensing the child part had her needs met, I invited the therapist to bring her focus back to her room and be present with me. The therapist expressed she felt clearer, stronger, and now had the clarity that she had been triggered by her clients' struggles with being alone, isolated, and afraid from the pandemic.

With this knowledge, the therapist learned she needed to warm up before her sessions by focusing her energy more consciously. She planned on giving herself 15 minutes before her first remote therapy session to sit quietly, reflecting on how she was doing physically, mentally, and spiritually. This quiet time allowed her to get in touch with her 9-year-old part, which needed resourcing so that her competent therapist part felt stronger and more capable of being present with her clients. By giving herself this room *to breathe, move, and add any sounds that were intuitively speaking to her, she was able to feel more grounded, centered, and focused. By developing a strong warm-up she practiced daily, she felt more confident, less afraid, and more effective with her therapeutic skills.*

....

Focusing Energy

The following warm-up practice, Focusing Energy, is a way for you to check in with yourself physically, emotionally, mentally, and spiritually before sessions. This practice invites you to slow down and be present with any images, thoughts, feelings, and body sensations that may be dysregulating your nervous system. The first part of this practice is discovering if you have any personal issues that may be distracting you, making it challenging to show up for your clients.

Once you become aware of any issues that might be distracting you from being present with your client, you can use another practice called Holding to help focus you back into the present moment. I first learned this practice in EMDR therapy called Containment, which I have adapted to help clients contain distressing traumas between sessions so that they feel safe through the process (Shapiro, 2018). This practice involves imagining something that can hold the disturbing or distracting material until you're ready to consciously look at it and give it the attention it needs to process. You can put disturbing issues, traumas, problems, dreams, memories, thoughts, pictures, feelings, and/or body sensations in this holding place. Some therapists have imagined a big wooden box buried in their backyard, a large freight container on a train, or downloading a file on a computer and sending it into the cloud. There are endless ideas for places to hold disturbing material, so don't worry about comparing yours to anyone else's. Let your imagination be creative and trust your intuition of what feels right to you. When your holding place is working, you'll know when you stop thinking about the disturbing material. You'll feel ease and relaxation throughout your body, allowing you to be aware, awake, and present. If this imaginal holding practice is difficult for you, try bringing your focus to your five senses. Notice what you see, hear, smell, taste, and sense in your office until you feel entirely present with no distractions. The practice of Holding has been life-changing for many therapists, helping them put away their distress so that they can be more present in their remote therapy sessions.

The second part of Focusing Energy is to take a moment and notice if you are experiencing any matching traumas with your clients, to the point where you may have enmeshed with the client's experience too much. Enmeshment is where you have lost your boundary with your client. As a result, you will take on too much responsibility for the client's success in therapy, experience moments of feeling helpless, and find it challenging to support your client's experience. You'll know you're enmeshed with your client if you struggle to feel separate in your own energetic body. By having a clear boundary, you will sense and feel where you begin and end energetically, providing a safe environment for both you and your client. In response, a sense of rapport and connection with your client deepens even though both of you are in separate rooms connected by a computer screen.

If you sense enmeshment with your client's trauma, you'll need to find a way to reestablish your energetic boundary. Some therapists have found it helpful to imagine a transparent bubble around themselves and one around their clients. Each bubble is permeable yet strong, allowing for connection by feeling empathy and compassion without overextending what you have to give. This boundary setting will support your nervous system by allowing you to see what's similar to your client's experience while holding onto the differences in order to differentiate your experience from theirs. You'll know this is working when you can take a deep breath and feel more solid in your being, ready to face your client once again.

In the third part of Focusing Energy, you will check to see if any of your clients are triggering your unresolved childhood traumas. A sign this may be happening is if you feel vulnerable, overwhelmed, and out of control when working with a particular client. Taking time to name and resource the young, wounded part of yourself who experienced that trauma by finding supportive allies is essential before sitting with this client. Remembering that your competent therapist self is the one who's engaging in the treatment allows the young, wounded part to be resourced, helping you feel more grounded, centered, and capable of doing the therapy session.

The last part of Focusing Energy involves your creativity leading the way to what may feel nourishing, supportive, and enlivening, which could include breathing, movement, and sounding. Listen to your body for what feels right to you at this moment, allowing your intuition to guide this exploration. Remember, there is no right or wrong. You simply need to become aware of how focused and ready you feel to begin your remote therapy sessions for the day.

This warm-up practice Focusing Energy can take as little as 5 to 15 minutes, depending on how much resourcing you need before seeing your clients. Give yourself enough time to listen quietly in order to hear what your bodymind needs without any distractions or interruptions. This practice aims to warm you up by stretching your affect tolerance, supporting your nervous system, and building your capacity to be present. Think of this practice as a daily ritual that will focus your energy by using resources to help you be more dynamic and present as well as become a strong psychobiological regulator for your clients. This ritual does not have to be elaborate; in fact, it's preferable it be something you can rely on that connects you wholeheartedly to your embodied therapist self. Through this practice, your energy will sustain throughout each session, helping you prevent remote fatigue. In practicing the Focusing Energy script below, adapt any of the words I suggest so that you feel grounded, natural, and at ease through the process.

....

PRACTICE: FOCUSING ENERGY

Take a moment to feel yourself in your chair with your feet solid on the ground. You can do this with your eyes closed or with a soft gaze looking at something soothing in your remote therapy office. Bring your awareness to your breath. Is your inhale and exhale the same pacing? Is the inhale or exhale longer than the other? Is it harder to inhale or exhale? Just observe without any judgment so that you can determine a baseline of how you're breathing without purposely changing anything.

Now slowly focus your attention to the top of your head, your shoulders, torso, legs, and finally, your feet. Can you sense your entire body? Is there any part of your body that wants attention? If so, take a moment, send your breath into that area and notice what happens. You can also bring your hands to this area and gently touch, hold, or massage it until the area feels you have given it enough attention.

Next, see if anything is going on in your personal life that might be distracting you today, including things around health, money, or your family. How do you feel you're handling these issues? Do you feel stressed, out of control, or that you can't deal with whatever is going on? Is there anything distressing you as a result of watching social media, the news, or even reading your emails? How is this impacting you right now? Bring your awareness to your body and notice how this feels when you think about these issues.

If anything is distressing, take a moment to imagine a holding place that would be strong enough to consciously put the distressing images, thoughts, feelings, or body sensations until you have time to give it the attention it needs. Once the disturbing material feels contained, focus your energy back on your body and see what you notice now. Does this bring more ease and relaxation to you? If you are struggling with imagining a holding place, slow down and explore what else you might need. You may need to make it larger, send it farther away, or surround it with protective allies. Keep exploring until you can take a breath and sense more ease in your body.

Now focus on your clients you'll be working with today. How do you feel when you think about each client? Notice if you have any issues, symptoms, or traumas that match what any of your clients are currently experiencing. What happens in your body when you sit with this information? Are you able to stay separate from each client, or are you enmeshing with their struggle? Have you been ruminating about this client and their issues? Are you struggling to find rest and ease in your nervous system? Are you having a hard time feeling present with other clients because one client is taking up too much of your energy and attention?

If you're struggling, ask yourself what kind of boundary you need to help you feel present, focused, and capable of being with these clients. It may help you to imagine a transparent bubble around yourself and one around your client. These energetic bubbles can help you feel separate while still providing you with the capacity to feel empathy, compassion, and kindness toward your client. See what feels just right in your own body until you feel more relaxed, at ease, and present.

Next, see if any of your clients are triggering your unresolved traumas. Is this trauma coming up during your sessions, making you feel incompetent, incapable, or inadequate? See if this is a young, wounded part crying out for attention. If so, what does that part need right now? Protection, nurturing, guidance, support, or grounding? See if you can imagine allies that can provide the missing experience for this part. When you find the allies, put them in a circle around the young, wounded part so that the part senses and feels this support. Notice what happens in your body when you let the support be present.

Next, allow the circle of support to take this child part to its safe place where it can play, laugh, or even rest. Let the child part know that it does not have to be in charge of the therapy session, that the adult therapist will be in control. See how this feels in your body. Next, bring your focus back, in the present moment, to your adult therapist self, who is highly skilled, confident, and capable of running therapy sessions. Feel how solid, connected, and grounded you feel in your body.

Last, see if you need to add anything else to your Focusing Energy warm-up practice that would feel nourishing, supportive, and enlivening, including movement, journaling, sounding, or sitting longer in silence. Listen to your body for what feels just right to you at this moment, focusing your energy, preparing yourself to sit with our clients. In ending this practice today, scan your body from head to toe while taking a deep breath. Has anything shifted from when you started this practice? Take a moment to look around the room, feeling your feet on the ground, focused and ready to start your day.

....

DURING SESSIONS: FLOWING

Trust

Once you've taken the time to warm up your bodymind, it's time to find ways to keep your energy flowing during remote therapy sessions. As a professional dancer, much of my work involved preparing my bodymind so I could flow with the choreography from an embodied place once I was in the performance. I spent hours learning intricate choreography so that my bodymind would be finely tuned, prepared, and ready to execute each step precisely. The discipline required to show up and practice every day—with the intention and care directed into every moment of the dance—was critical to each performance's success.

When we traveled across the nation to perform, we would arrive at the theatre the day before the performance to see the uniqueness of each stage. Every stage I performed on had various nuisances I had to quickly get to know because its size and dimensions would significantly impact the choreography. I would have to learn where to enter for my parts, where to exit safely, and how to position myself to hit specific lighting cues. This preparation time was quite stressful and required tremendous focus to be adaptable, flexible, and open to all the nuanced changes.

Part of this rehearsal was learning how to trust my bodymind from practicing for months, which allowed me to rely on my instincts to carry me through the performance. Each performance was unique and felt completely different, even though I was executing the same steps every night.

Some performances, it would feel like everything went like clockwork, while others felt like each step was a complete failure and took tremendous effort just to complete the dance. The hours of practice and preparation created a foundation in my bodymind that I could rely on if something went wrong. I was ready to respond, be creative in the moment, and not let the audience know that I was worried about what was about to happen.

One particular performance comes to mind. I was wearing a strapless, tight-fitting gold lame cocktail dress with matching gold high heels, clip-on earrings, and a microphone. In the dark, I would quietly slink onto the stage without the audience being aware of my presence as dancers moved in front of me. When it was my moment to be seen, the spotlight would focus on me as I spun around to face the audience lip-syncing to Leslie Gore's "You Don't Own Me" (1963). I looked like a lounge singer ready to entertain for the evening.

One night I spun around, and one of my clip-on earrings went flying across the stage. My heart started pounding as I realized this earring was now a hazardous object that could seriously injure other dancers. My mind was racing a hundred miles per hour, and I had to quickly and seamlessly resolve this issue so that no one would get injured. As I devised a plan in my mind while continuing to lip-sync, I slowly began to slink my way over to the earring. As I got closer and closer, the dilemma of how I was going to retrieve this earring without anyone noticing was worrying me. The dress I was in was so tight and unforgiving it was like I was a baby swaddled; I couldn't move, let alone breathe. I imagined myself bending over to pick up the earring, but that just wasn't possible. The only way I could resolve this dilemma was to do a backbend, keeping my torso straight, praying that I wouldn't fall on the floor. As I slowly began this contorted backbend, I extended one of my arms long behind me to balance my body's awkwardness. I had to trust that my hand would find this earring without me looking as I hoped and prayed I didn't make a fool out of myself through the process.

Low and behold, a miracle happened, and I was able to retrieve the earring seamlessly while swiftly hoisting my body back up to vertical, spinning around with a flourish as I had done in my entrance. I was amazed I had pulled off this acrobatic moment in just the blink of an eye. My fellow dancers were entirely in the dark and had no idea what I was up to the entire time. The choreographer was furious with me until he found out what I'd done had prevented a disaster on stage. He was ultimately grateful that I took care of this problem without the audience having a clue what had just happened.

There was no way to rehearse and prepare for a moment like this. All of my months of practice, knowing the choreography inside and out, allowed me to trust that I could respond in the moment, take the necessary action to keep myself and everyone else safe. That practice took care, attention to detail, and a total commitment to trusting my bodymind to lead the way. My nervous system was flexible, adaptive, and responsive in the moment due to all the earlier rehearsing. The foundation of my skills allowed me to be present, and not let anyone see that there was a problem.

Presence

My training as a dancer helped me learn that this kind of practice is also necessary for therapists in order to prepare their nervous systems to be responsive, flexible, and adaptable during every session. Through developing your presence, you're setting the stage for your nervous system to be ready to handle whatever happens, just like in a dancer during a performance. The more you practice, the easier it is to trust your instincts to guide you with interventions as you help your clients move through their issues and traumas. When you see your bodymind as a wise instrument, you can then begin to trust that vital information is available to assist your responses and interactions with your clients using grace, ease, and the ability to tap into your creativity.

Your presence will become stronger through the repetition of practice, which clients will sense by feeling seen, heard, and valued throughout the session. By developing your presence, you'll help clients feel safer and build more trust in the therapeutic relationship, allowing them to be more vulnerable in their sessions. Having a strong presence also enables you to tune into your bodymind and sense your clients' somatic responses. Tracking the powerful energetic exchange between your nervous system and your clients will help guide you when something significant happens in your session. Tuning in and sensing somatic cues, such as tension in your shoulders, constriction in your throat, heat in your core, pain in your heart, or an opening in your chest will become vital information for you to pay attention to in your own bodymind. These somatic cures can be subtle, tiny, and almost imperceptible or they can be expansive, felt through your entire body, which can feel overwhelming, ungrounding, and challenging to manage. Either way, your presence in the dance lets you know that you need to stay curious about what's happening in your session. These shifts are your body talking to you so that you can sense and feel what's going on in the nonverbal somatic dance between you and your client. In these moments, you may feel the enormity of your client's pain, feel dysregulation in your nervous system, disconnect from your intuition, and lose your connection to feeling present with your client. These somatic cues can also indicate that you may be experiencing transference, countertransference, or somatic resonance during your sessions.

As you remain curious in this dance between both of your nervous systems, you'll need to find ways to ground, stay aware, and awake to what's happening in the present moment. You can do somatic practices immediately in your session to help strengthen your presence with your clients. You can use your breath to change your physiological responses, find ways to ground in the present moment, and learn to put distractions on hold. These steps can help you avoid interruptions in your ability to be present with your clients. As you put these somatic practices into place, you'll begin to feel more flow, ease, and connection to yourself and your clients throughout your remote therapy sessions. Remember, the more you trust your bodymind, the easier it is for the dance to proceed, which will decrease your sense of fatigue at the end of the day.

Let's take a look at three somatic practices to help strengthen your ability to stay flowing during sessions: Breathing, Grounding, and Holding.

Breathing

The first somatic practice that can help regulate your nervous system during sessions is to breathe consciously. Breathing is the foundation of life and acts as a bridge between the conscious and unconscious. Unconsciously, you breathe every day, which keeps you alive and moving without thinking about how this is happening. In therapy, you can consciously work with your breathing by shifting the rhythm, pacing, and intensity of each breath to directly impact your physiological response. By continually tracking your own bodymind throughout the session, you'll become aware of how you breathe and how it affects your nervous system responses.

Take, for example, a client who's talking rapidly and barely breathing. You may notice that your own breath starts to become shallow, short, and holding, reflecting the same pattern as your client. When you sense this shift in your body, you feel a spike in your sympathetic nervous system as it matches your client's activation. Without noticing and then changing how you breathe, you may remain in a hyperarousal state and start to feel agitated, overwhelmed, and frightened by your clients' experience. Over time, this activation will exhaust your bodymind, leaving you feeling tired, exhausted, and fatigued.

To prevent this kind of fatigue, you can use your breath as a tool to reengage your nervous system differently, which can significantly impact how present you feel with your clients. Slowing down and engaging in long exhales to release the tension built up in your body will automatically engage your parasympathetic nervous system to become calmer, more relaxed, and at ease. By remembering that you are the psychobiological regulator in the session, your nervous system will come back into the window of tolerance. This also invites your client's nervous system to do the same. You will feel more present and capable of being in the flow with your client's experience and consciously engage in the somatic dance, feeling connected with their nervous system.

Another example of how breathing can impact your nervous system is when your client starts to feel sleepy, sluggish, and depressed. When this happens, you might feel the need to yawn, take a nap, or end the session because it's just too hard to stay awake. Your client's nervous system may have dropped into a parasympathetic shutdown, impacting your nervous system to regulate to theirs, mirroring the sleepy sensation in your bodymind. Without changing how you're breathing, you may remain stuck in a hypoarousal shutdown state where you may feel heavy, tired, and dreading the rest of your sessions. Over time, this sluggishness can impact your overall vitality, sense of value, and ability to feel effective as a therapist, ultimately contributing to a sense of remote fatigue.

When this powerful energetic exchange happens, it can help if you shift your breathing into your upper chest with rapid, short inhales to stimulate your sympathetic nervous system. Consciously changing your breathing will wake you up and allow you to feel present with your client. As the psychobiological regulator in the session, reengaging your nervous system to wake up will help you come back into the window of tolerance, which invites your client's nervous system to do the same. From this new activation, you will feel alive, flowing, and present, capable of helping your client with their distress.

With this awareness, the power of using your breath as an intervention to help center, ground, and support your nervous system is essential for you to feel connected and flowing during your sessions. Without this awareness, you may feel tired, depleted, and exhausted, contributing to your sense of remote fatigue. Consciously working with how you're breathing in a session will help strengthen your presence, help you feel capable of handling your clients' dysregulation in their nervous systems, and keep you connected to yourself and your clients during sessions.

Grounding

As you begin using your breathing techniques, it's also helpful to consciously ground in your body throughout your sessions to strengthen your sense of presence. As energetic beings, you and your client impact each other's nervous systems, and it's easy to lose your connection to the earth and feel less anchored in your bodymind. Sometimes during sessions, the energetic exchange can be so powerful it can uproot you with no warning. When clients become dysregulated in their nervous systems, it can feel overwhelming to your nervous system, ultimately leaving you feeling ungrounded, fuzzy, and incapable of tracking what's happening in your body. Once this has occurred, some therapists have felt breathing just wasn't enough to ground them. Finding practices that quickly reengage your nervous system, calming and soothing you, can make all the difference in helping you feel centered, connected, and flowing throughout your sessions.

It can help if you identify tools you can use during your sessions to quickly reconnect somatically to the felt sense of being calm, centered, and rooted in your body. Some therapists like to hold a unique rock, crystal, or favorite piece of jewelry. Others like looking at a painting, photo, art, or favorite words, quotes, or poems to remind them to stay centered and believe in themselves. This can also encourage therapists, reminding them they're capable of being lovable, strong, and courageous. Some therapists have pictures of their allies that they can easily see to remind them that they're never alone, always supported, and are capable of handling whatever is happening in the session. Make sure to place these tools in a place for easy access during your remote therapy sessions so you can quickly use them to ground if you become uprooted during your session.

Another way to ground yourself during your sessions is using your body as a tool that can easily reset your nervous system to help you feel solid, rooted, and anchored to the earth. Simply push your feet into the floor, engaging your leg muscles. Your body becomes a beautiful resource, helping you feel more in control of what you're experiencing while remaining present, aware, and capable of handling the dysregulation in your bodymind. This simple action helps stimulate your awareness of the ground, supporting your body to energetically manage the emotions and sensations you feel running through your body.

As you develop what feels grounding and helps you stay present, give yourself time to explore, experiment, and find what works for you. Notice what soothes your nervous system and find ways to integrate it into your remote therapy sessions. Remember, this process is yours and yours alone, so listen to your intuition to guide you as you find what feels right. These simple grounding tools will help you have the support to find flow, increase your ability to stay present and connected, and guide you to listen to your bodymind throughout your sessions. By staying grounded, present and awake, your energy level will remain steady and strong, decreasing your risk for experiencing remote fatigue.

Holding

During your remote therapy sessions, distractions can be expected and can interrupt your sessions' flow. Clients' children may want their parents' attention, dogs may bark, dumpster trucks may create loud noises, your home projects may stare you in the face, or incoming emails may call out to you to answer immediately. As these distractions occur, you may become irritated, impatient, and long to stop the session so you can attend to your own needs. In these moments, it's essential to hit pause and use your practice of Holding. Remember, this practice involves imagining a container strong enough to hold the distracting material until you have time to consciously return to it. Once you've contained the distraction, bring your awareness back to your bodymind to refocus your energy. The power of Holding, when practiced regularly, can help you focus more quickly when you become distracted so that you remain present with your clients and sustain your energy throughout your sessions.

Attentional Dance

As you develop your presence by using somatic tools to ground, support, and center yourself, your attention between you and your client needs to remain fluid, rhythmical, and dynamic, creating an energetic dance between you and your client during your sessions. This dance requires you to freely move your attention from your own bodymind to tracking your client's nonverbal somatic cues. This back-and-forth action is what I call the Attentional Dance of witnessing your client from a place of being grounded, curious, and remaining in a state of connection with yourself and your client.

If you are afraid of harming your clients because they're in separate rooms, this may impact how embodied you may feel during your remote therapy sessions. When you come from a place of fear, you may feel your eyes pushing through the computer screen, trying to make better contact with your client. Your gaze will become narrow and fixated, hypervigilant that you may miss your client's nonverbal somatic cues. Remaining in this heightened state of fear can cause strain on your eyes and body as you try to "see" everything, even when you can't actually see your client's entire body. This frozenness will lead to tiredness, aches, and pains, along with exhaustion by the end of the day. As you begin to become aware of how you're "seeing" your client, try instead to perceive from your whole body, trusting your intuition as a guide. When you trust that you have all the skills necessary to do remote therapy, your eyes and body will begin to relax, allowing you to more readily tap into your bodymind wisdom. Your energy will be more balanced and sustain you throughout your sessions.

Tracking your client's somatic cues can help you assess if the client has an emotional charge about what they're sharing. Take time to notice your client's posture, gestures, facial expressions, and eye contact. You'll also need to track the nonlinguistic components of their voice volume, tempo, pitch, intensity, timing, and their use of pauses between words. Notice any micro-movements in their face, such as an eye twitching, lips pursing, breathing shifts, or skin color changes, which can indicate your client is moving into tender material. Some of these somatic cues are obvious and easy to see in remote therapy. Other cues are more subtle and take practice to perceive the shifts—try not to discount what you're sensing and perceiving.

The Attentional Dance becomes effective when you notice the nonverbal somatic cues in your clients while also tracking your own bodymind. You let your attention move back and forth, allowing the Dance to unfold naturally. As you become more aware of this Dance, you may begin to notice when you get stuck with your attention in one place, which can cause distress in your nervous system, thus creating distance between you and your clients. When this happens, you will feel out of sync with your client and struggle to remain connected, supported, and flowing in your session. If you get stuck in your Attentional Dance, you'll need to find ways to reconnect, center, and balance yourself to keep your energy alive, vibrant, and flowing during remote sessions.

Let's take a look at how you may get out of sync with your client and get back into the flow of the Attentional Dance.

Out of Sync

As you move your attention back and forth, you may feel out of sync with your client by focusing too intently on one nonverbal somatic cue the client's experiencing. An example of this would be observing a repetitive movement, such as the client twirling their hair, pursing their lips, or biting their nails. You may become irritated with the client, anxious and impatient, wanting to make the client stop even though you can't look away. If you're hyper-focusing on this gesture, your client may feel exposed emotionally and want to push you away, shut down, or avoid difficult topics. When you become aware that you're hyper-focusing on one somatic cue, see if you can expand your awareness to sense the client's overall state. See how much energy the client has, whether they are rigid or collapsed in their musculature, how grounded they are in their body, allowing your gaze to soften, relax, and recenter in your body.

You may also step out of sync in your Attentional Dance by feeling your client's energy invading your space, even in remote therapy. The client may be pushing towards you to connect, making you feel like their energy is overtaking yours. You may feel anxious, afraid, and ungrounded, making it difficult to connect to your own bodymind. When this occurs, you may feel exhausted, drained, and depleted after your sessions. It's possible you'll also find yourself dreading working with this client because their energy is overwhelming your nervous system. When you feel inundated like this, take time to bring your attention back to your own body in order to ground and support what you're experiencing. Scan your body to identify what needs to happen so that you can ground, center, and get back into balance before returning your gaze to your client. Your somatic tools of Breathing, Grounding, and Holding may be helpful in this situation.

You can also step out of sync with your client when you have a body sensation that's so distracting you can't put your attention anywhere else. An example of this was when I had sciatica, and I found sitting in a chair excruciatingly painful. The pain in my body was so distracting that I had trouble feeling empathy for my client's pain. I struggled to pay attention and found myself short with my reflections, just wanting to get the session over in a hurry. When a physical sensation is this distracting, see if you can shift your attention back to your entire body. Use your somatic tools of Breathing, Grounding, and Holding to support your nervous system. You can also imagine a supportive ally that's there to support, nurture and take care of you. As you allow the support to come into your body, it will make it easier for you to shift your attention back toward your client.

Be careful to notice when you get stuck in your overall state, especially when you're experiencing personal issues that are emotionally challenging, such as a death of a loved one or pet, a divorce, community fires, floods, or a pandemic. After my mother died, I had trouble allowing my attention to move towards my clients because my grief was all-consuming. I had to rely on my somatic tool, Holding, to set my grief aside during sessions so that I could coax my attention out back into the world. If I brought my attention to my overall state of being, I would again feel my grief consume my attention, making it difficult for me to stay connected with my client. My Attentional Dance needed to be more directive to help me stay present, aware, and grounded throughout each session until I felt stronger and capable of sensing my entire body without dropping into my grief.

In Sync

When you become familiar with allowing your attention to move back and forth between you and your client, you will feel in sync with them, and they will respond by feeling seen, heard, and sensed on a profound somatic level. I recently experienced being in sync with a therapist in one of my trainings as I was doing a live remote demonstration. I found my intuition guiding me because I was aware of our Attentional Dance. I sensed the therapist was feeling tension in their heart area as they contracted forward to protect it. The energy seemed stuck and not flowing through their body to support what they were feeling. As I witnessed these somatic cues, I brought my attention back to my body and sensed tension building in my heart area. I intuitively said to them, "Let your big, beautiful heart have this feeling." As they heard my words, their energy began to shift, and their heart began to expand, opening up to this new sensation. I gently guided them to allow room in their body in order to undergo this experience without having to fix it, change it, or try to make it go away. As they slowly let themself breathe into this new, unfamiliar place, they became aware of new feelings and sensations that surprised them.

As I watched this therapist's energy expand and grow, I brought my attention back to my experience, trusting our connection. I could feel the energy start to flow through my entire body. I allowed my attention to move back and forth between us, sensing the expansion and supporting the therapist's new awareness. Our nervous systems were dancing together, and we were in sync with each other's experiences. As we shared this beautiful Attentional Dance, joy ran through my body; we both smiled at each other, feeling each other's presence. Even though we were in separate rooms, our bodies resonated with each other, sensing, feeling, and flowing. The therapist was aware that I was fully present with them, supporting their newfound experience. After the training, I received a handwritten note from this therapist expressing how powerful this experience was for them. They'd felt the power of the energetic exchange between us even though we were in separate rooms connected by a computer screen. My Attentional Dance helped guide me to sense my client's somatic experience as well as my own.

As you become familiar with the Attentional Dance, you will start to trust your intuition to guide you throughout the session. Your knowingness will come into play as you gently guide the client into more profound and meaningful work. Clients will express that they feel seen, heard, and sensed in meaningful ways beyond words. When you embrace this Dance, you'll feel more freedom in connecting with your intuition, have more vibrancy in your presence, and perceive from your whole being versus straining with your eyes. As you flow with your clients, you'll begin to trust the connection available between you and your clients. You then can begin to trust that remote therapy can be just as powerful as in-person sessions, leading you to feel satisfied, vital, and committed to your life as a therapist.

The following flowing practice, Attentional Dance, can help you begin to feel, sense, and experiment with seeing with your entire body rather than just your eyes. Do this practice when you have the time and space to explore without any distractions. As you do this practice, imagine sitting with one client at a time. Make notes as you move your attention back and forth, noticing when you feel connected and in the flow or when your attention gets stuck and how that impacts your bodymind. As you reflect on different clients, see what feels similar and what feels different in your dance. Give yourself permission to explore different ways of shifting your attention whenever you get stuck.

Repeat this practice as many times as you need, imaging one client at a time to see if you are noticing any patterns that are similar to your other clients. Take notes of any information that might distract you in your sessions. Be sure to use your somatic tools, Breathing, Grounding, and Holding, when necessary to keep your energy flowing in sessions.

As you get comfortable with this practice, bring it into your sessions and notice if your energy level changes, how your clients perceive you, and if you are enjoying your remote therapy sessions more fully. As your Attentional Dance grows more fluid, your energy will sustain throughout the day, and you'll feel the flow lessening your symptoms of remote fatigue. If you're struggling with any particular client and can't find your flow in this practice, take this information into your consultation, supervision, or your own therapy to explore this material more deeply.

....

PRACTICE: ATTENTIONAL DANCE

Take a moment to find a comfortable position for this exploration. You can do this with your eyes open with a soft gaze or closed, whatever feels best to you in the moment. Think about one of your clients that you're working in remote therapy. Begin to notice where your attention wants to intuitively go and allow it to rest there as you think about this client. Are you more aware of your client or yourself? Just notice what comes to you without judging or worrying if you're doing this right. You are just taking note of what you're sensing and perceiving in this moment.

Now consciously bring your attention to your client. What

overall perception or impressions do you have about your client? Notice their posture, gestures, facial expressions, and eye contact. Listen to how they are speaking and how that resonates in your body. How loud is their voice tone, pitch, and intensity? Are there specific words they emphasize, or are there long pauses between each word or phrase? Notice if any micro-movements are catching your attention. What do you notice in your body as you perceive this information? Are you trying to push to "see" more? Are you trying to reach through the computer screen to connect more with them? Are you relaxed, calm, and at peace as you think about this client? There are no right or wrong ways of doing this; you're just gathering information for yourself.

Next, let go of perceiving your client and bring your attention to your body and experience. Scan to see if any particular sensation is calling out for your attention. What do you notice about this sensation in your body? Is the sensation sharp, hot, cold, open, tingling? There is no right or wrong; just become aware of whatever you are sensing without trying to put any meaning to it.

After exploring this sensation, bring your attention to your entire body. What is your overall impression of what you are sensing? Are you tired, alert, anxious, afraid? Notice if you have any personal issues coming into your consciousness and, if you do, what you sense when you think about them. See if you can refrain from adding meaning to what you're experiencing. You are just noticing, observing, and getting to know yourself better.

Now, at your pacing, let your attention shift back and forth between your client and yourself. See if any places hold your attention and if you find it difficult to shift back and forth. Notice if you're avoiding anything in particular or get fixated in a way that makes your body tight, still, or frozen. See what you are noticing, trying not to judge it or label it as wrong or bad for sensing this. Be gentle with this process. You're just getting to know your experience with this client to help you find where you are in flow with your Attentional Dance and where you may be getting stuck, which could be depleting your energy.

As you experiment with different ways of working in your Attentional Dance, see if you can imagine yourself changing how you interact with your client the next time you see them. What happens in your body when you think about this future session? Is there anything you need to feel more supported as you sit with this client? See what feels nourishing to your bodymind as you explore different ideas. Are there any places that you still feel stuck, frozen, or incapable of making another choice? If so, what else might help you resource yourself so that you can smoothly let your attention move back and forth between your client and yourself.

When you're ready to end this exploration, take a deep breath, and let go of imagining your client with loving care, thanking them for what they are teaching you at this moment. Gently bring yourself back into the room and center yourself. Take any notes that will help you remember what you discovered and see how this information impacts your next session with your client. Remember, if you are struggling with anything you discovered, take this information into consultation, supervision, or your own therapy to explore more deeply.

....

Off-Balance

As you are in the flow with your Attentional Dance, you may become ungrounded from the powerful energetic exchange, which can throw your nervous system off-balance. Clients may project uncomfortable feelings onto you as the source of their discomfort, or your own unresolved traumas may surface from witnessing your clients' nonverbal somatic cues, or you may experience somatic resonance where your body is mirroring your client's somatic experience. Any of these issues can impact you, causing you to lose focus, become ungrounded, and have strong physiological responses that can be disorienting. When this happens, your session's flow can become disrupted, rupturing your sense of connection. Let's take a look at how transference, countertransference, or somatic resonance may show up in remote therapy sessions.

Transference

Transference happens when a client unconsciously feels something toward another person but transfers those feelings onto you instead. When this happens, it's easy to feel off-balance, blaming yourself for the client's discomfort instead of working consciously with the transference.

Let's look at an example of a client struggling during the pandemic to handle the changes at work and how transference occurs in the session. The client arrives for your remote therapy session upset that their boss is making them work from home instead of at the office. They like working in their office better and feel more productive there rather than working from home because there are too many distractions. As your client expresses their frustration with work, they suddenly get angry at you for looking at them judgmentally even though you feel you didn't. This unexpected angry outburst toward you completely surprises you, causing your muscles to tense and making you feel frozen in your chair. You find yourself flustered, unable to find your words, and incapable of moving forward, completely thrown off-balance. Your mind races a hundred miles per hour, wondering what you did wrong, and then you find yourself apologizing without understanding what just occurred. You simply want to make things right with the client.

When this kind of interaction happens, it is essential to slow down the process and get yourself back in balance in order to respond to your client therapeutically rather than reacting out of fear that the client is mad at you. Use your somatic tools of Breathing, Grounding, and Holding to get yourself back in balance. Take a moment to scan your bodymind and see if you did something unconsciously that hurt your client without your awareness. If this happened, take time to own your mistake and repair it with the client.

On the other hand, if you didn't do anything to upset the client, you need to recognize that the client's transference is a way to distract you from getting too close to what's really bothering them. If you take the client's anger personally it will not help them consciously deepen into the unconscious material requiring their attention. Slowing down and guiding the client to reflect on what they are feeling and how they feel it in their body will begin moving the transferred feelings off of you. The client will then deepen into their experience and sense the anger towards the person they're actually angry at but are afraid to connect to those feelings. Often, clients will connect to unresolved childhood memories that are the underlying feelings that make it difficult for the client in the present moment.

By slowing down and balancing yourself somatically before responding, you can then find ways to remain therapeutic, helping the client deepen their process. Being in touch with your body on an intimate level and learning how to regulate yourself in uncomfortable moments will allow you not to take things personally. Transference is a normal part of remote therapy; learning how to remain present with your client by using your somatic tools will deepen your therapeutic interventions and help you work with transference more consciously. Your energy will remain more fluid, dynamic, and flowing throughout your remote therapy sessions, preventing you from holding onto your client's pain that is not yours to take on. Without flowing with your energy, you can have lingering somatic residue at the end of your sessions that can cause remote fatigue if not processed.

Countertransference

As you work with clients in remote therapy, you may also experience countertransference where your own unresolved childhood trauma may become active in the session, making it challenging for you to stay present with the client's experience. You may become aware that you feel small, fearful, and incapable of working with this client, wondering if you should transfer them to another, more qualified therapist.

Let's look at an example of countertransference with a client struggling with an abusive ex-partner who kept trying to connect with the client during the pandemic. As your client shared how upsetting the experience with their abusive ex-partner contacting them was, they expressed feelings of being out of control, fearing for their life, and desperately wanting to run away. As they share this tender material, you notice your body is tingling from head to toe, your heart is pounding, and all you want to do is end this session. So, you focus on these sensations in your body, becoming aware of a childhood memory of when your dad beat your mother right in front of you. Your counter-transference has reared its ugly head in the session from your own unresolved trauma. Your body is signaling to you that your past is here in the present moment, making it difficult for you to stay present with your client's experience because the dysregulation in your own nervous system is challenging to manage.

As you become aware of this dysregulation in your bodymind, you need to get yourself back in balance in order to remain present with your client. Using the somatic tool Holding allows you to contain the distress until you can process it in consultation, supervision, or your own therapy later. Once you are no longer thinking about this disturbing memory, you can then use your somatic Breathing and Grounding tools to bring you back to the present moment with your client. You'll know your tools are working when you can track sensations in your body, breathe easily, feel your feet anchored on the floor, and are able to be present with your client without thinking about your past. All of this can happen in an instance without your client ever knowing what you're experiencing. This process is necessary to help keep you in the flow with your clients.

When you recognize that you may be experiencing countertransference and feel thrown off-balance during remote therapy sessions, you'll need to find ways to ground, center, and focus. If you do not find ways to manage the distress from countertransference, you may feel distracted, uprooted, and challenged throughout your sessions. This can lead you to feel exhausted, drained, and dread showing up to work with your clients. Finding ways to regulate your nervous system will help you feel more centered and in control when countertransference occurs as well as help you remain balanced, centered, and in the flow during your remote therapy sessions.

Somatic Resonance

Somatic resonance is when you become aware that you're experiencing body sensations you weren't feeling at the beginning of your session—and that it mirrors your client's experience in the exact moment. When this occurs, you may feel constriction in your throat, heat in your core, or pain in your head while your client experiences the same thing. Often this kind of energetic exchange scares therapists who aren't trained in somatic psychology. These therapists will try to avoid, distract, or deny that somatic resonance is happening. When somatic resonance occurs, it can indicate that the client is touching upon tender material in therapy. By sensing your body, you can help the client become curious about what they are experiencing and guide them to become aware of their felt sense. Once you sense this energy, you'll need to find ways to move it through your body to reset, balance, and center yourself again.

Let's look at an example of somatic resonance when a client struggled to voice how hurt they felt because their partner was not giving them the attention they needed through the pandemic. As your client shares how distressed they feel, your body starts to shake, you feel dizzy, and want to throw up. You are thrown off-balance and realize that you're struggling to remain present with your client. As you scan your bodymind, you're clear that nothing is coming up for you or reminding you of anything from your past. You realize that somatic resonance may be happening. In this moment, you become curious about what's happening for the client and gently turn your focus to your client's experience. Ask the client what they are noticing in their body as they're expressing their distress. They might say something like, "I feel shaky, dizzy, and want to vomit." You now have validation that somatic resonance is happening.

As the client becomes aware of their felt sense, see if you can breathe yourself into your body using your somatic tools Breathing, Grounding, and Holding to support your nervous system. See if you can make more room in your body to allow the energy to move, flow, and release. As you support your nervous system, you'll will become the psychobiological regulator inviting the client's nervous system to resonate with your nervous system. Your finely tuned instrument is a source of wisdom to help you sense, feel, and connect with your client even during remote therapy sessions.

Once you know somatic resonance is just a part of remote therapy, it becomes easier to move, breathe, and stay curious, with this information strengthening your presence during a session. You don't have to tell your client about this phenomenon unless it feels therapeutic, safe, and can provide empathy and compassion for the client's experience. If you don't work with this energy in your own body, you may experience lingering somatic residue, which can lead to feelings of anxiety, fear, and exhaustion.

As you grow more trusting that a powerful energetic exchange can occur in remote therapy, you'll begin to open to the possibility of experiencing transference, counter-transference, and somatic resonance during your sessions. Frequently, I hear therapists say they can't feel their clients somatically while doing remote therapy since it's cold, distant, and can't provide intimacy in the same way as in-person sessions. You have to remember that you are not doing therapy with a computer; instead, you connect with a live, vibrating, energetic being who can sense and feel you as much as you can sense and feel them. The more connected you are to your bodymind, the more its wisdom can guide you throughout the process during remote therapy sessions.

As you practice finding ways to regulate your nervous system, it will automatically begin to regulate your client's nervous system. If you struggle to figure out if you're experiencing transference, countertransference, or somatic resonance, don't get too worried about it. Recognize that your body is experiencing something, and you need to find a way to regulate your nervous system to be more present with what's happening for the client. Once this powerful energetic exchange comes into your awareness, use your grounding tools Breathing, Grounding, and, if needed, Holding to help you remain present during your sessions. Remember, the more you bring your bodymind into balance, the more you'll be flexible, adaptable, and flowing in your remote therapy sessions. You will strengthen your connection to yourself and your clients, preventing the debilitating effects of remote fatigue.

END OF SESSIONS: COOLING DOWN

Toxins

As you finish your day of experiencing this powerful energetic exchange in your remote therapy sessions, you'll need to cool down your bodymind just like a dancer must after performing. When I danced professionally, after every rehearsal or performance, I needed time to let my body cool down from all the physical exertions. While dancing, my sympathetic nervous system was engaged so that I could run across the stage, leap through the air, or gracefully fall onto the floor and find my way back up to standing once again. My heart pumped blood throughout my entire body, increasing my heart rate, breathing, and use of energy output. Once the dancing was over, I had to engage my parasympathetic nervous system to give my body time to recover from its exertion. Without this cooling down process, toxins would collect in my muscles, causing pain, stiffness, and rigidity the next day. Part of my post-dancing routine included drinking lots of water, stretching, and slow rhythmical breathing. My muscles would start to relax, lengthen, and rejuvenate from all the exertion.

As you increase your presence and embodiment during your remote therapy sessions, you may experience lingering toxins that need to be released at the end of a session or the end of your day. Finding ways to work with these toxins is essential to remain energetically vital, emotionally stable, and spiritually centered. Even if you have a consistent Warm-up Practice and use somatic tools during your sessions to stay connected with your client, you may still experience a toxic build-up of lingering images, disturbing thoughts, feelings, or uncomfortable body sensations. These toxins can feel like you've been slimed all over your body, causing feelings of disgust, repulsion, and nausea. Or you may discover that you are taking on too much responsibility for your client's wellbeing, where you feel like you're carrying the weight of the world on your shoulders. Any or all of these toxins can leave you feeling tired, worn-out, and cause you to dread showing up for your clients, adding to your sense of remote fatigue. To mitigate remote fatigue, you'll need to create a routine that you practice daily to flush out any toxic build-up. With this routine, you'll learn how to let go of what happened in your sessions, find easier transitions into your personal life, and rejuvenate yourself to sustain your sense of purpose and vitality in the field of psychotherapy.

Routines

To create and maintain a cooling down routine, you will need to schedule time for it. Without putting this practice into your schedule, it's easy to rush onto your next activity without reflecting on what just took place in your remote therapy sessions. Carve out 5 to 15 minutes for yourself after you've finished all your notetaking so that you can flush the toxins and recenter your energy before transitioning on with your day. Without time to consciously check in and become aware of your bodymind, it may be more challenging to reengage with your family, remaining present, aware, and awake to what's happening in your personal life. Your cooling down routines need to be simple, effective, and something that soothes your nervous system. Giving yourself the gift of time to reflect, release stuck energy, and reset your nervous system will go a long way in preventing remote fatigue.

The following practices—Holding, Calming, Releasing, Cleansing, and Soothing—are suggestions for releasing any toxins that may have built up during your remote therapy sessions. Allow yourself to adapt any of these ideas in whatever way helps you feel at ease, relaxed, and rejuvenated to continue with your day. You may find that one of these practices is all you need or that you want a combination of practices to help you balance your bodymind. There is no right or wrong; just keep checking in with yourself for what feels nourishing and supportive to your nervous system. If you're struggling with cooling down and flushing toxins at the end of the day, it's advisable to take this information into your consultation, supervision, or therapy to be explored and worked on later.

Holding

As you sit quietly after your sessions, reflecting on what occurred, notice if any disturbing images, thoughts, feelings, body sensations, or memories are lingering. Once you've named these toxins, use your Holding practice to help you create distance from this disturbing material. You'll then imagine putting these toxins into your Holding space by setting an intention to come back to this disturbing material at a later date when you can give it your full attention. If you are struggling with this cooling down practice of Holding, see if you need any support to help facilitate this process. You might imagine allies helping you put the toxins away and being in charge of them until you're ready to work on them. Once you feel the disturbance gone, bring your focus back to your bodymind and see if you can take a deep breath, feeling your feet firmly rooted on the floor. An excellent way to end this practice is to see if you can think of something positive about yourself while taking a couple of deep breaths. Repeat this positive statement; breathing it into your body from head to toe before transitioning to your next activity, allowing yourself to feel more refreshed and connected. As you practice Holding, be kind to yourself; a therapist's job can be challenging, dysregulating, and activating in your nervous system. You are human, with human feelings, so be aware of your own vulnerabilities and be kind to yourself.

....

PRACTICE: HOLDING

Take a moment to finish all your clients' notes for the day and sit quietly in your chair. You can do this practice with your eyes open with a soft gaze or closed. Scan your bodymind to see if you have any lingering images, thoughts, feelings, body sensations, or memories that are distressing or uncomfortable. Once you sense these toxins, imagine sending any of them into your Holding space where they will remain until you can review them at a later date. Make sure to give the toxins a boundary, letting them know when you will come back and review this material more thoroughly. Once you feel complete, bring your focus back to your bodymind and see if you can take a deep breath, feel your connection to the floor, and sense if your energy is refreshed and rejuvenated. Now see if there is a positive statement about yourself that makes you feel strong, competent, and capable when you hear it. Repeat this phrase to yourself a couple of times, making sure you connect to the felt sense in your body. Throughout this process, be kind to yourself, remember you are human, you experience human feelings, and the work you do as a therapist matters in the world. In ending this practice, take your time to slowly look around the room, reorienting to the present moment, preparing yourself to move on with your day.

....

Calming

Calming is another cooling down practice that can help soothe your nervous system at the end of a day in remote therapy sessions. In this practice, you'll want to make sure you've put away all your work-related items before proceeding. Sit quietly and take a couple of breaths to center and focus your bodymind. Imagine a place, real or imaginary, where you feel calm, relaxed, and at ease in your body. Once you can visualize this place, tune in to all the sensory information, such as what you see, hear, smell, taste, and touch as well as colors and temperature, helping you connect to the felt sense in your body. If anything negative arises, use your Holding practice to contain the distress and return to your sense of calm. This practice aims to soothe your nervous system so that you no longer hold any tension in your body from the day.

....

PRACTICE: CALMING

Begin by sitting comfortably in your chair with your feet on the ground. You can do this practice with your eyes open, using a soft gaze, looking at one of your pictures that centers you, or you can hold an object that helps you feel more grounded. Take a moment to imagine a real or imaginary place where you feel calm, relaxed, and at ease. Scan the picture in your mind's eye and notice what you're seeing. Are there any colors, objects, or other beings that are comforting to you? Do you hear any sounds, words, or melodies that warm your heart? Do you smell anything that brings you joy? Do you taste anything that calms and soothes you? What's the temperature in this place? Take a moment and notice what happens in your body. Bring your focus to your breathing, and with every exhale, see if you can let go of a bit of tension in your body, releasing it into the earth. Allow your body to sink more into the chair with every exhale you take. Give yourself time to enjoy the ease this special place brings to you at this moment. Once you feel complete, bring your awareness back to the room and gently look around, feeling present, aware, and awake, ready for your next activity.

....

Releasing

In this cooling down practice, you'll scan your body for any residual toxic sensations after your remote therapy sessions. Notice if your body feels tight, rigid, or in pain from sitting for so many hours while doing remote therapy sessions. You may also become aware of some somatic resonance that's still lingering. Invite your intuition to guide you on releasing these toxins by tuning into your body and seeing how it wants to move. Your movement may be sharp, direct, and staccato or gliding in a soft, gentle way. There is no right or wrong. Simply let your body articulate whatever it needs at that moment. Through this movement, you can begin to release the toxic sensations and let them sequence through your body until you feel satisfied. Feel free to stand, move through space, or lie on the floor for support. If you feel vulnerable in any area of your body, you can bring your hands to that area to hold, caress, or massage until you feel supported. You can also add sound to your movement by humming, singing, or playing music to find some release. When you feel complete, you will know because you can breathe easily, feel solid in your body, and are ready to move on with your day. This practice will refresh you so that you have sustainable energy for the rest of your day, preventing remote fatigue in the long run. Feel free to change any language that doesn't feel good to you. This is your practice, so make it work for you.

....

PRACTICE: RELEASING

Sit quietly in your chair after you have finished your work for the day. You can do this practice with your eyes open with a soft gaze or closed. See if you can slow down your breathing as you connect your feet on the ground. Take a moment to reflect on your clients that you worked with today and see how you feel about each session. As you think about each client, tune into your body, and see if you feel any toxic body sensations that were not there during your Warm-up Practice. Has your body become tight, sore, headachy from sitting in front of a computer all day? Are you feeling any specific sensations that are uncomfortable as you think about any of your clients? Take note of whatever is causing you pain, discomfort, or uncomfortable body sensations—now begin to listen to your intuition and how your body may want to move right now. As you move with these sensations, pay attention to how the movement feels in your body and release any stuck energy. Don't try to figure out how to move; see what your body wants you to do and follow your impulses. There is no right or wrong with this; just keep moving until you feel a sense of release and ease in your body.

Remember, you can stand and switch your weight from one foot to the other, or maybe your arms want to reach, stretch or push, or perhaps you just want to shake your whole body like a wet dog trying to dry himself. Notice if you feel vulnerable and allow your hands to help support you with these sensations. You may want to hold, gently caress, or massage the area until the area can take in the support and find release. See if you want to use sound to help move these toxins by singing, humming, or dancing to some music. Keep exploring whatever your body is asking of you until you feel satisfied, calm, and peaceful. Bring your focus back into the room and reorient to the present moment.

....

Clearing

Another beneficial practice for cooling down after a long day of remote therapy sessions is imagining a color which can magically clear away any residual toxins from their bodies. To start this practice, you'll imagine a vibrant healing color that streams through the top of your head all the way down your body, streaming into the earth. Give yourself time to slowly let the color stream through one body part at a time so you can melt away anything uncomfortable, painful, or anything making you feel ill as you work with this color. Remember that anything negative you want to let go of can transform in your mind's eye by seeing the energy change and become healing. In ending, make sure you feel present, grounded, and ready to transition by finding an intention of how you would like to move through the rest of your day. This practice is an adaptation from Francine Schapiro's "Light Stream" exercise (2018).

. . . .

PRACTICE: CLEARING

Find a comfortable position in your chair. Take a moment to feel your feet on the ground and take a deep breath. You can do this with your eyes open with a soft gaze or have them closed. Imagine a healing color for today that feels soothing to you when you think about it. This color represents energy, and this energy is from the Universe. The more energy you use, the more abundant it is. Imagine this healing color coming in through the top of your head, slowly bathing your brain, eyes, jaws, and entire face clearing away any residual toxins remaining from your day.

Now, allow the color to move down your neck, across your shoulders, into your arms, cleansing and clearing any stuck energy that may be causing you any pain or discomfort. Allow this healing energy to stream out through your fingertips like beams of light shining all around you. Next, take your time letting this color move down your back and spine as if it were a waterfall. Let this healing color melt away any tension in your back and let it flow down into your pelvic bowl. Now bring the color to the front of your body, filling your heart, lungs, stomach, and all your organs until your entire torso is full of this beautiful healing color.

When you are ready, bring your focus to your hips and let the color pour down through your legs, lower legs, into your feet. Imagine opening up the bottom of your feet to let the color stream down through the floor, through the building, into the earth. Give this energy over to the earth to transform it to become fertilizer for the trees, plants, and flowers.

Take a moment and let this color stream through your entire body, clearing away any of the somatic residues that you want to let go of in this moment. Keep sending the toxins down into the earth to be transformed into helping rejuvenate the earth. Once you feel complete, scan your entire body from head to toe and see if anything had changed from when you started this practice. Notice if you feel lighter, at ease, and ready to move on with your day. Slowly bring your focus back to the room and feel your feet firmly planted on the ground. Take a moment and set an intention of how you would like to transition to your next activity. You may want to flow, glide, or find ease as you continue with your day. There is no right or wrong with this practice, only what feels nourishing to your bodymind.

....

Resting

The last two practices for your cooling down involve taking care of your sensitive eyes, which may have strained by looking at a computer screen all day. Remember, ignoring your eyes can lead to more severe problems down the road, so giving them the rest they need is essential in preventing remote fatigue. The first practice, Yielding, is an adaptation from Marc Grossman, "Palming" in his *Magic Eye* book (2004). In this practice, you can start by sitting or lying down, whichever is more convenient and feels better for your body. Begin by rubbing your hands together to create some heat. Then gently place your hands over your eyes, letting the warmth from your hands soak in, bathing and soothing your tired eyes. As you feel this warmth, allow your eyes to yield into their eye sockets, taking away any effort in the muscles. As you continue to feel the warmth and yield, add some slow, rhythmical deep inhales and exhales to release any tension. Give yourself 5 to 10 minutes to let this yielding action take place so that you feel a sense of ease come over your eyes and body.

When you have more time, this second practice, Soothing, can give your eyes even more support to provide them with rest. Start by making a compress and soak it in chamomile or eyebright tea, which can be warm or cold depending on what feels best for your eyes. Lay down and let the compress rest across your eyes to soothe them. Make sure you're comfortable throughout this process. Feel the weight of the compress helping your eyes yield, rest, and relax, releasing any strain they may be feeling. As you feel this yield, take a moment and let your whole body give into this process while taking deep, calm, and relaxing breaths to support your nervous system. To finish, bring your focus back to your entire body and reorient it to the present moment. Give yourself 10 to 15 minutes for this part of the practice.

....

PRACTICE: YIELDING

Take a moment to put all your work away and feel your body in your chair or lay down if that's more comfortable. Rub your hands together until you feel heat building up between them. Now, gently place your hands over your eyes like a hot compress that bathes and soothes your eyes in comfort. Allow the warmth to soak into your eyes, letting your eyes yield into their sockets, releasing any strain or effort. Imagine your eyes are resting on soft clouds that support your eyes to rest, yield, and give into letting go. See if you can slow your breathing down, allowing any tension to melt away. As you continue to feel the warmth and yield, add some slow, rhythmical deep inhales and exhales to release any tension. If this feels good, you can repeat this process as many times as you like until you're ready to move on with your day. Take a moment and thank your eyes for all the hard work they have done for the day, letting them know it's okay to continue to relax.

PRACTICE: SOOTHING

Take a moment and lay down on your bed. Get comfortable by placing a compress over your eyes and bringing your awareness to your breathing, observing your inhale and exhale. As you deepen your breath, allow your body to yield into your bed, feeling the support beneath you. As you let this tension release, allow any negative thoughts, feelings, or other body sensations to melt away. You're allowing any residual toxins to release out of your body.

Now, bring your awareness to your eyes and allow them to sink back into your eye sockets as if there were clouds behind them, gently supporting them. Take a moment and thank your eyes for all the work they did today and tell them to stop working, to just relax. See if you can give into this process, feeling the weight of the compress and allowing it to help you deepen into this moment. Let your breathing support you, letting go and finding rest in your bodymind.

After you feel complete with this exploration, bring your focus back to your whole body and take a deep cleansing breath. Stay as long as you like taking in this calm. When you are ready, gently roll onto your side and give yourself time to slowly come into sitting, reorienting yourself back into the present moment.

WRAPPING UP

As you embrace remote therapy and discover that these sessions can be just as powerful as in-person therapy, finding daily practices to sustain your bodymind are essential. Taking time to acknowledge there are stressors inherent in remote therapy will help you become aware of the need for daily practices that can rejuvenate, support, and help you enjoy seeing your clients. Find ways to schedule your sessions so you have time to incorporate a thorough warm-up before getting into the flow with your clients. Recognizing that even the most skilled therapists have to find ways to take care of themselves is essential to preventing remote fatigue. Practicing daily will help support your nervous system, build your capacity to tolerate more sensation when you sit, and work with your clients' traumas. As you develop this capacity, it will help you handle adversity, to be in the flow with clients and find your balance with less effort. As you support your nervous system, finding ways to Breathe, Ground, and, when necessary, Hold, can keep you connected to your own felt sense experience, which allows you to be more available to sense your client somatically. Watching when you may be overextending, giving too much, and taking on your client's responsibility will wear you out quickly without recognizing what's happening. When you are in the sessions' flow, you'll feel the dance be creative, intuitive, and satisfying throughout the day.

And last, taking time for a proper cooling down routine will be essential to let go of any residue from the powerful energetic exchange that occurs during remote therapy. By warming up your bodymind, staying in the flow of being present, and ending by releasing anything that doesn't serve you, you'll remain vibrant, alive, and vital in the field of remote therapy. Remote therapy can impact you in powerful ways, and if you don't take care of yourself through daily practices, you may end up feeling remote fatigue, compassion fatigue, and even burn-out. If you are struggling with this material, bring this information into consultation, supervision, or your own therapy to get more support.

SAFETY

··········

The more prepared the therapist is for remote therapy, the more the client will be prepared for remote therapy.

··········

VALUE

One of the most significant challenges therapists faced during the pandemic was learning how to talk about remote therapy's value with their clients since they too struggled to see its value. Remember, most clients barely know what in-person therapy looks like, let alone what remote sessions entail. Think about all movies and television shows you've seen where actors depict therapists. It's hard to find a realistic portrayal of what goes on in therapy because you'll see these fictional therapists breaking all kinds of professional codes of ethics. The therapists cross boundaries by having a sexual relationship with their clients or acting stupid, incompetent, or revealing confidential information. Along with the depicted therapists causing harm to their clients, you have characters struggling with the idea of going to therapy because only "crazy" people would do that. Therapy has gotten such a bad rap for so long; no wonder people are afraid of therapists and the therapeutic process.

With the pandemic impacting people on such a pervasive level, the ongoing stigma around therapy has made it difficult for some people to reach out and get the help they need. Now that the world is experiencing a mental health crisis and therapy is needed now more than ever, we're seeing more positive articles and reports about therapy. As suffering continues, remote therapy has been a blessing by providing connection, support, and safety in a time of crisis. You likely know this firsthand.

As you switched your clients from in-person to remote therapy sessions, many of your clients' fears soared. They desperately needed reassurance that remote therapy was safe, effective, and worth their time. If *you* had any reservations about remote therapy being of lesser value, it might have influenced your clients in terms of how safe they felt about changing their sessions from in-person to remote. Your struggles with your own fears and feeling like an imposter while trying to convince your clients that remote therapy is safe may have unconsciously told your clients you didn't believe your own words—"trust me, this is effective"—

while your nonverbal communications said something different. What your posture, gestures, and tone of voice may have told your clients is, "I'm not sure this is going to be effective, and I'm afraid I'm going to hurt you." Typically, your clients will trust your nonverbal communications more than your words, and, in this case, may have led your clients to express some resistance to the process. Clients found excuses to discontinue therapy, leaving therapists feeling confused and frustrated. Many therapists, maybe including you, blamed remote therapy as the problem instead of looking deeper at how your own fears may have directly influenced your clients.

For clients to find safety in remote therapy, you must discover if you have any fears or reservations that may unconsciously influence how willing your clients are in engaging in the work. You have to become aware of your fears around technology, hurting your clients, or losing connection to your competent therapist self because you feel like an imposter. Along with these fears, you need to believe in and see the benefits that offering remote therapy provides to your clients. By building safety into this work that feels so scary, you'll build the confidence to help your clients trust an unfamiliar process. When *you* value remote therapy, you're communicating to your clients, "This is worth your time, money, and effort to continue to get the help you need." I've seen this with therapists repeatedly: when they truly believe remote therapy has inherent value, their clients are more open to making the switch with them.

During the pandemic, many clients experienced extreme trauma just in dealing with the enormity of what was happening globally. Clients struggled mentally, emotionally, physically, and spiritually, needing support but afraid it wasn't possible because of quarantines. One of the most significant benefits of remote therapy is that clients could either continue getting the support they needed or could reach out and get help for the first time. They were able to find validation in what they were grappling with, feel a connection with another human being, and find reassurance they were not alone in what they were experiencing.

Clients who grew up in communities where they felt safe, secure, and had no worries about the world's dangers before the pandemic, found they were feeling overwhelmed, fearful, and unable to cope. For the first time in their lives, they were having to wear masks, keep six feet distance from others, wash their hands more frequently, and work from home. All while trying to keep their families safe. The strain on their nervous systems left many feeling helpless, unable to cope, and fearful of the unknown. If these clients had unresolved childhood traumas too, many experienced those traumas activated as well, making it challenging to decipher and cope with what they were feeling. Some of their usual coping skills were ineffective, leaving them lost, afraid, and in need of extra support to handle these new difficulties thrust upon them.

For those clients who grew up in communities where they *never* felt safe, accepted, or valued, the pandemic caused even more distress for their nervous systems. Their fear levels were out of the window of tolerance. Some were constantly on high alert, never finding any rest in their boydminds, while others shut down completely, unable to sense or feel anything. It was as if the pandemic became an accelerant, rendering handling even day-to-day stressors impossible. Many of these clients felt confused by what they were experiencing because their unresolved traumas were mixing with their current traumas, making it hard to know what they were sensing and feeling. The isolation became unbearable due to being quarantined, isolated with excruciating pain and a sense of hopelessness, and, in some cases, suicidal ideation.

Another struggle many of these clients experienced was finding a culturally competent therapist who could understand, connect, and make them feel safe in a world in complete chaos. This was especially difficult if they didn't already have a therapist. My husband is a perfect example of a person who felt severely impacted by the pandemic without a safety net to help him navigate what he was experiencing. Over the past 10 years, he had tried unsuccessfully to find a therapist who could understand his lived experience as an Asian in America. He had several therapists wound him more deeply from their very first encounters, making it impossible for him to trust the therapist or the therapy process. As he took the risk to introduce himself with his name Young, these therapists would get uncomfortable and not know how to respond. Some would make a joke out of his name— "Guess you will never have to grow old!"—or try to pronounce his name in a way they thought sounded more Asian-*ish*, like "Jung," or putting his last name, Kim, first. Whenever this happened, he felt alone, different, and hopeless that *anyone* could understand his reality and his experiences. An energetic forcefield would encase him, shutting down all conversations, sharing, and openness. Once this shutdown happened with these therapists, he would never return to them because there was no safety for him to connect with them. His fears and wounds compounded from the lack of the therapist treating him with respect.

Even in our business interactions with therapists, Young has felt misunderstood, belittled, and devalued. When he worked as the customer support person for our business, therapists struggled with his name in emails or phone calls. They addressed him as Ms. Kim Young; they talked slower, assuming he wasn't fluent in English; or they accused him of undermining them when he enforced a policy, and, thus, demanded to speak to someone "higher up."

We tried to convince ourselves for years that biases and racism weren't a part of these interactions because therapists are highly educated professionals. When Young moved onto higher responsibilities, we hired someone to take over customer support, who happened to have a name of European origin. We noticed right away how differently therapists interacted with this new person compared to how they interacted with Young, even though the quality of service was identical, realizing that our worst fears were true.

As Young suffered such excruciating racism during the pandemic, these past experiences made it challenging to reach out for the help he desperately needed. The pandemic was so overwhelming that he shut down emotionally, spending hours in bed, feeling incapable of interacting, let alone having the energy to search for a therapist. I watched him become a shell of the man I knew; I worried for the safety of his well-being. His past traumas around the interactions with therapists made it difficult for him to reach out because he was certain that they would misunderstand him again.

My only hope was my belief that somewhere on this planet there existed a therapist who not only understood him but would show honor and respect, and work with him so he didn't feel so alone in his excruciating pain. Another major roadblock to Young finding a therapist was that he had to find someone who had no personal or professional relationship with me and since I teach so many therapists in our community, this was not an easy undertaking. Because he felt so immobilized, I searched for qualified therapists outside of our community who I didn't know, hoping I could find a good match for him. As he looked over therapists' profiles, I could see his body tighten, preparing for the worst, meaning there wasn't any therapist he could trust. Through his resistance, he did identify a therapist of Asian descent who stood out to him as someone he thought might be a possibility. He pushed himself to make that difficult phone call, and I will forever be grateful that he took that risk.

To his relief and mine, he found a therapist who has helped him put into perspective that the racism he experienced is real, that his responses were understandable, and that he had learned to distrust his own intuition. He began to see that his instincts were accurate, honest, and informative, all of which he had negated for years. The gift the pandemic has given Young is that he could feasibly search for a therapist outside of our community. Remote therapy made the impossible possible. I'm not sure he would have reached out for help without remote therapy because it provides him the safety of remaining in his home, so he doesn't have to put himself in danger to attend his sessions. He has been able to connect with another human being in an intimate way that has been powerful, insightful, and changed his life forever. His constricted world has gotten a little bit bigger through remote therapy and it has helped him come alive once again.

My hope in sharing Young's story is that others who are experiencing the same thing might be relieved they can also benefit from remote therapy. Many clients like not having to drive to therapy and feeling safe in their homes while still receiving effective therapy. This convenience has helped millions of clients be more consistent with their therapy sessions. By not having to drive or take a bus to make in-person sessions, clients save time in their days. Many clients must arrange a time with work, childcare, transportation, and/or family to receive in-person sessions. For some clients who do not own a car, traveling by bus can add additional stressors to their day. If they miss the bus, they miss their session, rupturing the therapeutic process, and leaving therapists scrambling to help their clients when they don't show up. With remote therapy, the obstacles that can arise from transportation issues disappear, allowing clients to show up more consistently for their treatment, which adds value to their therapy experience.

However, some clients encounter a downside of not having travel time after remote therapy sessions because they don't have a clear transition between therapy and their next activity. Time alone while driving is essential to some people for introspection of what occurred in their therapy session. For others, the time in the car gave them an automatic boundary between therapy and their home life. The danger with remote therapy sessions is that many clients feel pressure to immediately interact with their family as soon as their session ends, leaving no time for their brainbody to integrate what they discussed.

With this in mind, you'll want to set up a plan that creates safety for your clients regarding how much time they need to themselves before interacting with work, family, and/or friends. Clients need time to settle, reflect and transition gently, especially if the material covered in your session was challenging for them. When clients have this safety plan in place, they find they like remote sessions better than remote therapy sessions because it feels more approachable, less scary, and creates a boundary that feels safe and secure.

In one of my consultation groups, a therapist shared that he struggled with a client in his in-person sessions before the pandemic. Every time the client started to talk about his childhood, he would shut down his emotions and quickly move onto another topic. The therapist was frustrated, felt ineffective, and worried that he wasn't the right therapist for this client. Once the pandemic hit, the client was reluctant to switch to remote therapy and was tempted to quit altogether, which, the therapist shared with me, deep down felt like a relief. I encouraged the therapist not to let this be why their sessions would end; instead, I suggested they try a couple of sessions remotely before making that decision.

The therapist reluctantly agreed to give it a try. After a few remote sessions, the client was pleasantly surprised to realize he felt safer, more open, and less threatened in remote therapy. He started naturally sharing stories from his childhood, found it easier to connect to his emotions and body sensations, and wanted to continue doing the work because he'd started feeling the changes he wanted in his life. The therapist was amazed that the remote sessions were less threatening than being in-person, that the client felt safer, more secure, and able to handle intimacy in a way he never felt during in-person sessions. After this experience, the therapist found a new respect for the possibility that healing can occur in separate rooms, as well as being intimate, profound, and providing long-lasting benefits.

FUNDAMENTALS

Once you embrace the value of remote therapy, you can then begin to focus your energy on the fundamentals of putting safety into your remote therapy practice. As your clients express apprehension, fears, and worries about trying remote therapy, you'll need to remember that they may feel like they're losing the safety of being with you in your office. Clients may feel insecure and inadequate to handle remote therapy as a viable practice because it's new and changes the security they once knew in your therapy office. Just as you prepare your bodymind for remote sessions, you also need to have some fundamental practices in place to help both you and your clients feel more secure when engaging in remote therapy sessions.

These fundamentals include putting things in place that create a solid foundation of support for both you and your client. This involves knowing what your license, insurance panels, and malpractice insurance covers as well as becoming familiar with your technology.

Before offering remote therapy sessions, make sure you check with your state licensure board to determine if you're allowed to offer this kind of work. Since the pandemic and the lack of safety in providing in-person sessions, state licensure boards have opened up restrictions so that therapists can practice remotely. Some therapists have questioned whether they can work with clients who live in different states. Check with your state licensure board and the state in which your clients live to see if your license has reciprocity. You may have to become licensed in the state your client lives in to be able to work with them remotely. Once the pandemic is over, be sure to check what regulations will be in place as they may change.

Next, check with any insurance panels you're on to make sure they will reimburse for remote therapy sessions. Insurance companies have been covering remote therapy during the pandemic but may change those practices later on, so make sure you're informed. Insurance companies are coming up with new policies and it is your responsibility to know how plans change or are updated. Clients have the right to know if they are responsible for out-of-pocket expenses when working with you. Also, contact your malpractice insurance to see if remote therapy sessions are in your policy should a client grieve you. It's especially important to verify you are covered if you're working with a client in a different state. You don't want any surprises down the road.

After you have put these fundamentals in place, your next step involves taking time to become familiar with your technology. Your sessions will go smoother with less fear, anxiety, and trepidation about being in separate rooms if you understand your technology more fully. Since technology changes at the speed of light—and what I share now may be out of date even by the time this book is in print—I want to focus on simple ideas that can provide safety and security in your remote therapy practice.

The first and most important thing is to use is a HIPAA compliant platform that can provide a solid foundation of privacy and security for your remote sessions. Take time to familiarize yourself with this platform so you know what it has to offer, how to use it efficiently, and what to do if something goes wrong. The more comfortable you are with your technology, the more you'll be at ease, competent, and secure during your sessions.

Getting to know your technology includes making sure you and your client have high-speed internet. The slower your internet connections, the more problems will occur, such as images being blurry, videos freezing, and, worst of all, the internet shutting down entirely, causing you to lose connection altogether. To help mitigate these issues, you and your client should make sure you each have *direct* access to your internet by plugging your computers directly into secure routers/modems rather than relying on your

WiFi connections, which can be shaky and unreliable. Take time to close any applications you're not currently using, which will also help strengthen your internet connection, ultimately leading to fewer disruptions in the course of your sessions.

During remote sessions, if disruptions do occur, make sure you have a solid, reliable backup plan for the specific steps to reconnect in your session. Part of your backup plan may be shutting down the platform, rebooting your computer(s), texting each other, or calling to reconnect as quickly as possible.

Make sure you have given your client detailed directions for this backup plan in your consent form, along with what they can expect if ruptures do occur. Let clients know that pictures can freeze, become blurry, and/or voices can get out of sync with the picture. In these cases, nonverbal somatic cues can be lost or misunderstood, disrupting your ability to attune to them. Explain to your clients that you may have to ask more questions to clarify what just occurred, what you were perceiving, sensing, and what you might have missed due to interruptions. Be aware that some of your clients may get triggered with abandonment issues when ruptures occur, causing them to feel that you don't care about them. Discuss with them that when ruptures in technology do occur, you will do your best to reconnect with them as quickly as possible because you care about their treatment. Having an honest conversation about the limitations in remote therapy can help build safety and rapport with your client. Both of you can relax when you have a plan you can trust to keep your connection even when technology fails.

To develop a solid backup plan, you'll need to practice what to do when things go wrong. Take time to develop a sequence of steps to handle issues when things go wrong, so you don't go into a freeze response; rather, you're adaptive in the situation to resolve the problem as quickly as possible. Your knowledge and confidence will help your clients be less reactive when things don't go smoothly, which will help build trust and rapport in your therapeutic relationship. When I switched my training sessions to remote during the pandemic, I had to get a new sequence into my body to handle working with a large group in a new way. I was already working with a HIPAA compliant platform with remote consultations, so I was familiar with the glitches that can happen and how to handle them. Unfortunately, the platform I was using for the consultations was incapable of handling the number of people I would be working with and allowing to practice skills during live remote trainings. I had to research and find a new platform with all the features necessary to teach in a meaningful, reliable, and secure way.

As I researched and found a viable platform option, I still struggled to imagine a live remote training that was as effective and meaningful as in-person training. My fears and insecurities were out of control, and all I wanted to do was hide in my little safe cave and avoid facing the music that I was going to have to learn a new way of teaching. My learning curve was overwhelming, and I felt incapable, insecure, and resistant to change. I knew deep down inside myself that if I didn't face my fears, I would have to shut down our business and call it quits until the pandemic was over. I just couldn't let this happen! I needed to find a way to resource myself so that I felt strong and capable enough to overcome this new challenge, which felt so debilitating.

As I sat with this uncomfortable feeling, a memory came to my mind that I hadn't thought of in years. When I was in a dance company in New York City rehearsing for 6 months to prepare for our annual performance, five male dancers and I were practicing a demanding move that involved a lot of coordination between us. Four of the male dancers stood side-by-side, precariously holding the fifth male dancer horizontally with their outstretched arms. The men needed tremendous strength and concentration to create the illusion that the horizontal dancer was floating in the air. As they precariously balanced this dancer, the four men would slowly start to sit back in unison, trying to reach the floor. The dancer they held looked as though he was gliding through the air like a leaf falling from a tree until it gently landed on the ground. As the men began to sit down, I swiftly moved behind them, lying down on the floor so that my body would cushion their descent. As I started to find my way to the floor, one of the men lost control of his body, creating chaos for the other dancers. They began to tumble like dominoes, colliding with each other and falling on top of me. My right ankle rolled over and made a loud "CRACK," sound that seemed like it could be heard from miles away. The five men collapsed on top of me, creating a pile of torsos, legs, and arms. Laughter roared on top of me as I laid underneath them, crying, injured, and frozen in pain. I was sure my ankle had broken into a million pieces and my dance career was over. As the pile of men dissipated and they realized what had happened, they quickly helped get me get to the hospital. Luckily, I learned I had only sprained my ankle, which was a huge relief, and my dance career was not over after all. Then the harsh reality set in that I may not perform as planned, which sent me spiraling into despair.

That night I felt sorry for myself; I was angry, sad, and hopeless that all my hard work had just gone down the drain. I felt shame that I had somehow ruined our upcoming performance and that all the other dancers would be mad at me because they now had to adapt and replace me in every dance. After crying myself to sleep, I woke up the next day determined that I would not let this setback ruin the performance. I would do whatever the doctors told me to do so I could get back on that stage and not let my fellow dancers down.

The doctors said I could perform by the end of the week, with the caveat of practicing strict protocols before, during, and after my performances to prevent further injuries. I followed this plan in detail and was allowed to perform after all. Many told me that my performance was more heartfelt, expressive, and driven than they had ever seen me dance before. My perseverance, commitment, and absolute faith that everything would be okay helped me overcome this giant obstacle that almost derailed me.

If I could overcome a sprained ankle and find a way to perform, I knew that I could learn how to offer remote EMDR trainings. I just had to approach my fears with the fortitude and knowledge that it would take preparation, rehearsals, and believing in myself as well as believing remote teaching was possible and that I could excel in it too. By tapping into my strengths, I could approach this problem as a piece of choreography that needed to be created from the bottom up. I created the dance by making a list of everything required before the live training. I designed each moment, paying careful attention to transitions so that the dance had a beginning, middle, and end. Each moment had to have a purpose, meaning, and coordination to embody the training's essence as if it were happening in person. I wanted each participant to have time to question, express, and explore what they were learning without sacrificing any content. Every day, I practiced as though I was now the artistic director, lighting designer, stage manager, and performer of every training. I knew these rehearsals were necessary because I wanted the training to feel seamlessly smooth for the participants.

This practice was essential before showing up and doing the actual performance of teaching EMDR therapy. The rehearsals built up my confidence so that when things happened in the middle of training that I hadn't practiced, I could adjust and adapt the best I could. Patience, perseverance, and believing in myself came into play during these more vulnerable moments when something didn't go as planned. Trusting that the dance's foundation was solid, I could hold onto the hope these blips would not ruin an entire training. Now, after months of teaching these 3-day remote extravaganzas, I know the sequence in my body, which enables me to be relaxed, have fun, and feel present and alive with the participants. To go from being utterly debilitated at the thought of remote teaching to being excited, thriving, and enjoying every step has been a blessing beyond my wildest dreams.

Just as I had to practice with my technology, learning the sequence to make things appear seamless in my trainings, so must you with your remote therapy sessions. Taking time to get to know your technology will lessen your anxiety, increase your confidence, and help support you during your sessions even if something goes awry. Tap into your wisdom from past experiences that help you feel strong, confident, and capable of handling whatever comes your way. Connecting to your strengths will help you remain present and dance with your clients more fully during sessions, no matter what obstacles come your way.

STAGING

After becoming familiar with your technology, focus your attention on establishing safety by taking the time to "stage" your remote therapy office. Many behind-the-scenes practices make or break the audience's experience in every dance performance. Each dance must be "staged" to fit a particular space, making the sightlines work for everyone. Props need to be placed accurately on stage so that dancers can access them at the right moment. Lighting needs to be precise to create the ambiance for the dance. Costumes need to be easy to move in while also conveying the essence of the dance. All these pieces must seamlessly come together to enhance the choreography and make the dance come alive. Let's look at how the staging for remote therapy needs to evolve so that the client's experience of safety feels seamless.

Reliability

As you stage your remote office, take time to find a designated place that is consistent, reliable, and workable for your sessions. You spent time arranging and placing whatever you felt would create a safe environment for your clients to do therapy in your in-person office. Now you need to put that same intention into your remote therapy office. Many of you who have children may have struggled to find a consistent space to offer remote therapy sessions because your children are the priority. During quarantine, their educational needs came first, putting you last on the list of an area to do your work. You may have found yourself scrambling trying to find a space to set up your office. Some of you are trying to do sessions in your bedrooms, kitchens, or living rooms without considering rearranging the space to accommodate your work needs. As you prioritize others in your household, you may find that you're rushing into your sessions, quickly turning on your computer, struggling with poor lighting and uncontrollable noises, and without adequate support for your laptop or your body. Consequently, you may be trying to position the camera to hide intimate objects, contorting your body on uncomfortable furniture, and giving up trying to fix your lighting situation.

At the end of the day, your body hurts from poor posture, you're frustrated, and then dread facing another day doing remote therapy because it doesn't feel good to your bodymind. By getting in touch with the impact of *not* having a designated space that's reliable and consistent, you can begin to see the toll it's taking on you physically, mentally, and emotionally. Checking in with yourself and finding out what your needs are is just as important as making sure your children have the support they need for remote learning. Without the proper staging of a private, quiet, and uninterrupted space, you'll end up fatigued by the end of the day and dreading remote therapy sessions.

Sight Lines

Once you have decided on a dedicated, private, and quiet space, take time to check the sightlines of what your client sees and experiences in your remote therapy sessions. Dancers must be aware of where they're positioned on the stage so that the audience experiences the dance the way the choreographer had envisioned. Special attention goes into entrances, exits, and sightlines to ensure that every audience member can get the best view of the dance possible. If a dancer misses any cues, you'll be left wondering what happened and not get the full effect of what was supposed to happen.

You also need to pay special attention to your sightlines and what your client experiences while doing remote therapy sessions. Part of the staging is making sure your sightlines are creating an intimate experience for your clients. Make sure your camera is at eye level, helping the client feel as if you are looking at and connecting with them. If you sit too close to the computer screen out of fear that you will miss the client's nonverbal somatic cues, the top of your head will be missing from the client's sightline. You'll look constricted, cramped, and restricted, as if there isn't enough space for you to move, breathe, and be comfortable. Many clients will feel uneasy but won't know why they feel this way.

If you position the camera on your computer lower than eye level, you will look like you are "looking down" on the client, creating an unconscious nonverbal power dynamic that can rupture the therapeutic relationship. Clients may end up feeling judged, criticized, and "less than" without you even knowing why. In some cases, if you position the camera up on a wall, you'll appear as if you are searching and longing for connection, making it disorienting to the client.

Any of these positions can leave clients feeling disconnected from you along with an unconscious sense of distrusting you. They could also not feel safe. Finding ways to position your computer so that the camera is at your eye level is imperative for your client to feel connected to you. If you're using a laptop, purchase a computer stand that positions the camera at your eye level. Taking time to set up your computer with correct sightlines will help foster your therapeutic relationship to feel safe, connected, and dynamic.

Once you have your computer set in position, take a moment, and reflect on what your client sees in the background of your remote therapy office. See if you feel professional, comfortable, and relaxed with whatever the client sees. Make sure to create enough space behind you that creates a sense of depth and that it allows for freedom of movement. If you don't have enough space behind you, clients may experience you as being trapped, frozen, and uncomfortable, which will make them feel tense, fearful, and worried about you. Bring in natural elements like plants or flowers and objects like crystals, books, and your favorite artwork as props to add dimension, color, and texture to your space. Be careful not to have too many things in the background as this can overwhelm the client and make it hard to connect with you. Watch out for too many colorful patterns, paintings hanging too high or too low that throw off the balance of the space, or crowded bookshelves full of too many objects that can overpower your presence.

You'll also want to be careful of being in a room with nothing on the walls. An empty space with nothing grounding you may wash you out from the starkness. Clients may experience you as cold, distant, and not easy to connect with because there's nothing to help soften this background's harshness. I have seen some therapists use their virtual background feature to counterbalance this starkness, choosing images of outer space, the beach, or scenes from television shows. While this remote feature is novel and fun for laughs, it does not make clients feel safe. The brain feels a cognitive dissonance and doesn't know what to focus on: you or the virtual background. The brain is unconsciously trying to orient in the present moment, thus straining the brainbody as it attempts to make sense of this cognizant dissonance. Just like Mister Rogers anchored his set in reality for children by having familiar objects that were easily identifiable, you want objects that clients can easily see and identify to allow the brainbody to relax. You need to be anchored in reality so the client can orient to you in the present moment.

Recently, I was holding a consultation group, and one of the therapists had a virtual reality background on to hide whatever was in their room. I found myself becoming anxious and uncomfortable, and I struggled to listen to what the therapist was sharing. I had to take a deep breath and ground myself to recognize that this virtual background was ungrounding me. I couldn't feel the therapist anchored in real life, and therefore, my nervous system was struggling to center and orient to them. Once I invited them to turn off that feature, I could reorient to them spatially, mentally, and emotionally. My body began to relax; I could listen to what they were presenting and could feel our somatic connection through the computer screen.

As you experiment with your sightlines, try to find props that present you in the best light. Set up a time with a trusted friend for a remote session of experimenting with your sightlines. Have your friend look around your space and see what they notice. Do they feel calm, relaxed, and able to focus on you? Keep moving objects around until you find what feels just right to you and your friend so nothing is distracting, and everything enhances the feeling of you both being grounded, secure, and safe.

Lighting

The next step in staging your remote office is determining what kind of lighting to use so you have a warm glow across your face. Whenever you see a live performance, the lighting enhances it by highlighting movement to create a mood and ambiance. Lighting has the power to make the dancers look like they're floating, create mystery and suspense, or even take your breath away. The lighting is essential in making the choreographer's steps turn into something magical.

You need to apply this same time and care into staging the lighting for your remote therapy office. Position yourself to be in the best lighting possible to foster your connection with your clients so they experience you as warm, open, and connected. If you have shadows or glare across your face, your clients may feel that you are cold, distant, and aloof. When I started offering remote trainings, I had to stage my office and the lighting became a problem that was challenging to solve. I needed help from my husband, who is a photographer and knows how to work with lighting issues. We had to let go of my office's current setup and start from scratch, finding where I would be in the best lighting.

I have large windows in the office, and we both thought positioning my desk closer to the natural light source would create a warm glow over my face. We moved my desk, trying different arrangements only to find a glare across my face, which washed me out. We settled on a place where we were sure the lighting would let me easily see my training materials and I would be well lit in front of my computer. At last, knowing everything was in place, I felt ready to do my first remote training.

We forgot to consider I was getting up two hours earlier than I normally do because of a time zone issue. I arrived at the office the following day only to discover there was no natural light at that time of morning. My heart started racing as I quickly had to come up with a "Plan B." I turned on my overhead fluorescent lights, only to have a harsh glare across my face. My heart sank in the disappointment and harsh reality that this wasn't going to work. I needed another solution immediately. I moved every lamp I owned closer to my desk, hoping to solve the problem. These lamps cast a shadow on one side of my face while the other side was well lit. I was lost, floundering, and by the time the training started, I still didn't have the perfect solution. I just had to make do with poor lighting, hoping the participants would have compassion for me as I tried to solve this issue. As the day progressed, the sun began to shine, reflecting off the cars in the parking lot. I was blinded by the glare, unable to read my training materials or see the participants. By the end of that day, my nervous system was frazzled, my body ached all over, and I had a headache that just wouldn't go away. I felt shame that the lighting made it difficult for me to teach, and I couldn't correct the situation.

Once the training was over, I went back to the drawing board with my husband to develop a viable solution to all the lighting issues I'd discovered while teaching. I had to be able to control the lighting so that I could count on it all day. We spent hours experimenting with where to place my desk, deciding to move it away from the windows into the center of the room. We worked with all the lighting sources available, including hanging two large pieces of white paper on the ceiling behind me to let the light bounce off them to create more glow across my face. Finally, I was able to see my training material and be well lit no matter what time of day I was working.

As you work in your remote therapy office, you'll need to put as much time and effort into the lighting as I did.

Finding the appropriate light source can be challenging but it is absolutely necessary. If you position yourself so that a window is behind you, a glare will come in through the window and blind the client through the computer screen, making them squint, contract, and pull away from connecting with you. On the other hand, if you don't have enough light, you'll be hard to see, and the client will struggle to connect with you. If you have a light source on only one side of the room, only half of your face will be visible, making it seem like you're trying to hide something. Lighting needs to enhance your face, in a way that clients can see your eyes as clearly as possible. If you are wearing blue blocker glasses, make sure there's no glare reflecting in your glasses, creating difficulty for the client to make eye contact with you. A good professional pair of blue blockers can help alleviate the glare, which makes it easier to connect with your client.

In all these cases, you can see attention to lighting is crucial to connect with your clients. Your lighting needs to be reliable, secure, and allow your client to see you clearly, which will help build trust and safety in your work. Staging this lighting source can take a lot of time, effort, and energy. I know this firsthand! And yet, it is worth all that effort because you're setting the stage for your client to see you presenting yourself in the best light possible. As you find the right lighting, your eyes can begin to soften, relax, and be present, bringing more ease into your body so that you can put your energy where it needs to be with your client.

Wardrobe

The last part of staging is to think about what you will wear for your remote therapy sessions. Every dance performance needs costumes, which can make or break the dance. I can remember my favorite dance costume, a unitard dyed in a beautiful green mosaic pattern. The costume designer hand-painted lines on top of the mosaic that enhanced my body, making me feel taller, leaner, and more powerful. Every time I put this costume on, I felt ready and excited to get on stage and perform.

In contrast, I wore another costume that was the most unflattering thing I could ever imagine. It was a nude unitard with a blue belt. I felt short, lumpy, and dumpy in this costume. I dreaded putting it on before each performance and tried to ignore how I felt while I was dancing. I couldn't wait to immediately rip it off my body once the performance was over. Wearing a costume where I felt good about myself—like that beautiful green mosaic pattern unitard—allowed me to be more relaxed in my body, less self-conscious as I performed, and capable of enjoying that I was dancing.

As you work from home in your remote therapy offices, think about what you wear and how professional it makes you feel. Boundaries have become blurred between work and home for many therapists. You may have found you're dressing more casually because you're home. However, wearing clothes that help you feel professional is essential to help you feel you're working and not at home hanging out with your family.

I, too, had to take inventory of how I felt with my wardrobe as I switched from in-person trainings to remote trainings. I used to wear little jackets when I was teaching in-person, which helped me feel professional, confident, and strong. When I switched to remote trainings, I still wore the same little jackets only to find I felt confined, rigid, and less approachable. I had to redesign my professional wardrobe so that I was comfortable sitting in front of a computer all day while still breathing, moving, and feeling relaxed. This switch in wardrobe helped me feel softer, more open, and approachable. Once work was over, I found that I needed to change my clothes to create a boundary that I am no longer working; rather, it's time to relax.

Take time to ask yourself how you feel about what you are wearing to your remote therapy sessions. Do you feel professional, comfortable, and prepared to see clients? Are you putting thought into how you look for your sessions or are you just showing up in your casual clothes because your client can't see your whole body? Are you making enough time to transition after your sessions to help you feel separated from work to home? This simple act of changing clothes can make a huge difference in defining a boundary between work and home life.

When you put all of this together for staging your remote therapy sessions, you'll create more safety in your sessions. Taking time to stage your remote therapy office can make the difference between scrambling by "making do," leading you to feel unprepared or unprofessional, and managing your days with calm and confidence. Remember that a dedicated space is not optional—it is essential and necessary. Take time to ensure your camera is at eye level and that you've staged the sightlines for what your client will see in your background. Figure out the lighting that creates a warmness across your face and dress professionally to define work-life and home life clearly. These steps may sound daunting, but they are worth it. The correct staging will create the ambiance for your therapy sessions, just like your in-person offices. By setting the stage, your clients will automatically connect with you, feel safe, and trust more in the therapeutic process.

CLIENTS' STAGING

After creating safety in your space through staging, now it's time to prepare your clients so they can have the best experience in remote therapy sessions. You need to build safety from the ground up for clients. Part of creating safety is staging *their* space to be private and quiet for their sessions. Remember, clients are used to therapists' offices being a safe haven where they can share intimate details of their lives without interruptions. In remote therapy, you now need to help clients create that same feeling in their own space at home. Many clients struggle with this first foundational piece to feel safe. Some clients don't feel they have enough separation from their families and will try to do therapy from whatever space is available at the moment, including bedrooms, bathrooms, closets, and even in their cars. When clients don't have a dedicated safe space, they will be on guard throughout their sessions. Many clients will be fearful someone might overhear the most vulnerable parts of their lives, or they'll be interrupted abruptly or be distracted by family needs. Without your guidance, clients won't know that they need a reliable, quiet space with no distractions. The following are sample questions you can ask your client to help them figure out what space will support their treatment in the best possible way.

- Do you have a room that feels private and secure where you won't be interrupted? If not, what would help you create such a space?

- If you have (roommates, partners, children), where are they during your sessions so they know not to interrupt you? What kind of boundary do you need to set with them to help facilitate this?

- Where is a good place to set up your computer at eye level? Let's explore different options until the computer feels secure and you feel relaxed in your body.

- Do you have lighting that's comfortable on your eyes and bright enough I can still see you?

- Is there is anything in your space that is distracting for you? If so, how are you going to deal with this distraction?

- Are you positioned to have the best internet reception in this space, so our connection is the strongest that it can be?

- Do you have a charger by your computer or phone if your battery has low power?

- Do you have our emergency plan by you so if we lose connection, you know what to do?

These questions are essential when working with your client to begin setting the stage for their remote therapy sessions. Explain the importance of consistency in their space, how it helps you to connect with them, and that you want to support them to have the best experience possible, knowing ruptures can occur.

As clients grow more comfortable with this process, they can share more intimate pieces of their lives, such as introducing family members, beloved pets, meaningful objects, toys, stuffed animals, or photos. One therapist shared in a consultation group that his client's cat would scamper around the client's room during sessions. In one particular session, the client was processing a very tender piece of trauma from her childhood around being abused by her father. Right in the middle of this work, the cat curled up gently on the client's lap as if creating a shield to protect the client from her emotional pain. The cat was calm, anchoring, and supportive throughout the process. As the client found the resolution to this past trauma, the cat gently disappeared without a fuss, somehow knowing instinctually that the client no longer needed this support. The client's cat was a fantastic grounding tool and support during a difficult moment in therapy, which would have never happened in an in-person therapy session.

Making time to explore with your clients the space they can use for their therapy can help build safety, ground them in their bodies, and create a more supportive environment for your remote therapy sessions. As you're putting attention into your own preparation, think about translating everything you're doing into something practical for your clients to do. This preparation will make a difference in the long run for how your client can deepen their remote therapy experience.

Spacing

Once your client has a safe place to do remote therapy, you and the client need to explore the proxemics between the two of you. How close or far away you and the client sit from your computer screens can influence the bodymind connection between the two of you. Remember, the computer is bringing the two of you together in a magical way, and where you sit will either create connection or defenses. A somatic response will occur as soon as you start your session, so being aware of this phenomenon and working with it consciously will help build safety and rapport with your clients. Taking time to explore how close or far away each of you is to your camera will begin to connect your client and yourself to your bodymind. If you or your client are sitting too close to the camera, the other person may feel invaded, perhaps feeling their body retreat, which can lead to a feeling of disconnection, defensiveness, and even dissociation. If either of you sits too far away from the camera, it can create a sense of coldness, distance, and aloofness for the other person. Remember, 60%–70% of our communication is nonverbal; taking the time to experiment with spacing for both of you is a simple way to build safety. It takes only a minute to make a profound change in your therapeutic relationship.

In addition, take time to set up an experiment of how

close or far away you can sit from the camera with both of you feeling comfortable in your bodies. I often recommend that you and your client pretend to sit in the same room and let the computer screen melt away. Act as if you are in an in-person session to help you remain fluid, dynamic, and available to feel and sense your client fully. You'll know when both of you have found the proper distance when each of you can take a deep breath, relax, and be comfortable with each other.

The following practice, Spacing, is to help clients explore proxemics during remote therapy. This practice may take less than a minute but can significantly impact creating connection, safety, and support for both of you. As you work with this script, pause after every sentence. Give time for each of you to dialogue what each of you is sensing and feeling in your body. Both of you will explore what happens to your breathing, posture, and gestures as you become more embodied through this practice. You'll know this practice is complete when you both feel grounded, supported, and present, ready for your session to begin.

....

PRACTICE: SPACING

I'm wondering if we can take some time to explore where we're both sitting. Would that be okay with you? Let's start by noticing how it feels to sit in our current positions. Bring your awareness inside and see what you are thinking, feeling, and sensing in your body. Take a moment and ask yourself if you're comfortable with where I am seated, or would you like me to sit closer or farther away from the camera. Let's experiment until you feel relaxed in your body, can breathe easily, and are comfortable with where I sit. There is no right or wrong answer to this; just notice what happens in your body and how you feel as we explore this. Now that you have gotten comfortable in your body, I'm wondering if it would be okay if we explore where you are sitting so that I can get grounded in my body too.

Note: Have the client explore different positions until you feel supported in your own body. Your client should be able to take a deep relaxing breath, feel at ease from head to toe, and be ready to proceed with your session.

....

GROUNDING

Now that both you and your clients have spent time preparing to have a safe and secure experience with remote therapy, you can switch your attention to providing clients with grounding practices. These practices will help clients feel centered, more in control of their emotional states, and capable of handling life's stressors. By preparing your client with grounding practices, you can help them regulate their nervous systems more throughout the session, giving you peace of mind your client knows how to handle what they're experiencing. The skills you use for in-person sessions will easily apply to working in remote sessions.

During the pandemic, clients struggled emotionally, coming into remote sessions feeling chaotic, irrational, and disconnected from reality. Old unresolved traumas were resurfacing and making clients feel out of control and incapable of handling what's happening in the here and now. Many clients were dissociating, fueling some therapists' fears that something terrible would happen to clients because they weren't in the same room to control what was transpiring. You must get comfortable with dissociation. Remind yourself that the process is normal and natural during therapy. Clients' nervous systems are ever-changing, and it's your job to help clients regulate and come into their window of tolerance. Helping your clients develop a curiosity about their nervous systems will empower them and help them feel more in control. Educate your clients so they understand dissociation is a protective mechanism which helped them survive pain that was too big to handle at that moment. Teach your clients that part of dissociation helps them disconnect from their thoughts, feelings, and body sensations even if they are safe in the here and now. As clients become familiar with the window of tolerance, they can begin to make sense of why they feel so out of control with their emotions.

By helping clients develop grounding practices, they'll learn to tolerate feelings and body sensations, learn how to be uncomfortable without running away or shutting their experience down. Teaching your clients to slow down and be aware of signals in the body that indicate they are about to dissociate can empower them to learn how to regulate their nervous systems. Getting familiar with dissociative signs can help with this process. Dissociative signs include things such as their hearts racing, feeling overwhelmed, terror, panic, or the opposite, such as feeling numb, disconnected, and unable to feel emotions. Once your client becomes aware of these dissociative cues, they can learn to work with their bodymind to repattern their nervous system and have different responses in the present moment. Each person has unique cues; you and your client need to learn theirs intimately.

Remember, no two clients are the same, so let yourself be in the dance with your clients finding what feels grounding to them. Every client you work with is like being with a new dance partner. When I danced Argentine tango, different partners would ask me to dance with them throughout the night. Everyone knew the foundational steps in tango, and yet, with each partner, I felt like I was in a completely different dance. I had to listen, respond, and adapt to my partner's nonverbal cues. If my mind wandered or I resisted the flow, we would stumble, trip, and get out of sync. Each partner had their flourishes, ways of cueing, and rhythms they wanted to create. Even though I was doing the same steps, the result felt utterly different and unique. I had to step into a new relationship with each partner and stay present, connected, and curious about what this dance would be—and what was about to happen.

The same process happens with your clients. No two clients are the same, respond the same, or have the same experiences. They need you to be present, curious, and open to helping them find what feels right in their bodymind. Work with these practices early on in your remote therapy treatment with a client to provide safety for them when challenging material arises. Your clients will have ways to regulate their nervous system. Use these practices to help your clients get curious about what's happening in their nervous systems, what they are feeling, and to sense what's happening in their bodies. Each practice invites the client to connect to their body, ground in support, and feel more capable of handling distressing emotions and body sensations.

The word "practice" is so that clients will learn these skills in your remote sessions and practice them at home so that they become ingrained as resources they can rely on during challenging times. Just like learning how to ride a bike, the first time you try to balance on those two wheels, you may feel wobbly, unpredictable, and even hopeless that you can learn something new. With practice, the ability to balance on this precarious frame while simultaneously pedaling becomes second nature and you're no longer thinking about it; instead, the body takes over and remembers how to do it. Through repetition of the movement, the body will remember the action, creating muscle memory. This same process occurs when you learn how to brush your teeth or play an instrument or learn in therapy how to regulate your nervous system.

Some of the practices also involve visualization to increase the client's ability to regulate their nervous system. Many clients are concerned that visualization is "make-believe," therefore, it's not actually reality, which causes clients to refuse to believe it will be helpful. When clients struggle to accept visualizing as a valid part of therapy, I often turn to research in sports psychology to support the concept of visualization being so helpful in remote therapy. There are two theories of why visualization works in sports psychology: Symbolic Learning and Psychonueromuscular Learning.

The first theory is Symbolic Learning which hypothesizes that when you see yourself doing an activity, the brain lays down a neural pathway. This pathway contains information on the movement's coordination, such as brushing your teeth, driving a car, or even doing something fancy like a double pirouette in ballet. The more you repeat this movement in your imagination, the more automatic and easier it becomes to perform. This neural pathway begins to support the muscle memory, which is essential for athletes, dancers, musicians, public speakers, teachers, and, yes, clients in therapy regulating their nervous systems.

The second theory, Psychonueromuscular Learning, states that when you visualize an activity, the brain will send signals to the muscles to contract, which fires neurons so that you can complete the action. Essentially, when you visualize the movement of doing a double pirouette, the brain is firing neurons as if you're doing this activity even though you just imagine it. Colorado psychologist R. M. Suinn experimented with a skier visualizing an upcoming ski race. He observed that the racer's leg muscles were contracting, and the neurons were firing precisely at the same time, mimicking the terrain the skier was visualizing through the entire race (Ungerleider, 1996). The brain and body were remembering what it felt like and fired the neurons to perform it as if it was happening.

When I was a professional dancer, we had to learn choreography very quickly. Various choreographers would create dances that we had to learn to perform in a week. Complex combinations of steps would be given to us every day and often changed the next day. At the end of each day, I would be exhausted and felt my body just couldn't do one more thing, so I turned to visualization to help me learn. In my mind's eye, I'd go over the steps we learned that day, repeating them over and over, seeing myself performing the steps the way the choreographer had intended. I would eventually fall asleep completely drained, hoping and praying that I could remember the steps the following day. When I showed up for rehearsal the next day, I was surprised at how much I could remember. My visualization from the previous night had helped me. The repetition of the steps in my mind started laying down the neural pathways, making it possible for me to perform each sequence.

Just like I used this visualization technique to help me learn complex sequences of choreography, you can use this same process to learn how to ground your clients in their bodyminds. Through practice and rehearsal, neural pathways will strengthen and help clients execute the grounding practice faster and easier from muscle memory. Then you can begin to trust that if your client becomes triggered, dissociates, or becomes disconnected during remote sessions, they know how to regulate, calm, and soothe their nervous system.

Grounding Practices

The following ten practices are to ground and support your clients' nervous systems to create more safety as they experience challenging feelings and body sensations. By using these practices your clients will feel more in control as dissociation arises, enabling you to help facilitate and regulate their nervous systems, just as if you were in the same room with them. These practices are ideas to jump-start your creativity and to find ways to help ground your clients into safety. Feel free to change the language, find different ways to approach this, and tap into your creativity when using these scripts. There are endless ways you can help stabilize, ground, and support your clients. Give yourself permission to explore, experiment, and try new things. These practices are not sequential; instead, use them throughout your sessions to facilitate whatever the client needs in the moment.

Go slowly, assisting clients in exploring, experimenting, and learning what is helpful, supportive, and nourishing to their nervous systems. Help clients discover what's familiar about what they're sensing and what is unfamiliar, which can connect clients to conscious and unconscious material. There are no right or wrong answers the client can give you; instead, explore what's working and adapt the practice if it is not. The key is assisting your client to find a dance that helps them feel regulated, grounded, and ready to do the work. For those of you who are trained in EMDR therapy, you can add short sets of bilateral dual attention stimulation (BLS) at the end of each practice to enhance the body's felt sense. Repeat the BLS sets three to five times to strengthen the neural network and make it easier for the client to sense and feel grounded.

Support

Early on in your treatment with remote therapy, help the client find items that stimulate their senses and are grounding, calming, and supportive of their nervous system. This external support connects clients to feel more present in their bodymind, helping prevent dissociation. To find this support, have your client look around their home to locate items that stimulate the five senses: touch, sight, smell, sound, and taste. Assist clients as they find soothing objects, such as smooth rocks, crystals, fidget toys, stress balls, blankets, pillows, or stuffed animals. Next, have them gather photos of family, friends, spiritual figures, artwork, and places they love so they can easily access them during sessions easily. Clients can also use words, quotes, or inspiring poems that anchor them in their bodies and/or find smells such as lavender, cinnamon, or a fresh orange that feel supportive to their nervous systems. Many clients like to have their favorite song, hear ocean waves, or maybe even listen to a sound from a chant-like "om." Last, clients can find things to taste that can quickly bring them into the present moment, such as a piece of hard candy, a mint, or even chocolate. As clients find their items, have them slow down and sense what warms their heart, centers their soul, and brings joy to their bodymind.

Remember, there is no right or wrong to this process; instead, you're guiding clients to trust their gut to lead what feels right to them. Each client is unique and individual; what works for one client may be triggering to another. So, go slow with this gathering process to ensure the client has connected to their experience and that each item is supportive, nourishing, and grounding. Once clients find their special grounding items, remind them to have the items with them during your remote therapy sessions so that they can be used at any time. This way, if the client gets triggered, dissociates, or the technology fails in the middle of a session, the client has resources available to help them ground, center, and regroup as quickly as possible. Therapists have reported that this practice has been reassuring for them, too, knowing that their client has the resources to handle the distance they feel during remote therapy sessions.

The following practice, Support, helps you guide your clients in finding items that stimulate your client's five senses. These items help ground, anchor, and support the client before, during, and after sessions. You can make this gathering process a part of your session or give the client homework to find the items on their own if they feel rushed. The key is to ensure that the client has enough time to determine if each item is supportive and grounding. Remember that each client is unique and let the client's wisdom guide what feels right to them. Ask your clients to bring their supporting items to their remote therapy sessions and to use them as often as needed throughout the week.

....

PRACTICE: SUPPORT

I'd like to invite you to find items that feel supportive, nourishing, and safe to your bodymind. These items can be helpful to you so you can ground yourself in the present moment if your emotions feel too big, or the technology fails, and you don't know what to do. Would this be okay with you? Remember, there's no right or wrong way to do this practice, and you are the one in control. If something doesn't feel right, just say so, and you can let go of it. If something feels good, supportive, and worth exploring, then you can continue to use that. This practice is special and unique to you, so let your gut tell you if an item is working or not. You may use something today that feels just right, and tomorrow you need something else. You can keep adding new things as you discover them over time. Keep checking in with your body and let your gut lead the way of what feels supportive to you in each moment.

Begin by looking around your room and find something to hold that feels good to you. That might be a smooth rock, crystal, fidget toy, stress ball, blanket, pillow, or stuffed animal. Notice what happens in your body when you hold this item. Does it help you feel calm, centered, and safe? Notice what happens to your breathing when you are holding the item. Would it feel good to have this with you during our sessions?

Next, see if you can find a photo of your family, friends, spiritual figures, artwork, or places you love. What happens inside your body when you look at the item? See if you can feel your body relaxing and releasing tension as you gaze upon the photo. Notice what happens to your breathing when you see the item. Would it feel good to have this with you during our sessions?

What if you had a quote, word, or phrase, or even a poem that had special meaning to you that you can look at any time during our session? Would it feel comforting to have these words somewhere where you could see them? When you see these words, does it make you connect more to yourself in a way that feels good? Are you able to take a deep, calming breath? Would it feel good to have the item with you during our sessions?

Next, see if you can find a smell that pleases you. If you can't think of one now, take some time this week and explore different scents until you discover something you like. You may have a beloved incense, a lotion that you love, a favorite aromatherapy, or maybe even a preferred smell from your kitchen spice rack. There is no right or wrong; just see what comes to you. As you connect to this smell, see what happens in your body. Do you feel calm, grounded, supported? If not, you may want to try and find a different smell. Once you identify it, use this smell anytime you need help to feel safe and connected to your body. Notice if it brings you more into the present moment. See what happens to your breathing as you take in the aroma from your smell. Would it feel good to have this with you during our sessions?

Next, is there a piece of music or sounds that make you soften in your body, relax, and feel calm? It might be a meaningful song, nature sounds, or a chant. Do you have the sound available to you? If not, can you imagine hearing this calming sound now? Whatever you chose, can you let the sound reverberate through your body? What do you notice when you hear this sound? Would it be helpful to have this sound with you during our sessions?

Last, think of having something with you that you can taste. It may be a piece of hard candy, a mint, or even a piece of chocolate. Notice what happens inside your body as you connect to this taste. Does it help you feel more present, or is it distracting to you? Remember, there is no right or wrong, just finding what feels right to you. Would it feel good to have this with you during our sessions?

Now that you have your items with you, remember that you can use them when things feel difficult, too overwhelming, or you just need to take a break. If we lose connection because the technology fails, use any of your items to recenter and ground before reconnecting with me.

....

Connecting

As you begin to help your clients ground, they will need to learn how to connect to their bodies. Many clients who have experienced trauma disconnect, disown, and disengage with their emotions and body sensations to keep themselves safe. This disconnecting process developed to help protect them from feeling too much pain in the past. Now, clients are often left feeling empty, lost, and fearful that if they connect to their body, they won't be able to handle what they are sensing and feeling.

Teaching your clients to connect with their bodies starts by having them sit in silence, focusing their attention on one body part at a time. Slowly give the client time to sense and feel the area they focus on and what sensation they are noticing. Help the client learn how to observe the sensation without making it good/bad or right/wrong. Learning how to feel the sensation without any judgment and describing it in vivid ways will help stretch the client's ability to tolerate sensations without running away or shutting down. It's especially important to assure the client that there is no right or wrong way to answer any of these questions. Clients can quickly assume what they're noticing is wrong, judge it as bad, and/or feel shame that they are experiencing this.

Take time to pause after each direction, giving the client plenty of time to sense, reflect, and connect to their experiences. Dialogue with the client as they're going through this process to help them find ways to sit with the sensation without changing it, fixing it, or making it go away. It's okay to have the client linger in one area more than others to explore it on a deeper level. You can specifically ask how big the sensation feels; if there is a color, shape, or texture to it; or does it need support in any way, such as their hands gently holding this area.

The first time you offer this practice, clients will need to get used to it and learn how to tolerate the sensations. It can be just as uncomfortable as learning how to ride a bike, but with patience, perseverance, and practice, they will start to relate to their bodies more easily. Some clients are not ready for this entire practice in one session. They will quickly go through the motions, acting as if they feel something when they don't; shut down their experience by saying it's not working; or try to distract you by talking about something else. Clients who are highly traumatized will experience this disconnect from their body, and it's the therapists' job to help them reconnect to what they are sensing and feeling. Often clients who are asked, "What are you notching in your body?" lack a vocabulary for how to describe what they're sensing. Most people did not grow up in households where they learned how to describe the sensations they felt in their bodies. A simple solution to rectify this language deficit is giving your client a list of descriptive somatic words that depict different sensations. Words like *tight, tingly, constricted, open, light, heavy* begin to provide the client a vocabulary to understand what they're being asked to notice. As clients get more comfortable with this language, they'll start to connect easier to their bodies, gain a deeper understanding of who they are, what they feel, and how different events in their lives have shaped them. You will need to explore this with your client to help them develop the skill to tolerate sensations in their body and know that whatever they are experiencing is just fine. Break this practice down into bite-size pieces so your client can begin to tolerate sensation in one area before moving onto another place in the body. Then you can keep exploring other areas of the body as the client is ready, building up to sensing and feeling the entire body from head to toe. Be open to changing this practice by listening to your client, sensing what they are experiencing, and adapting to what you feel would best serve the client in the moment.

The following practice, Connecting, is a great way to start every remote therapy session as it focuses your client on connecting to their bodymind. Starting your session with this practice provides consistency and safety that the client can trust and rely on to begin your remote therapy sessions. As you lead this practice, you'll see how easy or hard it is for the client to connect to their body. As the client learns how to tolerate more sensation, they'll become aware of their perceptions of their external experiences and their internal experiences of what they think, feel, and sense in their body. Developing this awareness will help clients witness themselves more gently and compassionately. Carefully pay attention to pacing this practice so that the client can tolerate, connect, and be with what they're sensing. Remember that each client is unique and let the client's wisdom guide them. You are a guide that supports this process, making it safe for the client to reconnect and trust the essence of who they are: a breathing, feeling, soulful human being.

....

PRACTICE: CONNECTING

Take a moment to get comfortable in your chair. You can do this with your eyes open or closed. If you have your eyes open, find an object in your room to gently gaze at, making you feel calm inside. See if you can shift your awareness to sensing your body on the chair. Can you feel what parts of your body are touching the chair and which parts aren't? Now shift your attention to your breathing. Notice what happens on your inhale and exhale. What are you aware of with your breath? Pay attention to your inhale. What sensations do you feel coming in through your nose to your belly? Then pay attention to your exhale and see what you notice. Try not to change anything as you do this; you're just noticing whatever you sense without judging it.

Now bring your awareness to the top of your head, notice how it feels. Then let your awareness travel to your neck and down your shoulders. If you want to add any subtle movements to increase the sensation, follow that instinct. What are you noticing?

See if you can bring your focus to your face, eyes, jaw, mouth, tongue, throat. What are you noticing in these areas? Again, there is no right or wrong; you're just becoming aware of whatever you observe today.

Now let your awareness travel down your arms, forearms, and into your hands. Notice what the quality of energy is in your arms and hands. Is the right side feeling the same as the left side? Just allow your body to be, merely observing it without any judgment.

Next, bring your awareness to your shoulders, shoulder blades, upper spine, lower spine, and entire back. Does your right side feel the same as your left side? What are you noticing?

Notice what happens when you bring your attention to the front of your body. Notice your upper chest, lungs, and diaphragm, your heart area, then your belly. What are you noticing now? See if you can keep any judgment at bay and describe what you are aware of right now.

Bring your awareness down into your hips and feel your pelvis. Is it tilted forward, backward, or is it neutral? You can move your pelvis with slow, intentional micro-movements to help increase your awareness if that feels helpful.

Now bring your attention down your legs, lower legs, and feet. Notice if both sides feel the same or different. See what sensations you're aware of without judging or trying to make meaning out of what you notice.

Last, see if you can sense your whole body at once. Does the right side feel the same as the left? Does your upper half feel different from your lower half? How about the back of your body versus the front of your body? Be gentle with what you are noticing. See what you're aware of at this moment.

To end this practice, bring your awareness back to your breathing. Has it changed or stayed the same? Do you feel different from when you started this practice? Slowly prepare yourself to come back into the present by bringing your awareness into the room. You might need to move a little bit, stretch, yawn, or whatever feels good to you to shift your attention.

....

Breathing

One of the key ingredients to helping a client ground and regulate their nervous system is working consciously with *how* they are breathing. Breathing is essential to life, and we do it all the time unconsciously, every day. In therapy, helping clients become consciously aware of how they are breathing can help support difficult emotions and body sensations so they don't run away or shut down what they're experiencing. You can invite clients to work with different breathing strategies to impact their nervous system immediately. Slowing the breath down will have a calming effect for clients in a hyperarousal nervous system state while quickening the breath will stimulate and wake up clients in a hypoarousal nervous system state.

If a client is anxious, overwhelmed, and panicky, their sympathetic nervous system will go into the fight or flight action, sending them into a hyperarousal nervous system state. Their breath becomes short and shallow, and all they want to do is escape from what feels dangerous. Helping the client learn how to slow down their breathing in these moments will automatically tell their nervous system to CALM DOWN NOW. Slowing down the breath will help bring the client back into the window of tolerance, reorient the client to the present moment, and help them see there is no immediate danger; it just feels that way. The client will observe what they're thinking and feeling in a more controlled way, allowing room for awareness of what might be triggering them into this fearful state.

A therapist shared a story about one of her clients

struggling during a walk on a trail while wearing a mask for the first time during the pandemic. The client walked by several people who were not wearing masks. She felt uncomfortable, anxious, and afraid that she was going to contract the virus from them. Without any warning, she felt her mask suffocating her to the point where she couldn't get any air in to breathe. Her heart was racing, and she felt jittery from her head down to her toes. Everywhere she looked was full of danger. Her rational brain went offline, and her survival brain kicked in to protect her. Then suddenly, she remembered that her therapist had taught her about breathing and regulating herself when uncomfortable feelings arise. She heard her therapist's words, "Slow down your breathing." As the client started to deepen her exhales, she became aware of a memory from when she was 5 years old and having her tonsils removed. She was in the hospital all alone, surrounded by people wearing masks, afraid that something terrible was going to happen to her. The client recognized that her current fear of people not wearing masks triggered this past unresolved trauma from her childhood. Acknowledging what was happening allowed her to continue to slow down her breathing and ground in the present moment. Once she was able to steady herself and regulate her nervous system, she was able to finish her walk, remembering she was safe in the moment and had a choice of how close or far she could position herself from other people not wearing masks. The client reported to her therapist that she was grateful for knowing how to handle such a scary feeling and was proud of adapting to the situation.

While this client felt panic, fear, and out of control, other clients may feel stuck, numb, and have difficulty engaging in activities. Their nervous system is in a hypoarousal state, and if you do slow, calm breathing practices with them, they'll only feel more tired, sluggish, and unable to move or be motivated. In these cases, quickening the breath into the upper chest will stimulate and activate the client's nervous system to come into the window of tolerance. The client will then begin to connect to their feelings and body sensations to feel more alive, present, and awake with their experience.

During the pandemic, this process of shutting down feelings became apparent with one of the therapist's I consulted with as he shared his struggle with one of his clients. The client's children were home doing remote education, his partner had lost his job, and he was also trying to work from home. He felt overstimulated by all the activity in his home, and he found himself feeling tired, grumpy, and no longer caring what others were experiencing around him. He had little energy and felt numb; he was disengaged from his work as well as from being a parent or a loving partner. This client was in a hypoarousal nervous system state and would dissociate from his feelings and body sensations.

His therapist taught him to do three quick upper chest breaths to see if this would bring more charge to his body. The client did feel a shift immediately and was able to experience moments where he connected to his emotions without trying to shut down, disengage, or escape uncomfortable feelings. The client started to recognize when he was about to shut down his feelings and learned to apply this breathing practice to help bring him back into the window of tolerance. It took practice for the client to sense and feel when his nervous system was trying to shut down, and the quick breathing gave him a skill that he could apply during sessions or while he was at home. As the client began to wake up, he learned to set healthier boundaries with his family and work to feel more engaged in his life once again.

As you can see, learning how to work with the breath to support the nervous system can be a life-changer for clients. When practiced regularly, clients' nervous systems become more adaptable, increasing their ability to handle difficult emotions and body sensations in, during, and between remote sessions. The following practices, Slow Breath and Quick Breath, are easy ways to help regulate clients throughout your remote therapy sessions. Once you teach your clients these practices, make sure to instruct them to use Slow Breath and Quick Breath daily to repattern their nervous systems so they have a greater capacity to handle life's challenges.

. . . .

PRACTICE: SLOW BREATH

Begin by feeling your body sitting in the chair. You can do this breathing practice with your eyes open or closed, and if they are open, have a soft gaze. Becoming familiar with how you breathe can help you feel more in control of what you're feeling and sensing in your body. Take a moment to scan your body. What you are thinking, feeling, sensing?

Now, bring your hands to your belly and imagine a balloon there. Without force, allow air to come in through your nose down into your belly, expanding your belly like a balloon. Now, on your exhale, let the balloon lose all its air, deflating your belly as the air releases. If it is helpful to you, you can add a slow count of four on your inhale and a slow count of four on your exhale, letting the rhythm from the counting help you slowly control your breathing.

Continue to notice your slow inhale and exhale for a couple of minutes, remembering not to force your effort during this practice. When you stop, scan your body from head to toe. Has anything changed from when you began? What are you thinking, feeling, sensing in your body?

Remember that anytime you feel overwhelmed, panicky, or out of control, you can slow down your breathing just like this, and it will help you feel more grounded, safe, and secure to handle the situation.

....

PRACTICE: QUICK BREATH

As you become aware of feeling tired, slow, and/or sluggish, take a moment to feel your body in the chair. You can do this breathing practice with your eyes open or closed, and if they are open, have a soft gaze. Becoming familiar with how you breathe can help you feel more in control of what you are feeling and sensing in your body. Take a moment to scan your body. What you are thinking, feeling, sensing?

Now, place your hands on your upper chest. Take in a quick sip of air through your nose and then quickly push the air out of your mouth as you exhale. Repeat this process two more times. Be careful not to do this too many times because you might begin to feel lightheaded. After you complete the three quick breaths, scan your body from head to toe. Has anything changed from when you started? What are you thinking, feeling, sensing in your body?

Remember that you can quicken your breathing anytime you feel sluggish, and it will help you feel more energized to go on with your day.

....

Centering

One of my favorite practices, Centering, is a quick and easy way to ground your client when they struggle to handle difficult emotions and body sensations; feel like they will dissociate; or become distracted and unable to focus. Centering involves guiding the client to focus outside of themselves by engaging the senses: what they see, hear, smell, and touch. This process allows the client's distress to fade into the background, letting them feel more grounded in the present moment. Go slow and gently guide the client to keep naming what they're sensing until they can take a deep breath, feel their body grounded, and report being 100% present with you. Give the client plenty of time to explore, so don't rush the process. You'll know that the client is present with you when they are able to make eye contact as well as report feeling calmer and capable of handling their emotions and body sensations. Once the client becomes familiar with this process, they can practice it between sessions when they feel distressed and need to let go of pain from the past or worries about the future. This will help them become centered in the present moment. The more they use this practice, the sooner their muscle memory will take over, making it easier to center without thinking so hard.

....

PRACTICE: CENTERING

I notice that you are having a hard time staying present with what you're feeling. On a scale of "0 to 10," where "0" is not present at all and "10" you are completely present, how present do you feel with me now? Take a moment, look around your room and say out loud what you see: colors, shapes, objects, patterns, whatever comes into your awareness. Can you take a deep breath and feel your body? What are you noticing? Now see if you notice any sounds in the room. As you hear the sound, what do you notice in your body? Next, see if you smell anything. What do you notice in your body as you take in this smell? Now, can you feel your feet on the ground? Can you sense your body in the chair? Is there any movement that would feel nourishing to you in this moment? Let yourself follow any movement you want until you feel complete.

Can you take a deep breath? On a scale of "0 to 10," where "0" is not present at all and "10" you are completely present, how present do you feel with me now?

Note: Continue having the client say out loud what they see, hear, and sense in their bodies until they feel 100% present and centered with you.

....

Calming

Another helpful grounding practice, Calming, is where you help your clients visualize a real or imaginary place that's soothing to their nervous system when they think about it. I first learned this practice, called Safe Place, in EMDR therapy and I've found it extremely helpful for clients to regulate their nervous systems (Shapiro, 2018). The word Safe can be triggering for some clients who have never felt safe in their lives, so the word Calming is an easier language for clients to understand and embody. By doing the Calming practice, clients will feel more grounded, relaxed, and at ease in their bodies. While the client visualizes this place they've chosen, take time to help them explore any sensory pieces they are aware of, such as the temperature, colors, time of day, sounds, smells, objects, or allies. These sensory pieces help make the imagery more dynamic, alive, and vibrant for the client. As the client connects to this place, make sure they feel the embodiment of the felt sense as they connect to relaxation in their body. You don't want your clients simply thinking about this, you want them to feel it as they do it. Watch tension melt away, making sure the client can take a deep breath without any effort.

Some clients will struggle to do Calming because they have experienced severe trauma that's impacted their ability to feel safe, relaxed, and grounded in the world. In these cases, try to allow the client to find a picture of nature that is soothing; or pick a place in a movie or book that sounds calm; or maybe use a piece of music that helps them achieve this same feeling. Allow your creativity to come into play to find what has meaning to your client so they can connect to this calm sensation in their body. Go slowly through the script, giving the client plenty of time to focus, reflect, and engage with this imagery, ensuring that they connect to the felt sense in their body. Let the client share what they're noticing throughout the practice to ensure that it's soothing and not bringing up any anxiety, fear, or worries.

If the client becomes anxious, overwhelmed, or fearful, then this place they've chosen will not help them achieve the desired goal. In those cases, have the client let go of that imagery and start again, making sure the client feels safe, secure, and ready to proceed until they find something soothing and grounding. Once the client finds this calming sensation, have them choose a cue word or phrase representing it. Use the cue word or phrase anytime to help the client return to this calming sensation in their body. The more the client practices Calming, the easier it will be for them to sense the state of peace once again.

....

PRACTICE: CALMING

Begin by sitting comfortably in your chair. You can have your eyes open or closed when doing this practice. Think of a real or imaginary place where you feel calm, relaxed with no worries. Just let an image come to you and see if it feels relaxing when you think of this place. Only you know what feels calming and relaxing, so make sure you sense and feel this in your body. As you picture this calm place, see what you notice. What time of day is it? What are the colors that are pleasing to you? What is the temperature? Are there any smells that you're aware of that you like? Do you hear any sounds that are calming when you hear them? Notice what makes you feel grounded, calm, and relaxed in this place. Scan your body from head to toe. What are you sensing in your body? Bring your awareness to your inhale and exhale. See if you can let tension melt on every exhale, allowing your body to sink deeper into the chair. As you sense this in your body, let your posture reflect how you feel right now.

As you experience calm in your body, see if you can give this place a name. This name can be a word or a phrase that helps you connect to this place easily. What would you like to call this calming place? Repeat the name of your calming place a couple of times and see how it feels in your body. When you think of your calm place can you connect effortlessly to the felt sense in your body? Take your time sensing and feeling what it's like to imagine this calm place. When you're ready, bring your focus back to the room, look around gently and slowly, and feel how grounded you are in your body. Know that this calm place is yours to have any time you want so that you can feel grounded in your body. Use it every day to help you feel safe, secure, and calm so that when life stressors come around, you have a skill that you can rely on to help you manage this feeling.

....

Rooted

In Japan, *shinrin-yoku* (森林浴 - "forest bathing"), which involves going out into nature and taking in the forest atmosphere through the senses for relaxation, is a practice that helps people receive immediate health benefits. Research has found the trees release antimicrobial essential oils that boost moods, increase the immune system, lower blood pressure, reduce the heart rate, and decrease stress and anxiety (Qing, 2018). I have a favorite tree I go to when I feel anxious, afraid, and overwhelmed. When I stand by this tree, it feels as if my pain is absorbed and processed energetically. This tree recently helped me grieve a dear friend who unexpectedly died in an accident. When I heard about his death, I felt a shock wave run through my body, making it difficult to tolerate the sensations. I struggled with this news especially because I was by myself and had no way to grieve with my fellow friends. I decided to visit my tree and see if I could get support from nature to handle the pain running through my body. When I arrived at my tree, I felt relief from the pain immediately come over my body. I hugged the tree, allowing the energy exchange between us, allowing the tree's lifeforce to bring more ease and comfort to me. Then I sat at the roots of the tree and looked out into the horizon. Spontaneously, I started singing a song in honor of my friend. I didn't know this song I was singing; rather, odd sounds came out of my mouth that were low, haunting, and expressed my pain. These sounds were guttural, spontaneous, and flowing from a place deep inside me. I had never heard anything like this in my life. Through these grieving sounds, my body opened, my heart expanded, and I felt connected to my friend even though he was gone from this earth. Once the song was complete, I was able to leave my nature spot feeling grounded, centered, and at peace. I was grateful the tree provided support for me to express all my grief safely so that I wasn't so alone and, instead, I felt love and compassion for this friend who will always hold a special place in my heart.

As people struggled through the quarantine, many did not have access to connect with nature and feel the benefits from trees. This next practice, Rooted, is an excellent solution for clients to feel grounded by visualizing a strong tree with deep roots connected to the earth. Once the client has a tree in mind, they can begin to imagine stepping into the tree to embody its essence. The client's legs and feet become the roots, their torso the trunk, and their arms and head the branches and the leaves. As the client finds this connection to the earth, their energy drops into their body, helping them feel more solid, anchored, and rooted to the ground. As you invite the client to connect with this grounding practice, read each line slowly, allowing them to share with you their experience as they feel, sense, and connect with the tree energy. Clients love this practice so much that they often come into sessions requesting to do it.

....

PRACTICE: ROOTED

You can begin this practice standing or sitting, whatever inspires you as you get rooted. You can do this with your eyes open or closed, and if your eyes are open, have a soft gaze, looking somewhere in the room that feels good to you. Now scan your body from head to toe and notice how you feel right now. There is no right or wrong; just be aware of what you are experiencing. You might be aware of some tension in your body, or you might feel open and receptive. Whatever you're experiencing is okay at this moment.

Now, imagine a big beautiful, strong tree in front of you. You love looking at this tree, and it brings you joy when you see it. See yourself walking up to the tree and then magically stepping into the tree. Notice how your feet and legs become the roots; your torso, the trunk; and your neck, head, and arms become the tree branches. Take a moment to let your body posture move and reflect how it feels to be one with this tree.

On your next inhale, see the energy from the Universe, enter the branches of the tree, and stream down into the trunk. On your next exhale, let the energy stream down from your trunk, releasing it into the earth. On your next inhale, see the earth's energy come up through the roots and into the trunk of the tree. On your next exhale, see the energy in the trunk move through the branches streaming out into the Universe.

At your own pace, allow energy from the Universe to flow down into the earth, and let the earth's energy rise out into the Universe. Feel the power, frequency, and aliveness the tree has to offer you. As you breathe in the nourishment from this tree, notice if any tension is releasing from your body.

Now, ask the tree if it has a gift for you today. It may be something like *strong, grounded, rooted, flexible*. See if you can receive the gift the tree has to offer you and feel it from your head down to your toes. Take a couple of deep breaths to enjoy this feeling and then thank the tree for the gift it has given you today. When you're ready, see yourself gently stepping out of the tree and feel anchored to the earth. Take a moment to look around your room while still feeling connected and rooted to the earth's energy. Take a moment and see if anything feels different from when you started this practice. Remember that you can sense this support anytime you want, especially if you feel overwhelmed, panicked, and unrooted by what's happening in your life. You can tap into feeling rooted anytime you need or want.

....

Edges

As clients felt overwhelmed from the changes created by pandemic, many felt they could not set boundaries that would keep them feeling safe, strong, and capable of handling new stressors every day. Boundaries are essential to create an edge of where you begin and where you end physically, mentally, and emotionally. They are on a continuum from being open, permeable, and receptive to being shut off, rigid, and closed, not letting anything in.

Healthy boundaries are meant to be adaptable, flexible, and responsive to different situations—and they are intended to change based on what's appropriate for what's happening at the moment.

Growing up in a small town in Ohio, I had no clue what I was walking into when I first moved to New York City. It was a hot, muggy summer day, and I was naively walking to my first dance class, making eye contact with people as I had always done in the past. Without my being aware, a group of men surrounded me on the sidewalk, taunting me about my blue eyes while blocking my path to my class. I was in shock, not knowing what to do or how to handle this situation. I felt alone, afraid, and hopeless, fearing I was in extreme danger and that it was rapidly escalating beyond my control. Suddenly, out of nowhere, another man broke through the group putting his arms out to block the danger while he shouted at me, "RUN!" Everything in my body kicked into action, and I ran away as fast as I could, never looking back.

Once at my dance class, I had difficulty focusing on the steps because I was afraid to go back outside once again and face the potential danger. I learned that making eye contact in New York was dangerous and that my boundary was too open for this city. From that point on, I walked in a straight path with my eyes directly ahead of me, avoiding making direct eye contact unless I knew someone personally. My boundary became more rigid, strong, and no-nonsense whenever I was walking down a street. I never had a problem like the group of men ever again. I am grateful to this angel of a man who kept me safe when I had no idea of the dangers of New York City. I hold in my heart that he experienced no harm trying to save me and that life has treated him well for doing this good deed.

After living in New York City for 8 years, I decided to move to Boulder, Colorado. As I started to explore the beautiful walking trails available, people would look at me and smile warmly, saying, "Hi." At first, my body would tighten, and I wondered what they wanted from me. Over time, I learned they were being friendly and thus I could relax my boundary and remain safe in this new environment. As you can see, boundaries need to be adaptable, flexible, and responsive to where you live, who you're with, and how safe you feel in every moment.

For many clients struggling during the pandemic, their sense of safety collapsed when dealing with the unknown dangers caused by an invisible, very contagious virus. Their edges were pushed by being quarantined with their families, hearing distressing news every day, and dealing with their unresolved childhood traumas. The collective pain from their families, communities, and the world became too big to manage. This pain came flooding through their bodies, causing them to feel out of control, panicky, and lacking clarity in their sense of self. Their boundaries were lost, sensing too much at once, overwhelming their nervous systems. Many felt inundated by too much stimulation or felt abandoned, alone, and isolated, unable to connect through their loneliness. By losing their boundaries, their edges became too permeable. They needed to reestablish and strengthen as well as practice establishing new boundaries to help them develop a stronger sense of self, capable of handling whatever comes their way.

This next practice, Edges, allows clients to use their imagination to set new energetic boundaries so they can feel their sense of self become more solid and adaptable, better to handle life's stressors. In the beginning, you can have a client imagine a transparent bubble outside of themselves that's strong enough to hold anything disturbing, that creates a defined edge and separation from their energy. Many clients use this bubble to hold an argument they had with a partner, their fear of the unknown, or even the collective trauma of grief and pain people are experiencing worldwide. Whatever feels like too much for the client to handle, they can imagine putting that distress into the bubble temporarily until they're ready to engage with the material once again.

Once the distress is contained safely in the bubble, the client can send the bubble as far away as they need, making it smaller, less scary, and more manageable. Have the client check in with their bodies to see if this visualization has helped them feel a separation from their distress and more at ease in their bodies. If the client has more than one distressing thing, repeat this process of creating as many bubbles as the client needs until they report feeling calmer and more in control of their emotional state.

The next step in this practice is for the client to imagine a bubble around their entire body so they have a way to contain their energy. Let clients know this bubble is permeable: it can let whatever is nourishing in, and it can keep out anything that feels distressing. Have the client check in with their body again and see if they feel centered, grounded, and capable of handling their emotions.

The last step of the practice is for the client to imagine filling up their bubble with a beautiful healing color that's soothing, relaxing, and heals any distress in their nervous system. Make sure the client feels this energetic force field in a way that allows them to be nourished, replenished, and supported throughout their body, mind, and spirit.

Feel free to adapt, adjust, and make this practice work for the client in whatever order the client needs. Trust your gut to let you know how to start this practice as well as complete it. There is no right way to do this, only what works for the client to create resiliency in their bodymind. Take your time when reading this practice so that the client can tell you what they are experiencing. You're invited to adapt the script as needed. You'll know this practice is working for your client when they report having a different perspective of what they are struggling as well as feeling more grounded and centered. Have the client practice setting bubbles throughout the week to create defined edges of their energetic body releasing anything that feels too big to handle. By doing this practice, the problem does not go away; instead, it helps a client ground in their own body before engaging with the outside world.

....

PRACTICE: EDGES

Take a moment to get comfortable wherever you're seated. You can do this with your eyes open or closed. If you have your eyes open, find an object to look at that makes you feel calm inside, keeping your focus soft with as little effort as possible. Now see if you can shift your awareness to sensing your body. Notice if there is anything that is feeling overwhelming or too much to handle. What are you noticing?

Now imagine a big bubble outside yourself that's strong enough to hold the distress. See if you can allow the distress to move into the bubble in whatever way feels right to you. Take as much time as you need to contain the distress in the bubble. Let me know when you feel complete. Notice how it feels when you have the distress in its bubble. Check in with your gut and see if you need to move this bubble farther away from you. Find where it feels just right to have the bubble in relationship to yourself. There is no right or wrong when you do this, just allow your intuition to guide you. Once you have sent the bubble away, scan your body, and see if anything has changed. Did you get all the distress in the bubble? Is there anything else you're aware of that needs to go in another bubble?

Note: Repeat the process of creating as many bubbles as the client needs to contain all the distress.

Now, imagine a bubble that goes around your entire body. This bubble is permeable and can let in what feels right to you but keeps out things that feel distressing or toxic. See how it feels to have your energetic bubble. What are you noticing in your body? Does this feel strong, solid, and supportive of your nervous system?

Next, imagine a healing color that can fill your entire bubble. As you see this color coming into your bubble, allow it to dissolve any tension, pain, or upset you may still be feeling. Breathe this healing color into all parts of your body so that it nourishes, rejuvenates, and replenishes your body, mind, and soul. What are you noticing?

When you're ready, slowly prepare yourself to come back into the present, bringing your awareness back into the room. You might need to move a little bit, so let yourself stretch, look around the room, staying connected to the felt sense in your body.

....

Holding

Another way to help clients feel more solid in their bodies and control their emotional states better is using the practice of Holding. Often in remote therapy sessions, issues may arise around dealing with the pandemic, families, work, remote traumatization, or unresolved traumas, leaving a client feeling ungrounded and incapable of handling the distress. Disturbing images, thoughts, feelings, and body sensations can become very distracting, making it challenging for clients to function throughout their daily lives. Developing a way to consciously set aside the distress until the client is ready to process it is essential in remote therapy. By doing this practice, clients will feel more present, grounded, and safe throughout the therapeutic process.

The following practice, Holding, helps clients visualize something that's strong enough to hold any distressing images, thoughts, feelings, or body sensations that may be difficult for the client to handle. This practice can help clients learn they have more control and choice over how they feel, act, and respond. Having the client imagine a holding space that's strong enough to contain what's distressing and distracting can help them focus and be more present. A few examples of what clients have used in this practice include a bank vault with a tumbler lock, a spaceship that goes to Mars, or a cave where they can bury their distress and cover the entrance with a large rock. Let your client's creativity and imagination figure out what feels best in their nervous system. There is no right or wrong with this practice; simply stay out of the way and let your client find what has meaning to them.

Once the distressing material is in the imaginal holding space, have the client set a boundary with the disturbing material, letting it know when they will come back and process it. By setting a boundary with the disturbing material, the practice of Holding honors the disturbing material as important with a commitment that it *will* be reviewed at a later date when the client has time to focus and work on it more fully. You'll know Holding practice is working when the client can take a deep breath, feel grounded in their body, and be present with you.

As clients use their holding space, you can begin to trust that your client has a way to manage challenging feelings and remain safe between sessions. By trusting this practice, you can then let go of taking on too much responsibility for your client's experience. If the holding space isn't working for the client, explore changing the size, color, or distance until the client can take a deep broth and feel grounded in their body. Try to end all your remote therapy sessions with this practice of helping clients contain any distress before moving on with their day. Have your client practice Holding daily to get it into their muscle memory so they can use it to feel safe between sessions.

....

PRACTICE: HOLDING

Begin by feeling your body connected to your chair and your feet on the ground. You can have your eyes open or closed as you explore, finding a way to feel more in control of what you're feeling. Begin to imagine a holding space that's strong enough to hold whatever is distressing to you until you have time to come back to it and review later. See what comes to your mind. Some clients have visualized bank vaults with a tumbler lock, treasure chests buried in the ocean, or rockets sent into outer space. There is no right or wrong; just see what comes to your mind that feels strong and secure when you think about it. What are you noticing? Is your holding space big enough to hold what's disturbing to you? Is it close or far away? Does it feel capable of holding this distress and giving you some relief? Let the distressing material know when you will come back to it, whether it's tonight, tomorrow, or maybe not until our next session. What do you notice in your body when you give this material a boundary? Can you take a deep breath and feel grounded? Now see if you can find a word or a phrase that can name this holding space so that when you hear the word, it helps you connect easily to it so you can use it whenever you want. What's the name of your holding space?

Now let's test your holding space and see how well it works for you. Try thinking about something that has been recently disturbing: a memory, email, text, conversation, picture, thought, feeling, or body sensation. What is this disturbance? Now imagine putting the disturbance into the holding space and see what happens. Is the holding space strong enough, big enough, protective enough to contain this material until you're ready to process it? Does the holding space need to adapt, adjust, or have more protection? See what feels right and give the holding space whatever it needs. Notice what happens in your body when you feel the disturbance securely held. Can you breathe easily and feel grounded, secure, and in control of what you're feeling? There's no right or wrong with this practice; your holding space must work for you and no one else. Practice using your holding space throughout the week as different situations arise that might distress you. The more you practice Holding, the more effective it will be to help you feel more in control of whatever may be disturbing you.

....

Stretching

If your client struggles with any of the practices already discussed in this chapter, it may indicate that the client has experienced complex trauma. These clients will report feeling uncomfortable, incapable of feeling good, and afraid that something is inherently wrong with them. Sometimes they will resist the practices because they have learned that it's not okay to feel good, positive, or even neutral.

An example of this is a show I recently watched on Netflix, *Bridgerton* (2020), about a little boy whose mother died when he was born. He was a smart, inquisitive little boy who worked hard to learn as much as he could. His father was a wealthy, powerful man in the community and demanded perfection from his son. There was just one problem: the boy stuttered when he spoke, and his father felt his son was an imbecile, bringing shame to the family lineage. The father disowned his son, keeping his distance, leaving the son abandoned from his father's love. As this boy grew up, he learned how to speak without any speech impediment, was bright, intelligent, and became a powerful man in his own right. Unfortunately, through his father's abandonment, the son felt that he was never good enough, unworthy of love, and doomed to a life of pain. These interactions left this man with a limited capacity to tolerate positive feelings and body sensations. As soon as he started to feel the intimacy of love, he would pull away and put up barriers as well as harden his bodymind into a wall of shame and unworthiness. This man needed to stretch his capacity to tolerate the good feelings so he could start healing the wounds his father had inflicted upon him. Over time, this man learned to tolerate the sensation of love and accept it into his life, at last repairing this deep wounding that caused him so much pain.

This kind of deep pain can show up with clients. The therapist needs to work with it consciously to begin to repattern and stretch the client's ability to tolerate the uncomfortable emotions and body sensations. The following practice, Stretching, is an intervention to help the client stretch their window of tolerance and repattern their ability to safely feel neutral or positive without running away or shutting down the feeling. This practice has the client move their attention back-and-forth between a state of neutral or positive and distress. When the client begins to feel emotions and body sensations that are too hard to tolerate, have them bring their attention outside of the body and find something in the room that feels grounding, calming, and soothing to their nervous system. The client's focus can be on something in their room, such as a plant, photo, artwork, or even their water bottle—anything that will quickly orient them into the present moment that feels grounding, connected, and safe. You should see the client be able to take a deep breath, feel more ease in their body, and gain a sense of control of what they are feeling.

Once your client senses more ease, gently guide them back to the distress, letting them know they will only touch this for a few seconds and then return to safety with what was grounding. Keep repeating this process to see if you can stretch the client's length of time to tolerate the distressing feelings and body sensations while remaining in the window of tolerance. This back-and-forth motion will help the client build their emotional muscle to handle more powerful emotions or uncomfortable body sensations without running away, shutting down, or making the feelings go away.

Without this back-and-forth motion to stretch the client's capacity to tolerate uncomfortable feelings and body sensations, the client will continue to dissociate from the feelings, which recapitulates their original trauma rather than developing a new neural pathway of change. As the client learns how to move their attention away from that which does not feel safe to something that's grounding and supportive, the nervous system will find rest and ease, bringing safety back to the client. When the client is ready to return to the distressing emotion or body sensation, they will feel more in control, ready to sense and feel them, knowing that "now" can be different than "then." Now the client can explore an emotion or body sensation feeling safe, which is a different experience from their past. Through this back-and-forth motion, the client will handle sitting in distress for longer periods, which begins to stretch their capacity to manage uncomfortable emotions and body sensations easier. It's like the body's energy stretches and becomes a larger container to hold more emotions and body sensations for the client. Therapists have been surprised that when they help their clients stretch their capacity for tolerating emotions and body sensations through this process, their clients make progress faster in a safer way.

....

PRACTICE: STRETCHING

It looks like you're feeling overwhelmed right now and having trouble focusing. Let's slow things down and help you feel more grounded, solid, and in control of what you are sensing right now. Look around the room and find something that feels calming, grounding, and centering to you when you look at it. It can be a plant, a photo, a piece of artwork, or even your water bottle. There is no right or wrong; just find what feels okay to you at this moment.

Now that you see something that feels grounding, can you describe what you like about what you see? What brought your attention to this grounding object? Can you take a couple of deep breaths? What's happening in your body now? Does this feel good or neutral as you focus on this grounding object?

Note: Do not proceed to this next step if the client cannot get grounded in their body.

Now that you feel calmer, are you ready to touch back into the distress you felt earlier? You will only touch the distress for a brief moment, and then you can bring your focus back to your grounding object. Are you okay with this?

Note: Make sure the client feels ready to move back into the distress before leading them there.

Bring your focus back to the distress. Where are you feeling this in your body? How big is it? Is there a shape, color, temperature? Can you handle what you're feeling right now?

Now that you have touched the distress, bring your focus back to your grounding object so you can let go of the distress. See if you can take a couple of slow deep breaths while you ground yourself. Take a moment and scan your body once again. What are you noticing? Has anything changed, or does it feel the same?

When you're ready, bring your focus back to the distress. Notice what happens now when you touch this tender area. Are you able to be with this sensation and breathe? Has anything changed, or does it feel the same? Is it okay to be with this feeling a little bit longer? Before the sensation gets too big to handle, bring your focus back to your grounding object.

Note: Keep having the client bring their attention back to their grounding object as much as they need. Try to stretch the client's length of time in the distressing feelings or body sensations as long as they can tolerate the uncomfortable feelings and body sensations. As you stretch the client's capacity, they will increase their window of tolerance and handle difficult emotions and body sensations better without dissociating.

....

Sustain

When ending your remote therapy sessions, have clients find something positive they have learned and can embody from their session. By focusing on the good from the session, clients can begin to sustain and appreciate the progress that they're making in therapy, even if they feel like nothing good is happening. Clients may find new insights about themselves; tolerate an emotion or body sensation; or touch on a new belief about themselves, such as being strong, competent, or smart enough. Having the client focus on the good feelings strengthens their positive emotional muscles, increases their capacity to feel good, and creates safety in ending your sessions.

The following practice, Sustain, helps clients review their session and see what they've learned that they can embody and take with them. As the client finds something positive, help them get the felt sense in their body so what they're saying is not just an intellectual exercise, but rather an embodied practice. If a client has difficulty reflecting on something positive, you can offer a moment you witnessed during the session, encouraging them to see the good from their work. Therapists have found this practice extremely helpful for clients who have experienced a lot of trauma. Their positive emotional muscle needs to develop through them giving it attention and learning how to sustain this feeling for extended periods outside the remote therapy office.

....

PRACTICE: SUSTAIN

In ending our session today, take a moment and reflect on what you experienced today. Is there anything positive that you learned about yourself that you could embody right now? Take a moment and let yourself connect to this positive feeling from your body from head to toe. What are you noticing? Are you able to feel, sense, and tolerate the sensations? How will this information help you as you go through your week? Take a moment and imagine seeing yourself leaving this office with this newfound feeling in your body. What are you aware of in this moment? Does this feel good and supportive? Do you think you can bring this feeling with you as your go through your week? How do you think it will be helpful to you? Take a moment and thank yourself for all the hard work you did in your session today. Can you feel this in your body? See if you can reflect on this good feeling throughout the week, and we can discuss what you're aware of in our next session.

WRAPPING UP

As you learn how to offer and/or maximize the effectiveness of your remote therapy sessions, having a solid foundation is essential for you and your clients. Taking time to lay down a solid foundation of knowing the ins and outs of the technology you're using will build your confidence that remote therapy has value, provides healing, and can be sustainable to your practice. Clients will start to see the value in this work when you model that to them. Put effort into staging your remote therapy office by finding a quiet, reliable space that you can depend on for your sessions. Design this space to create safety for you and your clients, so they have the best experience possible. Provide practices for your clients that are grounding, embodied, and give clients a sense of safety. These grounding practices will help clients feel more in control of their emotional states as well as stretch their capacity to tolerate uncomfortable feelings and body sensations without dissociating. By working consciously with your client's window of tolerance, you can let go of taking on too much responsibility for your client's wellbeing. As your clients practice their grounding skills, you can begin to trust that safety is possible to achieve in doing remote therapy. As you and your clients prepare more fully for remote therapy, you'll reduce your tendency of developing remote fatigue.

FINALE: SUSTAINABILITY

....

The dance between therapist and client
flows best when they are both listening
to each other's bodymind.

....

MOVING FORWARD

Now, as you reach this point in the book, you've had an opportunity to explore and try on each step of the remote therapy dance, ideally choreographing routines that work best for you and your clients. Many parts of the world, including the United States, have access to vaccines, which has enabled people to re-engage with their lives in ways similar to before COVID-19 brought us to a halt. However, we are still dealing with the effects on our mental health and the grief of losing millions of people around the globe to this terrible disease. And those effects are still impacting therapists on a profound level.

As you continue to move forward in helping your clients heal, your practices may have returned to all in-person sessions, all remote sessions, or a hybrid model. Your practice is *your practice*, so develop a schedule that works best for you and your clients. Many therapists have shared with me that if they are doing a hybrid model, they're scheduling all in-person sessions on one day and remote sessions on another day. This has helped them stay organized in their spaces, cut down on traveling, and helped sustain their energy throughout each day.

No matter what model you chose, the one thing that is *not optional* is taking care of yourself. This is an ongoing practice that will never end, a lifelong journey that's constantly evolving to keep your bodymind adaptable and sustainable. There will be days where you feel strong, grounded, and able to work with your clients because your life is flowing. And then there are times in life when everything can feel as if it's falling apart, and you're barely able to keep it together. Throughout the highs and lows in your personal life, you are the only one who can navigate your emotional, mental, physical, and spiritual world. That means you must take care of yourself every day on this journey called life.

In a recent training, I asked how many of the therapists take time to prepare themselves before, during, and after their sessions. In a group of 27 therapists, only 3 of them raised their hands. This tells me that therapists are not consciously taking time in their days to prepare their bodyminds for the challenges that can arise while doing therapy work. Therefore, the practices in this book are essential to your vitality and to helping you remain in a field where you are essential to the heartbeat of your community. I hope you've seen ways here to tap into your intuition so that you can nurture your body and soul. I'm asking you to dance with your purpose as a therapist and find how to move from one moment to the next by listening to your body's wisdom so it can guide you. Any time you find yourself feeling remote fatigue or struggling with an aspect of doing therapy remotely, I encourage you to revisit sections of this book to see if you may want to make any tweaks to your specific dance of taking care of yourself. Remember, you are not alone in your struggles, and it's okay to reach out for more support from your community of therapists whenever needed.

GRATITUDE

In ending, I want to thank all the therapists who trust me and who continue to reach out for support and guidance for their remote therapy practices. It takes a community to keep therapists functioning at their best, and I am honored to be a part of such communities. I know that I couldn't do the work I do if I didn't have a great support system myself. It has taken me years to find trustworthy guides who I'm grateful for because they help me see where I am limited in my thinking, triggered by others, and where I'm still holding unresolved traumas that interfere with me feeling strong, solid, and empowered. My daily practices continue to change, adapt, and be flexible to what I need from moment-to-moment, day-to-day, week-to-week, and year-to-year. This process is a dance I'm constantly choreographing so that I can be present, real, and authentic in my interactions, personally as well as professionally. If I don't nurture how I take care of myself, I'll go through the motions with little awareness and not feel the impact my actions have on myself or others. When I take time to connect with myself, it helps me be more present with others, so they feel seen, heard, and affected in ways they have never felt before. Having a strong presence with clients takes discipline and practice so that when times are challenging, the muscle memory kicks in and takes over. When you practice with intention, purpose, and care, people will feel the difference. So, put *care* into how you prepare for your sessions. Put *care* into how present you are with your clients. Put *care* in how you end your day of remote sessions so that you feel ready to be with your family and friends. When you put *care* into each part of being a therapist, your practice will become more sustainable for years to come.

I want to share one more practice that helps me keep my heart open and nourish my soul as well as helps keep me hopeful that I'm a resilient human being able to handle the ups and downs life offers. This last practice, Gratitude, can change how you feel instantaneously by connecting to your heart and helping you be grateful for special moments in your life. Often gratitude is discussed as being thankful for things you have attained. That is not the intent of this practice; instead, the purpose is for you to remember times when you felt pure joy and delight; or were being honored; or were in awe of the preciousness in your life.

I have felt this kind of gratitude when I'm dancing with my husband and joy explodes through my body; or when I am laughing with friends so hard tears start to stream down our faces; or when clients make profound changes that leave me feeling in awe and honored to be a witness to their transformation. These are the moments that make me feel grateful to be here on this earth, dancing with other human beings in the rhythm of life.

As you practice Gratitude, give yourself the space and time to be quiet and reflective. Practice this daily so your muscle memory will remind you of times when you have felt pure joy, delight, and wonderment—even when you feel your world is falling apart. As you connect deeper to your heart, your capacity to have compassion for yourself and others will increase and, at times, even overflow.

....

PRACTICE: GRATITUDE

Take a moment to feel yourself in your chair. You can do this with your eyes open or closed; if they are open, find a place to look with a soft gaze. Bring your awareness to your body and notice how you are breathing. Slowly let your attention move into your heart. You may want to gently place your hands over your heart to support this area if that feels right to you. Notice how your heart is feeling right now. Is it open, expansive, loving, or contracted, withered, and in pain? Try not to judge your heart; only observe what you are noticing.

Now, think of one moment in your life where you felt pure joy, delight, were being honored, or were in awe of the preciousness in your life. See what comes to mind. Do you get a picture of it? What are you thinking, feeling, and sensing in your body? There is no right or wrong; just be with whatever comes to you at this moment. See if you can allow yourself to connect to your heart without running away from it, shutting it down, or pushing it away. Can you let your heart expand, take in the goodness, and be with this gratitude? How big can this feeling get? Check in and see if your heart feels any different from when you began this practice. What has changed? How can you take this feeling with you as you go through your day? Let yourself have this moment, sense it deeply, and let it nourish your soul. Once you feel complete, gently come back to being present in the room, staying connected to this feeling of gratitude in your heart.

....

MAY YOU SOAR

As I tap into my sense of gratitude, I want to thank you for choosing to read this book to help support your journey in offering remote therapy to your clients. I hope by sharing my personal stories and those of fellow therapists' struggles that you could relate them to what you've experienced in switching your practice to remote therapy. Take time to reflect on what resonated with you throughout the book and how you can bring more practices into your daily life to help support, nurture, and sustain your work. The field of psychotherapy will never be the same, but we'll continue to be remote together, and learning how to dance with remote therapy can be a fun journey if you let it. Tap into your purpose of why you are a therapist and let that lead the way. Remember, you are the person people turn to in times of struggle, pain, and heartache. Let yourself be big, bold, and courageous with your work. Tap into your resiliency so you can help your clients find their own power and strengths. Be a dynamic force in your community because you are essential, vital, and the work you do matters—and will continue to matter for generations to come.

REFERENCES

Bridgerton, season 1, episode 2, Shondaland, December 25, 2020, www.Netflix.com/title/80232398.

Cardona, G., Garcia, C. Seres, C., Vilaseca, M., Gispets, J. (2011). Blink rate, blink amplitude, and tear film integrity during dynamic visual display terminal tasks. *Current Eye Research*.

36(3):190-7. Retrieved from http://doi:10.3109/02713683.2010.544442. Epub 2011 Jan 28.

Einstein, Albert , Zur Elektrodynamik bewegter Körper, *Annalen der Phys*ik, (4) xvii (1905), 891–92.

Grossman, M. (2004). *Magic eye beyond 3D: Improve your vision, reduce computer eye strain, stress & more.* Kansas City, MI: Andrew McMeel Publishing.

Keleman, S. (1987). *Bonding: A somatic-emotional approach to transference*. Berkeley, CA: Center Press.

Kubler-Ross, E. (1969). On death and dying. New York: MacMillan.

Madara, J. & White, D. (1963). You Don't Own Me [Recorded by Lesley Gore]. On *Lesley Gore Songs of Mixed-Up Hearts*. Chicago, Illinios: Mercury Records.

Mayer, E. (2018). *The mind-gut connection: How the hidden conversation within our bodies impacts our mood, our choices, and our overall health.* New York: Harper Wave.

Lucas, G. (1977). Star Wars Episode 1V: A New Hope, Twentieth Century Fox.

Porges, S. (2011). *The polyvagal theory: Neurobiological foundation of emotions, attachment, communication, and self-regulation.* New York, NY: Norton.

Qing, L. (2018). *Forest bathing: How tress can help you find health and happiness.* New York, NY: Viking Publishers.

Schore, A. N. (2012). *The science of the art of psychotherapy.* New York, NY: Norton.

Schwartz, R. (1997). *Internal Family Systems Therapy.* New York, NY: The Guilford Press.

Schwartz, A., & Maiberger, B. (2018). *EMDR therapy and somatic psychology: Interventions to enhance embodiment in trauma treatment.* New York, NY: Norton.

Sea Change Project, Fence, ZDF Enterprise, & Ehrlich P., & Reed, J., (2020). *My Octopus Teacher.* South Africa: Netflix Productions. www.netflix.com/title/81045007.

Shapiro, F., (2018). *Eye movement desensitization and reprocessing (EMDR) therapy: Basic principles, protocols and procedures.* (3rd ed.). New York, NY: The Guilford Press.

Sheppard, A. & Wolffscoh, J. (2018). Digital eye strain: Prevalence, measurement an amelioration. BMJ Open Ophthalmology. 3(1): e000146. Retrieved from https://dx.doi.org/10.1136%2Fbmjophth-2018-000146

Siegel, D. (1999). *The developing mind: How relationships and the brain interact to shape who we are.* New York, NY: Guildford Press.

Ungerleider, S. (1996). *Mental training for peak performance.* Emmaus, PA: Rodale Press, Inc.

van der Hart, O., Nijenhuis, E., & Steele, K. (2006). *The haunted self: Structural dissociation and the treatment of chronic traumatization.* New York, NY: Norton.

van der Kolk, B. (2015*). The body keeps the score: brain, mind, and body in the healing of trauma.* New York, NY: Viking Press.

Varker, T., Brand, R. M., Ward, J., Terhaag, S., & Phelps, A. (2019). Efficacy of synchronous telepsychology interventions for people with anxiety, depression, posttraumatic stress disorder, and adjustment disorder: A rapid evidence assessment. *Psychological Services*, 16(4), 621–635.

Vidor, K., Fleming, V. Cukor, G., Thorpe,R. Taurog, N. & LeRoy, M. (1939). The Wizard of Oz, Metro-Goldwyn-Mayer (MGM).

Watkins, H. & Watkins, J. (1997). *Ego states: Theory and therapy.* New York, NY: Norton.

ABOUT THE AUTHOR

Barb Maiberger, MA, LPC, is the founder of the Maiberger Institute, and the author of *EMDR Essentials: A Guide for Clients and Therapists* and the co-author of *EMDR Therapy and Somatic Psychology: Interventions to Enhance Embodiment in Trauma Treatment.* She is a Licensed Professional Counselor in the State of Colorado, EMDR Trainer and Consultant and has a Master of Arts in Somatic Psychology. Barb's knowledge, experience, keen sense of empathy, and strong presence have motivated thousands of therapists to incorporate somatic practices into their work.

Made in the USA
Monee, IL
19 May 2022

96732785R00213